Production and Logistics

Managing Editor

Horst Tempelmeier, University of Cologne, FRG

Editors

Wolfgang Domschke, Technical University of Darmstadt, FRG
Andreas Drexl, University of Kiel, FRG
Bernhard Fleischmann, University of Augsburg, FRG
Hans-Otto Günther, Technical University of Berlin, FRG
Hartmut Stadtler, Technical University of Darmstadt, FRG

Titles in this Series

Erwin Pesch
*Learning in Automated
Manufacturing*
1994. XIV, 258 pages.
ISBN 3-7908-0792-3

Rainer Kolisch

Project Scheduling under Resource Constraints

Efficient Heuristics
for Several Problem Classes

With 35 Figures and 88 Tables

Springer-Verlag Berlin Heidelberg GmbH

Dr. Rainer Kolisch
Institut für Betriebswirtschaftslehre
Universität Kiel
Olshausenstr. 40
D-24118 Kiel, FRG

ISBN 978-3-7908-0829-2   ISBN 978-3-642-50296-5 (eBook)
DOI 10.1007/978-3-642-50296-5

The use of registered names, trademarks, etc. in this publication does not imply, even in the absence of a specific statement, that such names are exempt from the relevant protective laws and regulations and therefore free for general use.

88/2202-5 4 3 2 1 0 - Printed on acid-free paper

Preface

This book is the result of my research performed at the University Kiel under the supervision of Professor Dr. Andreas Drexl. I am very grateful to him for suggesting the subject as well as for his guidance and support during the preparation. Professor Dr. Klaus Brockhoff deserves thanks for undertaking the task of the secondary assessment.

The Institut für Betriebswirtschaftslehre in Kiel and especially my colleagues Dr. Knut Haase, Carsten Jordan, Alf Kimms, and Dr. Frank Salewski provided a stimulating environment. Particularly, I am indebted to Dr. Arno Sprecher and Andreas Schirmer. The results of Chapter 2 and 3, respectively, are outcome of joint research with Arno; Andreas proof-read the entire manuscript.

Furthermore, I would like to express my gratitude to Prof. Dr. Erik Demeulemeester, Prof. Dr. James H. Patterson, Prof. Dr. Roman Slowinski, and Prof. Dr. Ramon Alvarez-Valdes for the valuable help they provided with suggestions, papers, and computer programs.

As to the technical realisation of this book, I owe thanks to Reimer Karlsen for coding and implementing parts of the algorithms, to Marc Schumann for drawing all figures, to Ina Kantowski who looked after the literature, and to Uwe Penke for providing a ready-to-use computer-laboratory.

The gratitude that I feel towards my family requires no further comments.

Rainer Kolisch

Contents

Chapter 1

Introduction

1.1 Fundamentals of Project Scheduling

According to Hax and Candea (1984, p. 325), **a project** is a complex and large scale one-of-a-kind product or service, made up by a number of component activities, that entails a considerable financial effort and must be time-phased, i.e. scheduled, according to specified precedence and resource requirements. Examples for projects are (cf. Levy et al. (1963) and Hax / Candea (1984)):

- Construction (of buildings, infrastructure, new plants etc.).

- Manufacture and assembly of large products (like ships, generators etc.).

- Repair and maintenance (of nuclear plants, oil refineries, etc.).

- Design, development, and marketing of new products.

- Development and launching of new complex systems (like space missions etc.).

Generally, the management of a project consists of three different phases (cf. McClain / Thomas (1985, p. 52)):

(*i*) **Acquisition of the data**, indispensable to manage the project, i.e. the types and number of available resources, the activities and their durations, resource requirements, and technological precedence relations, as well as the specification of the management goal.

(*ii*) **Scheduling of the activities** such that the pre-specified goal, i.e. the objective or performance measure, is met in the best possible way while considering the constraints as imposed by precedence relations and scarce resources. This phase will be covered in the subsequent chapters.

(*iii*) **Realisation of the plan** obtained within phase two.

As outlined, all projects consist of the three elements: activities, precedence relations, and resources. Nevertheless, there is a distinctive difference between projects w.r.t. the certainty of these elements. That is, some projects like the development and launching of a new complex system mainly consist out of probabilistic elements, others, e.g. the construction of a building, are generally made up of deterministic elements.[1] From the beginning in the late fifties of this century, project planning methods have been explicitly devoted to projects with either deterministic or stochastic elements:

The program evaluation and review technique (**PERT**, cf. Malcolm et al. (1959)) was developed to efficiently plan and produce the Polaris missile system subject to probabilistic durations of activities. The graphical evaluation and review technique (**GERT**, cf. Pritsker / Happ (1966) and Pritsker / Whitehouse (1966)) extended this line of research by additionally taking into account probabilistic precedence relations.

The critical path method (**CPM**, cf. Kelley (1961)), on the other hand, originally aimed at better planning the overhaul and maintenance of chemical plants which consisted, in general, of deterministic elements. Within CPM, the project is regarded as entirely deterministic. This assumption is made despite slight amounts of stochastic elements.

Notwithstanding that the methods mentioned do not take resource constraints into consideration, the line of reasoning as pursued by CPM is extended in here. That is, it is assumed that all data required for the planning

---

[1] Note that the five project examples stated above are sorted in the order of increasing probabilistic elements.

process is available, deterministic, and integer valued. Hence, neither problems with stochastic elements (cf. Neumann (1990) and Slowinski / Weglarz (1989, part III)) nor continuous problems (cf. Weglarz (1981, 1989)) nor dynamic problems where activities arrive at random (cf. Blazewicz et al. (1993, p. 246)) are covered in this work.

1.2 Treated Topics

As already outlined in the previous section, the first scope is on scheduling the activities of a project to meet a pre-specified goal in the best possible way. Thus, a question is what kind of projects and what kind of goals are taken into account? Four different **projects scheduling models** are considered. All of them are so complex that the computational effort to find an optimal solution grows exponentially with the number of activities (so-called *NP*-hardness of the optimisation problem). Furthermore, for two of the models an (in terms of the number of activities) exponentially growing effort has to be undertaken in order to find even a feasible schedule (so-called *NP*-completeness of the feasibility problem).

Hence, the second question is, how can the problems be solved efficiently? The focus is on **heuristic solution methodologies which make use of priority rules**. That is, within the planning process activities are considered deterministically in the order of certain attributes. It will be shown in the literature review that priority-rule-based heuristics are very popular for solving project scheduling problems. This is due to several reasons: They achieve a satisfying quality of solutions, they are fast in terms of the computational effort, and they proceed similar to the way decisions are made by people in charge of project planning.

Nevertheless, even if the deterministic decisions on the basis of priority rules tend to be good or are even local optimal, they generally do not guarantee good solutions for the overall problem. This is not surprising since on the basis of one priority rule, only one plan, i.e. schedule, out of the vast number of possible plans is selected. In this situation **biased sampling procedures** are considered. They perform the planning process several times and select activities not in a deterministic way but slightly biased. Hence, several solutions in the neighbourhood of the deterministic solution, i.e. the sample, are generated and the best one of these has - depending from the sample size - a fair chance of being better than the deterministic solution.

1.3 Chapter Synopsis

To cover the three outlined objectives, this work is divided into ten chapters: Chapters 1 gives an introduction to the treated topics. Chapters 2 - 4 provide the groundwork while Chapters 5 - 8 are devoted to heuristic algorithms for solving the problem classes introduced within Chapter 2. The Chapters 5 and 6 are the central ones of this work. Chapter 5 provides a detailed discussion and experimental investigation of different priority-rule-based solution techniques. Chapter 6 addresses a decomposition methodology which allows to tackle more general project scheduling problems. Chapters 7 and 8 serve to demonstrate how these ideas can be employed to solve related problems. Chapter 9 gives an outlook on the application of project scheduling to the management of production systems. Finally, conclusions are drawn in Chapter 10. More precisely:

Chapter 2 starts with a detailed introduction of the four components making up each project scheduling problem (PSP): resources, activities, precedence relations, and performance measures, i.e. optimality criteria. Thereafter, four different classes of the PSP are considered in detail: the single-mode project scheduling problem (SMPSP), the multi-mode project scheduling problem (MMPSP), the project scheduling problem with given deadline (PSPDL), and the project scheduling problem with setup times (PSPST). Each problem is outlined in terms of a verbal description and a formal 0-1 programming model, respectively. Furthermore, variants and special cases as well as complexity results are provided.

Chapter 3 is concerned with a classification of schedules, i.e. solutions, for project scheduling problems. A brief literature review shows that a precise classification does not exist for PSP's. On that account, formal definitions are derived which allow to classify schedules into feasible, semi-active, and non-delay schedules. The definitions are complemented by illustrative examples.

Chapter 4 is devoted to parameters for the characterisation of PSP's. Based on a thorough review of the relevant literature, parameters are taken over, are adapted, or are newly developed. As a result, a framework to generate benchmark instances for several problem classes of the PSP is developed which essentially relies on three concepts: a network construction procedure which is based on the definition of a network, the resource factor as a measure of the density of the coefficient matrix, and the resource strength expressing the degree of availability of the resources.

Chapter 5 tackles the most popular PSP, the single-mode project scheduling problem (SMPSP). At the beginning, a detailed up-to-date review of optimal and heuristic algorithms is provided. Afterwards, the chapter focuses on deterministic (single-pass) priority-rule-based heuristics which are introduced by a precise description of their two basic elements: scheduling schemes and priority rules. Based on the schedule classification derived in Chapter 3, deeper insight into these heuristics is gained. On account of a thorough investigation of one priority rule, two new priority rules are proposed. Then, alternative ways of altering the single-pass heuristics to biased random sampling approaches are presented. An in-depth computational study is performed which gives insight into the performance of scheduling schemes, priority rules, and sampling procedures w.r.t. different problem parameters. The conclusions drawn from the experimental results are then exploited in order to devise a hybrid solution procedure which is enhanced by lower bounding schemes. Finally, the new solution methodology is compared to heuristics recently supplied for the SMPSP.

Chapter 6 deals with a solution methodology for the probably most general and difficult PSP: the multi-mode project scheduling problem (MMPSP).

Again, a detailed and up-to-date review of exact and suboptimal procedures is given at the beginning. It makes clear that exact procedures can only solve very small instances while heuristic solution approaches quite often fail to generate feasible solutions. On account of the need for a good and reliable solution procedure, a new heuristic is proposed which consists of two parts: a local search procedure which assigns to each activity a mode, respectively, and the solution procedure for the SMPSP given in Chapter 5. An in-depth computational study is performed in order to tune the parameters of the new heuristic, to assess the performance w.r.t. different problem parameters, and to provide a comparison of suboptimal procedures recently proposed to solve the MMPSP.

Chapter 7 embodies the attempt to employ (parts) of the solution methodologies proposed in the two preceding chapters in order to solve the project scheduling problem with given deadline (PSPDL). A preliminary computational study is undertaken in order to assess the efficiency of the outlined solution approach.

In **Chapter 8** the heuristic for the SMPSP is extended to solve single-mode project scheduling problems with explicit consideration of setup times (PSPST). Again, only restricted computational results are presented.

Chapter 9 shows that the tools developed for PSP's are very much suited to tackle the problems which arise in the context of short-term production management. Especially, it is pointed out how models and methods of project scheduling play a vital role for two important modules of computer integrated manufacturing (CIM): Production planning and control (PPC) systems and so-called "electronic leitstand" or "Fertigungsleitstand" systems.

Finally, **Chapter 10** sketches out the main results and points out fields of further research.

Chapter 2

Description of the Problems

Chapter 2 provides in Section 2.1 the general assumptions and notations employed and introduces in Sections 2.2 - 2.5 four different problem classes of project scheduling problems. Each problem class is outlined in terms of a verbal description and a formal 0-1 programming model, respectively. Additionally, variants and special cases as well as complexity results are given.

2.1 Basic Notations and Definitions

Every project scheduling problem (PSP) consists of resources, activities, precedence relations, and performance measures (cf. Slowinski et al. (1991)). In the sequel, each component is introduced. It is assumed that all data needed is available, deterministic, and integer valued.

2.1.1 Resources

Scarce resources are classified along the following lines (cf. Blazewicz et al. (1986, p. 1) and Figure 2.1): **categories**, **types**, and **numbers**.

W.r.t. the **category**, resources are distinguished to be *renewable, nonrenewable* and *doubly constrained*:

Renewable resources are constrained on a period basis only. That is, regardless of the project length, each renewable resource is available for every single period (e.g. hour, day, shift, week, month). Examples are different sorts of machines, equipment, and manpower.

Nonrenewable resources are only limited w.r.t. the entire duration of the project. No limit for the consumption within one period is given. Examples are the capital budget of a project and overall pollution limits.

Finally, *doubly constrained resources* are limited on a period basis as well as on a project basis. Doubly constrained resources can be viewed as renewable resources which - dependent on the amount used within every period - are accessible for a limited number of periods only. Capital with restricted period cash flow and limited total cash is one example for a doubly constrained resource. Another one is a member of the project team, who can work only a limited number of periods on the project. Formally, each doubly constrained resource can be represented by one renewable and one nonrenewable resource, respectively, which has been shown by Talbot (1982). Hence, in the sequel doubly constrained resources are not considered as a separate resource category.

It should be quite clear that any categorisation of resources is not only a result of their nature but also depends on the practical situation at hand (cf. Slowinski (1980)). E.g., bricks for a housing project are renewable if a truckload is delivered for every period. Now, consider that there are two different types of bricks: a cheap type (small and heavy) and an expensive type (large and light). Naturally, the building progress is faster when the expensive type is employed. But due to the high price, only a limited amount of the expensive brick type can be used. Clearly, those bricks are - depending on the mode of delivery - a doubly constrained or nonrenewable resource.

W.r.t. the function to be fulfilled, each resource category can be distinguished in different **types**: For instance, the (category of) renewable resources can be classified into staff with different skills (e.g. civil engineers or bricklayers), machines with different functions (e.g. trucks and excavators) or dissimilar productivity (manual machines and numerically controlled machines) etc.

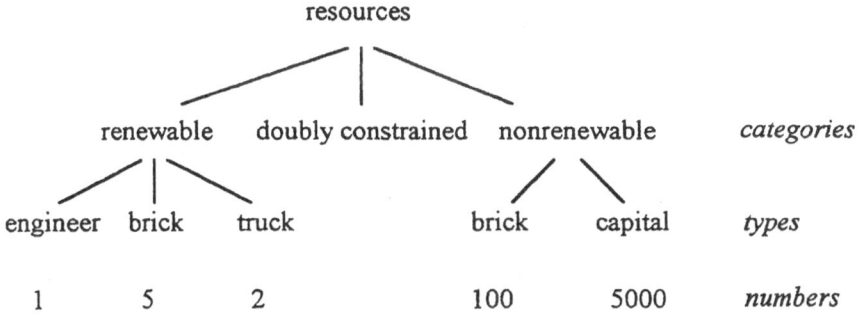

Figure 2.1: Classification of Resources

Finally, the **number** or amount of resources within each type is distinguished. E.g., in a housing project there are 1 civil engineer, 2 trucks, and 5 units bricks available per day while the overall amount of bricks is restricted to 100 units and the budget must not exceed 5000 units. Figure 2.1 displays the classification of resources.

For notational purposes the categories of renewable and nonrenewable resources are represented as the set R and N, respectively. Each element r of R or N denotes one resource type of the category under consideration. The number of type r resources available is indicated as K_r.

2.1.2 Activities

A project consists of a number of activities where synonymous terms are jobs, operations, and tasks.[1] In order to complete the project successfully, each activity has to be processed in one out of several modes, respectively.

---

[1] Generally, the term activities is used for project scheduling problems (cf. Moder et al. (1983) and Elmaghraby (1977)), the terms jobs and operations, respectively, are employed for (static) job shop and flow shop problems (cf. Baker (1974) and French (1982)), while tasks are referred to within processor scheduling (cf. Blazewicz et al. (1986, p. 229)).

Each mode stands for a different way of performing the activity under consideration. E.g., the activity "excavation" might be performed in three different modes: (*i*) by three workers in twenty days, (*ii*) by ten workers in five days, or (*iii*) by one worker and one excavator in five days.

The fact that the duration of an activity can be decreased at the expense of a larger resource demand is referred to as time-resource tradeoff (cf. Drexl / Kolisch (1993a) and Demeulemeester et al. (1993b)). The possibility to alter the resource types requested while keeping the duration constant is referred to as resource-resource tradeoff (cf. Drexl / Kolisch (1993a)). Hence, switching from mode (*i*) to mode (*ii*) is a time-resource tradeoff while changing mode (*ii*) to mode (*iii*) is a resource-resource tradeoff.

Associated with each mode of an activity is a *duration* measured in the number of periods, a *resource usage* w.r.t. every resource type of the renewable category measured in the number of resource units occupied during each period the activity is being processed, and a *resource consumption* w.r.t. each resource type of the nonrenewable category measured in the overall number of units consumed. Each activity is denoted with a unique activity label j. Thus, by beginning with the label $j=1$ and increasing it in steps of 1, the overall number of activities is J.

The number of modes for an activity j, $1 \le j \le J$, is denoted by M_j. Activity j, $1 \le j \le J$, performed in mode m, $1 \le m \le M_j$, has a nonpreemptable[2] duration of d_{jm} periods during which it requires k_{jmr} units of each resource type r out of category R. After activity j is completed, the k_{jmr} units are available to process another activity. Furthermore, activity j when processed in mode m consumes k_{jmr} units of each resource type r out of category N. Conse-

---

[2] It is assumed that once an activity is started, it has to be processed continuously until it is finished. Generally, preemption can be considered in two different ways: (*i*) In the discrete case, preemption is allowed at a priori defined points by splitting an activity into several subactivities with an integer duration of at least one period (cf. Davis / Heidorn (1971) and Remark 3.7). (*ii*) In the continuous case, preemption is allowed at any time moment, i.e. a continuous point in time (cf. Blazewicz et al. (1986, p. 163)).

quently, the number of available units is reduced by k_{jmr} units for the rest of the project. Without loss of generality it is assumed that the modes of each activity are sorted in the order of non-decreasing duration, i.e. $d_{j1} \leq d_{j2} \leq ... \leq d_{jM_j}$. This eases the notation for solution procedures which will be presented in the subsequent chapters.

2.1.3 Precedence Relations

Often technological reasons imply that some activities have to be accomplished before others can start.[3] This is handled by depicting the project as a directed graph where an activity is represented by a node and the precedence relation between two activities is represented by a directed arc.[4] Without loss of generality the graph has to meet the following requirements:

(i) It contains a dummy source, i.e. node $j=1$, without any predecessors and a dummy sink, i.e. node $j=J$, without any successors. The term "dummy" refers to the fact that both activities have only one associated mode with zero duration, zero resource usage, and consumption, respectively, i.e. $M_j=1$, $d_{j1}=0$, $k_{j1r}=0 \ \forall \ r \in R \cup N$, for $j \in \{1, J\}$.

Definition 2.1: Let $G=(V, A)$ be a graph with node set V and arc set A. An arc (h, j) is called **redundant**, if there are arcs $(i_0, i_1),...,(i_{s-1}, i_s) \in A$ with $i_0=h$, $i_s=j$ and $s \geq 2$.

(ii) In the sense of Definition 2.1, G does not contain redundant arcs.

---

[3] More elaborated temporal constraints to represent minimum and maximum time lags between starting times and / or completion times of any two activities (cf. Bartusch et al. (1988)) are not treated in here.

[4] Beside this activity-on-node (AON) representation, precedence relations can be depicted by the activity-on-arc (AOA) representation, which is not considered in here. Neither are the pros and cons of the two representations as well as the translation of AON to AOA networks subject of this work. For details refer to Elmaghraby (1977, p. 3), Kamburowski et al. (1993), Krishnamoorthy / Deo (1979), and Syslo (1984).

(*iii*) Finally, the nodes must be labelled in such a way that for every arc the tail-activity is always lower labelled than the head-activity. If the latter demand is met, the graph is called to be topologically ordered (cf. Moder et al. (1983, p. 121)).

For notational purposes, for each activity j, $1 \leq j \leq J$, four sets, i.e. P_j, the set of all immediate predecessors, S_j, the set of all immediate successors, $\bar{P}_j$, the set of all predecessors, and $\bar{S}_j$, the set of all successors are introduced.[5] An example of a project scheduling problem is provided by the network of Figure 2.2 and the data of Table 2.1, respectively.

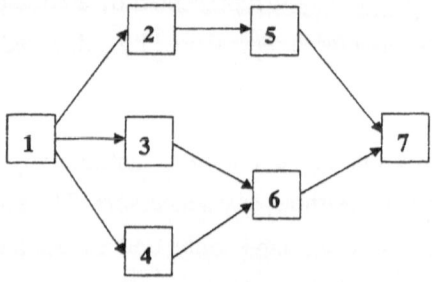

Figure 2.2: Network of a Project Scheduling Problem

j	1	2	3	4	5	6	7
m	1	1	2	1	1	2	1	1	2	1
d_{jm}	0	4	6	2	3	5	2	2	4	0
k_{jm1}	0	2	1	1	3	1	1	2	1	0
k_{jm2}	0	3	1	0	4	2	0	3	2	0

$R=\{1\}$, $N=\{2\}$, $K_1=4$, $K_2=8$

Table 2.1: Data of a Project Scheduling Problem

---

[5] Of course the following holds: $P_j \subseteq \bar{P}_j$ and $S_j \subseteq \bar{S}_j$ for all j, $1 \leq j \leq J$. E.g., w.r.t. the network depicted in Figure 2.2, associated with activity 3 are the sets $P_3=\bar{P}_3=\{1\}$, $S_3=\{6,\}$, and $\bar{S}_3=\{6,7\}$.

2.1.4 Performance Measures

Before continuing, the following definitions have to be introduced:

Definition 2.2: A **mode-assignment** M is a J-tuple $M=(\mu(1),...,\mu(J))$ which assigns to every activity j, $1 \leq j \leq J$, a unique mode $\mu(j)$, $1 \leq \mu(j) \leq M_j$.

Definition 2.3: A **schedule** S is a J-tuple $S=(FT_1,...,FT_J)$ which assigns to every activity j, $1 \leq j \leq J$, a unique finish time FT_j.

Definition 2.4: A **performance measure** is a mapping $\phi : (M,S) \rightarrow R_{\geq 0}$ which assigns to each tuple, viz. mode-assignment M and schedule S, a performance value $\phi(M,S)$.

Definition 2.5 (cf. Conway et al. (1967, p.12) and Rinnooy Kan (1976, p. 16)): If minimisation is considered and the performance measure ϕ monotonically increases w.r.t. component wise ordering of S, i.e. $\phi(FT_1,...,FT_J) > \phi(FT'_1,...,FT'_J)$ implies $FT_j \geq FT'_j$, $1 \leq j \leq J$, and $\exists j$: $1 \leq j \leq J, FT_j > FT'_j$, than ϕ is called a **regular performance measure**.

Using the definitions stated above, objectives, i.e. performance measures, can be classified as *regular* or *non-regular*. Probably the most frequently used (regular) objective for project scheduling problems is the minimisation of the makespan (cf. the vast literature which is partly reviewed in Chapters 5 and 6, respectively):

$$\text{minimise } FT_J \tag{2.1}$$

where the finish time of the sink J and thus of the entire project is minimised. The following reasons are advocating this objective (cf. Drexl / Kolisch (1993a)):

(*i*) The majority of income payments occurs at the end of the project. Hence, early finishing the project reduces the amount of tied-up capital.

(*ii*) The quality of forecasts tends to deteriorate with the distance into the future of the period for which they are made. Minimisation of the makespan reduces the planning horizon and thus the uncertainty of data.

(*iii*) Finishing the project as early as possible lowers the probability of violating the deadline. The latter will often result in the loss of good will as well as in penalty costs.

(*iv*) Finally, using resources as early as possible frees capacities in the future. This might be beneficial w.r.t. orders to come.

Another (regular) objective which plays a vital role within the (project) scheduling context is the minimisation of the mean flow time:

$$\text{minimise} \frac{1}{J\text{-}2} \sum_{j=2}^{J\text{-}2} FT_j \tag{2.2}$$

An example for a non-regular objective is the minimisation of the consumed amount of nonrenewable resources:

$$\text{minimise} \sum_{j=2}^{J\text{-}2} \sum_{r \in N} k_{j\mu(j)r} \tag{2.3}$$

Further regular and non-regular objectives for project scheduling problems can be found in Slowinski (1989), Patterson et al. (1989), Slowinski et al. (1991), and Domschke / Drexl (1991b).

Finally, Table 2.2 gives an overview of the notation introduced so far.

2.2 The Single-Mode Project Scheduling Problem

The single-mode project scheduling problem (SMPSP) arises when every activity j, $1 \leq j \leq J$, can be performed in one mode only, i.e. $M_j{=}1$, $1 \leq j \leq J$. Then, the overall consumption of resources is predetermined and solely the way resources are consumed over time pertains an open question. Since the classical SMPSP is exclusively concerned with the minimisation of the project's makespan, nonrenewable resources are not relevant any more and hence are not incorporated, i.e. $N=\emptyset$. For the sake of simplicity, the mode index m and the nonrenewable resource set N are omitted in the SMPSP.

Symbol	Definition
$j=1$ $(j=J)$	unique dummy source (sink)
ST_j	start time of activity j
FT_j	finish time of activity j
$S=(FT_1,...,FT_J)$	schedule
$M=(\mu(1),...,\mu(J))$	mode-assignment
P_j	set of immediate predecessors of activity j
$\bar{P}_j$	set of all predecessors of activity j
S_j	set of immediate successors of activity j
$\bar{S}_j$	set of all successors of activity j
$m=1,...,M_j$	modes of activity j
d_{jm}	(nonpreemptable) duration of activity j performed in mode m
$r \in R$	set of renewable resource types
$r \in N$	set of nonrenewable resource types
k_{jmr}	per period usage (overall consumption) of renewable (nonrenewable) resource r required to perform activity j in mode m
K_r	per period (overall) availability of renewable (nonrenewable) resource r

Table 2.2: Basic Symbols and Definitions

2.2.1 The Model

In order to set up a workable zero-one program for the SMPSP, earliest and latest finish times for each activity have to be calculated with a forward and backward recursive algorithm, respectively (cf. Domschke / Drexl

(1991a, p. 90)).[6] Using the end of period 0 as a starting point, the forward recursion (FR) determines for every activity its precedence-feasible earliest start and earliest finish time, respectively. More precisely, in the initialisation the earliest start and finish time of the dummy start activity is set to (the end of period) 0, respectively. Afterwards, the earliest start and finish times of the remaining J-1 activities are calculated in the order of the activity labels, respectively. The earliest start time for each activity j, $1 < j \leq J$, is determined as the maximum of the earliest finish times of all immediate predecessors of j. Then, the earliest finish time of activity j equals the earliest start time plus the duration of activity j.[7] Denoting the earliest start (finish) time of activity j, $1 \leq j \leq J$, with EST_j (EFT_j), FR can be described formally as follows:

$$\boxed{\text{FR}}$$

Initialisation: $EST_1 = EFT_1 := 0$;

FOR $j := 2$ TO J DO
BEGIN
  $EST_j := \max \{ EFT_i \mid i \in P_j \}$;
  $EFT_j := EST_j + d_j$;
END;

Stop: An earliest start and finish time has been calculated for every activity;

***

Given an upper bound T for the latest finish time of the entire project, the backward recursion (BR) determines precedence-feasible latest start and finish times for the activities. In detail, BR is initialised by setting the latest start and finish time of the unique sink to T. Afterwards, the latest finish and

---

[6] Note that in the literature the terms earliest and latest as well as early and late finish (start) times are used (cf. Moder et al. (1983, p. 74) and Talbot (1982)). Under the assumptions made, due to precedence constraints, no earlier (later) finish or start times exist when the project is started in $t=0$ or has to be finished at a pre-specified period. Hence, it is referred to "earliest" and "latest".

[7] Since the activities are topologically ordered, the earliest finish time of each activity preceding activity j, $1 < j \leq J$, is determined. Because of transitivity of the precedence relations, only the subset of immediate predecessors has to be considered.

start times of the remaining J-1 activities are calculated in the order of decreasing activity number, respectively. The latest finish time of activity j is set to the minimal latest start time of the immediate successor activities. Thereafter, the latest start time of activity j is calculated as the latest finish time minus the duration of activity j. Denoting LST_j (LFT_j) as the latest start (finish) time of activity j, $1 \leq j \leq J$, BR can be described formally as follows:

$$\boxed{\text{BR}}$$

Initialisation: $LFT_J = LST_J := T$;

FOR $j := J$-1 DOWNTO 1 DO
BEGIN
  $LFT_j := \min\{LST_i \mid i \in S_j\}$;
  $LST_j := LFT_j - d_j$;
END;

Stop: A latest start and finish time has been calculated for every activity;

***

In order to obtain the latest finish times for the zero-one program of the SMPSP, the upper bound T is set equal to a heuristically determined project's makespan.[8] Note that it is not necessary to calculate earliest and latest *start* times in order to derive the problem formulation. Nevertheless, earliest and latest *start* times are needed within the algorithms described in the subsequent chapters. Hence, the calculation of the latter is included in FR and BR, respectively.

To facilitate understanding, Table 2.3 provides the earliest and latest finish times which were obtained by applying FR and BR (with T=13) to the example problem introduced in Figure 2.2 and Table 2.1, respectively. Note that only the first mode of each activity was taken into consideration.

---

[8] A poor upper bound can always be derived by scheduling the activities in a serial fashion, i.e. $T = \sum_{j=1}^{J} d_j$.

j	1	2	3	4	5	6	7
EFT_j	0	4	2	3	6	5	6
LFT_j	7	11	11	11	13	13	13

Table 2.3: Earliest and Latest Finish Times of the SMPSP Example

The range $[EFT_j,...,LFT_j]$ can be interpreted as a time window (cf. Bartusch et al. (1988)) in which activity j, $1 \le j \le J$, has to be finished. Defining binary variables

$$x_{jt} = \begin{cases} 1, \text{ if activity } j \text{ is finished at the end of period } t \\ 0, \text{ otherwise} \end{cases}$$

as proposed by Pritsker et al. (1969), the following zero-one programming model for the SMPSP arises (cf. Patterson / Huber (1974) and Patterson / Roth (1976)):

$$\text{minimise } \phi_{SMPSP} = \sum_{t=EFT_J}^{LFT_J} t \, x_{Jt} \tag{2.4}$$

s.t.

$$\sum_{t=EFT_j}^{LFT_j} x_{jt} = 1 \qquad\qquad j=1,...,J \tag{2.5}$$

$$\sum_{t=EFT_i}^{LFT_i} t \, x_{it} \le \sum_{t=EFT_j}^{LFT_j} (t - d_j) \, x_{jt} \qquad\qquad j=2,...,J, i \in P_j \tag{2.6}$$

$$\sum_{j=1}^{J} k_{jr} \sum_{\tau=t}^{t+d_j-1} x_{j\tau} \le K_r \qquad\qquad r \in R, t=1,...,T \tag{2.7}$$

$$x_{jt} \in \{0,1\} \qquad\qquad j=1,...,J, t=EFT_j,...,LFT_j \tag{2.8}$$

The objective function (2.4) minimises the completion time of the unique sink and thus the makespan of the project. Constraint set (2.5) assures that to each activity a unique finish time within its time window is assigned. Constraints (2.6) take into consideration the precedence relations between each pair of activities (i, j), where i immediately precedes j. Finally, constraint set (2.7) limits the total resource usage within each period to the available amount.

Note the difference between time and period: Activity j, $1 \leq j \leq J$, with start time ST_j and finish time FT_j is scheduled in periods $ST_j+1,...,ST_j+d_j=FT_j$. E.g., in Figure 2.3 activity 3 with $ST_3=0$ and $FT_3=2$ is scheduled in periods one and two.

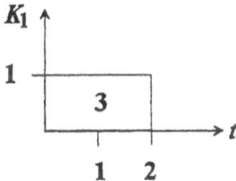

Figure 2.3: Relationship Between Time and Period

An optimal schedule for the SMPSP example (i.e. Figure 2.2 and Table 2.1, respectively, with $M_j=1$, $1 \leq j \leq J$, and $N=\emptyset$) is given in Table 2.4 and illustrated by Figure 2.4.

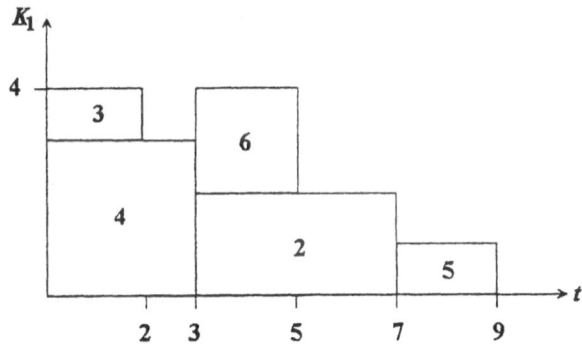

Figure 2.4: Optimal Solution of the SMPSP Example

j	1	2	3	4	5	6	7
FT_j	0	7	2	3	9	5	9

Table 2.4: Optimal Solution of the SMPSP Example

2.2.2 Variants and Special Cases

Two models associated with (2.4) to (2.8) are worth mentioning, to wit:

(*i*) Altering (2.7) to

$$\sum_{j=1}^{J} \sum_{\tau=t}^{t+d_j-1} k_{jr(d_j-\tau+t)} \, x_{j\tau} \leq K_{rt} \qquad\qquad r \in R, \, t=1,...,T \qquad (2.9)$$

gives way to the time-varying resource-supply / resource-demand case where K_{rt}, the number of renewable resources of type r available, is a function of the period t ,$1 \leq t \leq T$, and k_{jrt}, the number of renewable resources of type r occupied by activity j, varies for every period t, $1 \leq t \leq d_j$, of the entire duration d_j.

(*ii*) By relaxing the resource-constraints (2.7), the SMPSP reduces to the CPM-case (cf. Davis (1966)) for which the forward recursion provides an optimal solution in polynomial time.

The SMPSP is a generalisation of the classical static job shop problem (JSP). The JSP is the subject of considerable study and is, being *NP*-hard, one of the most difficult scheduling problems (cf. Barker / McMahon (1985) and Brucker et al. (1992)). Since the relationship of SMPSP and JSP plays a vital role in solution procedures for the SMPSP, it is examined in more detail:

The JSP originates from the scheduling problem arising in make-to-order companies where - on a short-term basis - a number of A jobs have to be processed through B different machines. Each of the machines is capable of processing at most one job at a time. Additionally, each job must pass each machine exactly once. The processing of a job on a machine is called an operation. Hence, each job a, $1 \leq a \leq A$, can be decomposed into $(a,1),...,(a,b),...,(a,B)$ operations. Due to the (job-)specific processing order, operation (a,b) has to be processed on machine $l(a,b)$ for $p(a,b)$ periods. The objective of the JSP is to finish the latest job as early as possible.

It has been shown by Schrage (1970), Baker (1974), Stinson (1976), Drexl (1990), and Sprecher (1994) that the SMPSP can be reduced to a JSP as follows: The number of activities equals the number of operations plus one dummy source and one dummy sink. To each operation (a,b), $1 \leq a \leq A$, $1 \leq b \leq B$, one activity j, $1 < j < J$, is assigned as follows: $j=(a-1) \cdot B+b+1$. The processing order of the operations is ensured by the precedence relations where for every activity j, $1 < j < J$, the only predecessor (successor) represents the preceding (succeeding) operation of the job under consideration. Furthermore, every machine is modelled via one (renewable) resource type with one available unit, i.e. $R=\{1,...,B\}$ and $K_r=1 \ \forall \ r \in R$. Finally, every activity j, $1 < j < J$, uses one unit of resource $r=l(a,b)$ for every period of its duration $d_j=p(a,b)$. On account of the fact that the SMPSP is a generalisation of the NP-hard JSP, it also belongs to the class of NP-hard problems (cf. Blazewicz et al. (1983)).

Two special cases of the JSP and consequently of the SMPSP are the flow shop problem (FSP) and the permutation flow shop problem (PFSP) (cf. French (1982, p. 14) and Potts et al. (1991)). For both problems - additionally to the assumptions already made for the JSP - every job has the same processing order. Furthermore, for the PFSP passing of jobs is permitted, i.e. every machine has to process the jobs in the same (a priori unknown) order. In addition, the SMPSP is a generalisation of many other scheduling problems addressed in the literature, e.g. a variety of single and parallel machine problems (cf. Baker (1974)) as well as open shop problem (cf. Sprecher (1994)).

The broad applicability of the SMPSP is further demonstrated by translating the bin-packing problem and the 2-dimensional packing / cutting stock problem into the SMPSP as well as by showing the strong analogy between the SMPSP and assembly line balancing.

The bin-packing problem (BP) can be stated as follows (cf. Garey / Johnson (1979)): Given a finite set $U=\{u_1,...,u_n\}$ of "items" and a rational "size" $s(u) \in Z^+$ for each item $u \in U$, find a partition of U into disjoint subsets $U_1,...,U_k$ such that the sum of the sizes of the items in each U_i, $1 \leq i \leq k$, is no more than C and k is as small as possible, i.e. the number of bins needed to accommodate the items is minimal. BP can be modelled in terms of the SMPSP as follows (cf. Garey et al. (1976)): Consider one renewable resource type where the number of resources equals the unique bin capacity C, each activity j, $1 < j < J$, represents one item u with duration 1 and the resource usage equals the size of the item $s(u)$. Furthermore, in the project graph each activity must have the sink ($j=1$) as unique predecessor and the source ($j=J$) as unique successor, i.e. there are no precedence relations between any pair of activities (i, j), $1 < i, j < J$, $i \neq j$. Then, the solution of the SMPSP (i.e. the makespan) yields the number of bins needed.

The 2-dimensional cutting stock problem (cf. Dyckhoff (1990)) can be formulated as follows: Given a finite set $U=\{u_1,...,u_n\}$ of rectangular "items" with length $l(u) \in Z^+$ and width $w(u) \in Z^+$ and a stock object of width W, find a pattern to cut the items out of the object such that the length L of the object needed is minimised. This problem can be represented as SMPSP in the following way (cf. Schrage (1970)): Consider one renewable resource type where the number of resources equals the object width W. Each activity j, $1 < j < J$, represents one item u with duration $l(u)$ and resource usage $w(u)$. In the project graph each activity must have the sink ($j=1$) as unique predecessor and the source ($j=J$) as unique successor, i.e. there are no precedence relations between any pair of activities (i, j), $1 < i, j < J$, $i \neq j$. The solution of the SMPSP (i.e. the makespan) now equals the length of the object needed.

The assembly line balancing problem (ALB) can be stated as follows (cf. Elmaghraby (1977)): Given a cycle time c, a set of tasks $\{1,...,i,...,I\}$ to be performed according to precedence relations; and given the processing time t_i of task i, find an assignment of the tasks to stations (where only one task can be processed at a time) so that: (*i*) each station consumes no more time than the cycle time c, (*ii*) the precedence relations are respected, and (*iii*) the number of stations is minimised.

The following analogy between the ALB and the SMPSP was pointed out by Elmaghraby (1977): within the SMPSP there is one (renewable) resource type with c units available per period. Each task of the ALB corresponds to one activity of the SMPSP with unit-time-duration and resource usage t_i while precedence relations of activities equal the ones of tasks. Furthermore, periods of the SMPSP correspond to stations of the ALB. Hence, by reducing the makespan of the SMPSP, the number of stations needed within the ALB is reduced as well.

The major difference between the ALB and the SMPSP is the fact that two tasks i, j, with i immediately preceding j, can be placed in the same station within the ALB whereas in the SMPSP the two corresponding activities cannot be scheduled in the same period (cf. Wee / Magazine (1982) and Davis (1973)). Sprecher (1994) showed that the ALB can be transformed into a SMPSP with time-varying resource-supply.

2.3 The Multi-Mode Project Scheduling Problem

2.3.1 The Model

The time-windows for the multi-mode project scheduling problem (MMPSP) are calculated with the forward and backward recursive algorithm as introduced above for the SMPSP with the following minor modification (cf. Talbot (1982)): To each activity j, $1 < j < J$, the mode with the smallest duration is assigned, i.e. $\mu(j){=}1$, $1 < j < J$.

Introducing the binary decision variables:

$$x_{jmt} = \begin{cases} 1, & \text{if activity } j \text{ is scheduled in mode } m \text{ to finish at the end of period } t \\ 0, & \text{otherwise} \end{cases}$$

the MMPSP can be formulated as follows (cf. Talbot (1982)):

$$\text{minimise } \phi_{MMPSP} = \sum_{t=EFT_J}^{LFT_J} t\, x_{J1t} \tag{2.10}$$

s.t.

$$\sum_{m=1}^{M_j} \sum_{t=EFT_j}^{LFT_j} x_{jmt} = 1 \qquad\qquad j=1,...,J \tag{2.11}$$

$$\sum_{m=1}^{M_i} \sum_{t=EFT_i}^{LFT_i} t\, x_{imt} \leq \sum_{m=1}^{M_j} \sum_{t=EFT_j}^{LFT_j} (t - d_{jm})\, x_{jmt} \qquad j=2,...,J,\, i \in P_j \tag{2.12}$$

$$\sum_{j=1}^{J} \sum_{m=1}^{M_j} k_{jmr} \sum_{\tau=t}^{t+d_{jm}-1} x_{jm\tau} \leq K_r \qquad\qquad r \in R,\, t=1,...,T \tag{2.13}$$

$$\sum_{j=1}^{J} \sum_{m=1}^{M_j} k_{jmr} \sum_{t=EFT_j}^{LFT_j} x_{jmt} \leq K_r \qquad\qquad r \in N \tag{2.14}$$

$$x_{jmt} \in \{0,1\} \qquad j=1,...,J,\, m=1,...,M_j,\, t=EFT_j,...,LFT_j \tag{2.15}$$

Using the upper bound $T = \sum_{j=2}^{J-1} d_{jM_j}$, the time windows for the MMPSP example problem of Section 2.1 are as presented in Table 2.5.

Again, the objective function (2.10) minimises the makespan of the project. Constraint set (2.11) ensures that to each activity exactly one mode is assigned as well as a unique completion time in its time window. Constraints (2.12) represent the precedence relations. The period capacity of the renewable resource types is maintained by constraint set (2.13). Finally, the constraints associated with (2.14) limit the total resource consumption of nonrenewable resources to the available amount. An optimal solution of the example problem is provided in Table 2.6 and by Figure 2.5, respectively. For the latter, the number in brackets stands for the mode $\mu(j)$ activity j is performed in.

j	1	2	3	4	5	6	7
EFT_j	0	4	2	3	6	5	6
LFT_j	13	17	17	17	19	19	19

Table 2.5: Time Windows of the MMPSP Example[9]

j	1	2	3	4	5	6	7
$\mu(j)$	1	1	1	2	1	1	1
FT_j	0	4	2	5	6	7	7

Table 2.6: Optimal Solution of the MMPSP Example

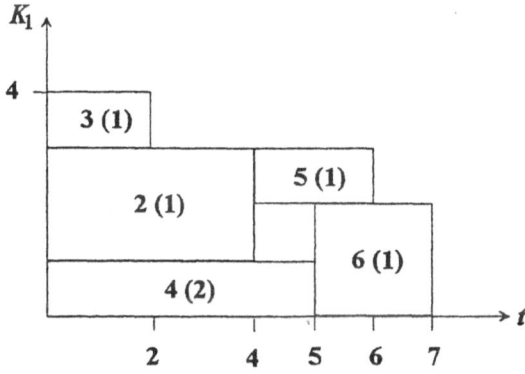

Figure 2.5: Gantt-Chart of the Optimal Solution of the MMPSP Example

---

[9] Note that since the modes are ordered by non-decreasing duration, the earliest finish times of the MMPSP example match those of the SMPSP, while the latest finish times of the MMPSP equal the latest finish times of the SMPSP example plus the difference between the upper bound of MMPSP and SMPSP, i.e. here 19-13=6.

2.3.2 Complexity Results

The MMPSP has the great benefit of representing different ways to perform a certain activity, i.e. the modes. Incorporating different modes into a given problem setting enlarges the solution space (cf. Ahn / Kusiak (1991) and Li / Willis (1991)) which gives way to possible better solutions. But at the same time the problem becomes much more difficult. In fact, the multimode problem is probably the most general and thus the most difficult (project) scheduling problem. As a generalisation of the SMPSP it belongs to the class of NP-hard problems. In fact, the feasibility problem of the MMPSP is already NP-complete. To prove this, the multi-mode problem is decomposed into two subproblems: the mode-assignment problem (MAP) and the SMPSP. Introducing the binary decision variables

$$x_{jm} = \begin{cases} 1, & \text{if mode } m \text{ is assigned to activity } j \\ 0, & \text{otherwise} \end{cases}$$

the MAP can be stated as follows:

Is there a feasible mode-assignment $M = (\mu(1),...,\mu(J))$, i.e. a vector of variables x_{jm} such that constraints (2.16) - (2.18) hold?

$$\sum_{m=1}^{M_j} x_{jm} = 1 \qquad\qquad\qquad j=1,...,J \qquad (2.16)$$

$$\sum_{j=1}^{J} \sum_{m=1}^{M_j} k_{jmr}\, x_{jm} \leq K_r \qquad\qquad r \in N \qquad (2.17)$$

$$x_{jm} \in \{0,1\} \qquad\qquad j=1,...,J,\, m=1,...,M_j \qquad (2.18)$$

Constraint set (2.16) assures that to each activity exactly one mode is assigned while the constraints (2.17) limit the overall consumption of nonrenewable resources to the available amount.

Theorem 2.1: The MAP is NP-complete for $|N| \geq 2$ and $M_j \geq 2$, $1 < j < J$.

Proof: The MAP is in NP since the feasibility of any mode-assignment $M=(\mu(1),...,\mu(J))$ can obviously be checked in polynomial time. To prove that the MAP is NP-complete, the knapsack problem, which is known to be NP-complete (cf. Garey / Johnson (1979, p. 247)), is polynomially transformed into the MAP.

The knapsack problem can be stated as follows: Given a finite set U with elements u, $1 \le u \le |U|$, a size $s(u) \in Z^+$, a value $v(u) \in Z^+$, for each $u \in U$, a size B and a size D, is there a subset $U' \subseteq U$ such that (i) $\sum_{u \in U'} s(u) \le B$ and (ii) $\sum_{u \in U'} v(u) \ge D$?

The transformation of a knapsack problem into the MAP is straightforward: Each non-dummy activity representing one element out of U has two modes, respectively, i.e. $J =|U|+2$, $M_j =2$, $1 < j < J$, and $M_j =1$, $j \in \{1,J\}$. The activities to which the first mode has been assigned, respectively, represent the elements in the subset U'. Furthermore, the two constraints of knapsack are depicted by two nonrenewable resource constraints, i.e. $|N| =2$. The first constraint can be employed straightforward. Hence, w.r.t. resource $r=1$, the availability is $K_1 =B$, and the resource consumption of the first (second) mode equals $k_{j11} =s(u)$ ($k_{j21} =0$), $1 < j < J$. The second knapsack-constraint has to be converted to the type "$\le$" by multiplying it with "-1" and adding $|U| \cdot \max \{v(u)|u \in U\}$ to each side. Hence, w.r.t. resource $r=2$, the availability is $K_2 =|U| \cdot \max \{v(u)|u \in U\}-D$, while the resource consumption of the first mode is $k_{j12} =\max\{v(u)|u \in U\}-v(u)$ and the resource consumption of the second mode comes up to $k_{j22} = \max\{v(u)|u \in U\}$, $1 < j < J$. Consequently, each instance of the knapsack problem can be transformed to an instance of the MAP. A solution of the latter re-translates to a solution of the further as follows: If the first mode has been assigned to activity j, $1 < j < J$, i.e. $\mu(j)=1$, the corresponding u is in U'. This proves the NP-completeness of the MAP (and hence of the feasibility problem of the the MMPSP). ∎

2.4 The Project Scheduling Problem with Given Deadline

An important issue within project scheduling are deadlines. Quite often a specific project has to be finished by a certain deadline (*DL*) since otherwise penalty costs may become due and good will of customers might be lost. Therefore, the most important goal of the project manager is to finish the project in time. Because both the SMPSP and the MMPSP are minimising the makespan of a project, solution procedures for them automatically create schedules which consider the deadline. However, a (new) problem arises when the best (or even the optimal) makespan exceeds the deadline. In this case the only way to finish the project in time is to cover peak resource demands of an in-time schedule by temporarily employing more resources. Additional capacity of such an in-time schedule can be supplied by either (*i*) working overtime or (*ii*) by subcontracting part of the resource demand (cf. Dervitiotis (1981)).

Assuming that an additional unit of the renewable resource r provided in period t is available at the cost of c_r and additionally is limited to o_r percent of the regular period capacity K_r, the objective is to find a feasible project schedule which satisfies the deadline and is associated with the least additional costs. This problem has been termed by Deckro / Hebert (1989) as project crashing problem. In here it is referred to as project scheduling problem with given deadline (PSPDL). While Deckro and Hebert modelled the single-mode case of the PSPDL, in the following the multi-mode version of the PSPDL will be discussed.

Using the notation summarised in Table 2.7, employing the binary variables of the MMPSP (x_{jmt} =1 if activity j is scheduled in mode m to finish at the end of period t, 0 otherwise) and setting $T=DL$, the following model arises:

$$\text{minimise } \phi_{PSPDL} = \sum_{r \in R} c_r \sum_{t=1}^{T} O_{rt} \tag{2.19}$$

s.t.

$$\sum_{m=1}^{M_j} \sum_{t=EFT_j}^{LFT_j} x_{jmt} = 1 \qquad\qquad j=1,...,J \tag{2.20}$$

$$\sum_{m=1}^{M_i} \sum_{t=EFT_i}^{LFT_i} t\, x_{imt} \leq \sum_{m=1}^{M_j} \sum_{t=EFT_j}^{LFT_j} (t - d_j)\, x_{jmt} \qquad\qquad j=2,...,J, i \in P_j \tag{2.21}$$

$$\sum_{j=1}^{J} \sum_{m=1}^{M_j} k_{jmr} \sum_{\tau=t}^{t+d_j-1} x_{jm\tau} \leq K_r + O_{rt} \qquad\qquad r \in R, t=1,...,T \tag{2.22}$$

$$O_{rt} \leq o_r K_r \qquad\qquad r \in R, t=1,...,T \tag{2.23}$$

$$x_{jmt} \in \{0,1\} \qquad j=1,...,J, m=1,...,M_j, t=EFT_j,...,LFT_j \tag{2.24}$$

$$O_{rt} \geq 0 \qquad\qquad r \in R, t=1,...,T \tag{2.25}$$

Symbol	Definition
DL	deadline of the project
O_{rt}	number of additional (renewable) resources of type r used in period t
o_r	factor limiting the amount of additional resources of type r to o_r percent of the regular per period availability of the (renewable) resource type r
c_r	cost per additional unit of the (renewable) resource r

Table 2.7: Additional Symbols and Definitions for the PSPDL

The objective function (2.19) minimises the cost caused by the use of additional capacity; constraint set (2.22) limits the availability of renewable resources to the sum of regular and additional capacity. Finally, additional capacity is restricted in constraint set (2.23) to a certain percentage of the number of regular resources. For the sake of simplicity nonrenewable resources were not incorporated into the PSPDL. Doing so, i.e. introducing the type of constraint as stated in (2.14), does not pose any modelling problems but renders the problems even more difficult.

Two problems related to the PSPDL are (i) the minimisation of the total cost associated by providing $K_r(1+o_r)$ units of each renewable resource (cf. Möhring (1984), Demeulemeester (1992)) and (ii) the minimisation of the variance of the resource demand in the case of unlimited resources availability (cf. Burgess / Killebrew (1962), Woodworth / Willie (1975)).

Of course, the PSPDL being a generalisation of the SMPSP is NP-hard. In fact, the following can be stated:

Theorem 2.2: The feasibility problem of the PSPDL is NP-complete.

Proof: By reduction of the PSPDL to the SMPSP, i.e. setting $M_j = 1$, $1 < j < J$, and posing the question, is there is a feasible schedule with makespan smaller or equal DL w.r.t. the maximum amount of renewable resources, i.e. $K_r(1+ o_r) \ \forall \ r \in R$.   ■

To illustrate the PSPDL, consider the example problem provided in Section 2.1 where only one renewable resource is taken into account, i.e. $R=\{1\}$ and $N=\varnothing$. Additionally, assume that a deadline exists at the end of period 6, i.e. $DL =6$. Capacity units in excess of the regular capacity of $K_1 =4$ cost $c_1 =1$ per period and unit and are limited to 50%, i.e. $o_1 =0.5$, of the regular capacity. Solving (2.19) to (2.25) of the example with LINDO (cf. Schrage (1991)) to optimality generates the solution presented in Table 2.8 and 2.9 as well as Figure 2.6. The optimal objective function value is $\phi^*_{PSPDL}=4$, i.e. an additional cost of 4 units will be due to meet the deadline.

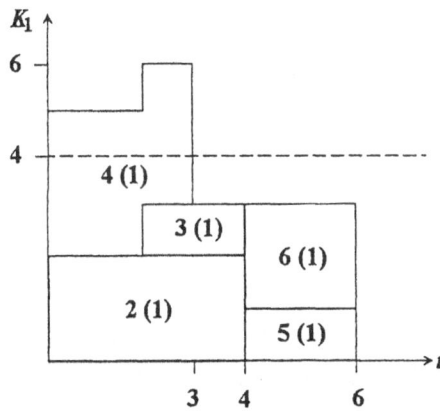

Figure 2.6: Optimal Solution of the PSPDL Example

j	1	2	3	4	5	6	7
$\mu(j)$	1	1	1	1	1	1	1
FT_j	0	4	4	3	6	6	6

Table 2.8: Optimal Solution of the Example - Modes and Finish Times

t	1	2	3	4	5	6
O_{1t}	1	1	2	0	0	0

Table 2.9: Optimal Solution of the Example - Additional Resource Units

2.5 The Project Scheduling Problem with Setup Times

Up to now it has been implicitly assumed that for the SMPSP the duration d_j of an activity j reflects setup (s_j) and processing time (p_j), i.e. $d_j=s_j+p_j$. This is a common assumption (cf. Rinnooy Kan (1976)) which does not have major drawbacks as long as setup times are small compared to processing times. But if some activities require the same (considerable) setup, the makespan can be reduced by batching these activities. In this case, modelling and solving such a problem as SMPSP might produce poor solutions.

Examples of setup times for project scheduling problems are abundant. E.g., for construction projects, excavators need to be equipped with different types of scoops in order to perform certain classes of activities. Heavy equipment in general (e.g. trucks, cranes, excavators) might be requested at different construction sites. Moving them from one site to the other can be viewed as a setup time. Examples of setup times for scheduling problems within production and operations management are provided by Conway et al. (1967, p. 53) and Monma / Potts (1989). Conway et al. give the example of producing different colours on the same machine where setup times occur for cleaning the machine. Monma and Potts report on flexible manufacturing systems (FMS), where rearranging and retooling is necessary before switching between different product types.

Thus, it is quite clear that considering setup times for project scheduling might be very important. Hence, in the sequel a zero-one programming formulation for a single-mode setup problem is presented. It applies the multi-mode concept in order to represent two modes for every activity: processing including and excluding setup. The crucial point is that these two modes differ only w.r.t. the duration of the activities while the resource usage is identical. Consequently, the mode index is included only for the duration.

The following is assumed: The set of renewable resources which have to be in an appropriate setup-state in order to process an activity are called setup-resources, denoted as R^S. Each setup-resource is available with one unit per period only, i.e. $K_r=1 \ \forall \ r \in R^S$, and can therefore process only one activity at a time. Correspondingly, each activity can at most use one setup-resource. The activities which have to be processed on setup-resource r altogether require r in $u=1,...,U_r$ different setup-states.[10] The information which setup-

---

[10] Note that the following holds: $U_r \leq \sum_{j=2}^{J-1} \sum_{r \in R^S} k_{jr} \leq J\text{-}2$, i.e. the number of setup-states required on setup-resource type r is bounded from above by the number of activities using resource r, which can be at most the overall number of non-dummy activities.

state on a setup-resource is required to perform a certain activity is provided by extending the notation of resource usage k_{jr} to[11]

$$k_{jru} = \begin{cases} 1, & \text{if activity } j \text{ has to be performed on setup-resource } r \text{ in setup-state } u \\ 0, & \text{otherwise} \end{cases}$$

For each activity j, $1 < j < J$, to be processed on a setup-resource r, i.e. $k_{jr} > 0$, $r \in R^S$, two modes are considered: mode $m=1$ represents processing only while mode $m=2$ stands for setup *and* processing. Table 2.10 provides the additional notation introduced for the project scheduling problem with setup times (PSPST).

Symbol	Definition
R^S	set of renewable resources where a setup is necessary
$u=1,...,U_r$	setup-states of setup-resource r
k_{jru}	1, if activity j has to be performed on setup-resource r in state u

Table 2.10: Additional Symbols and Definitions for the PSPST

In order to illustrate the multi-mode concept within the PSPST we present the following example with two types of setup-resources, the first one with 1 and the second one with 2 setup-states, i.e. $R^S=\{1,2\}$, $U_1=1$, and $U_2=2$. The project graph is as already depicted in Figure 2.2 while all other data is provided by Table 2.11.

---

[11] Of course the following holds: $k_{jr} = \sum_{u=1}^{U_r} k_{jru}$, i.e. if activity j requires setup-resource r, then it does so in exactly one of the $u=1,...,U_r$ setup states of r.

j	1	2	3	4	5	6	7
m	1	1 2	1 2	1 2	1 2	1 2	1
d_{jm}	0	3 4	1 2	2 3	1 2	1 2	0
k_{j11}	0	1	0	0	0	1	0
k_{j21}	0	0	1	0	1	0	0
k_{j22}	0	0	0	1	0	0	0
			$R^S=\{1,2\}$, $U_1=1$, $U_2=2$, $K_1=K_2=1$				

Table 2.11: Example for the PSPST

The fact that the two modes of activities to be performed on a setup-resource do only differ w.r.t. the duration would - within the context of the MMPSP - imply that mode 1 dominates mode 2 and hence should always be selected. In contrast, for the PSPST the choice of modes is controlled via the setup-state of the setup-resources. Defining the continuous variables

$$y_{rut} = \begin{cases} 1, & \text{if setup-resource } r \text{ has the setup-state } u \text{ at the end of period } t \\ \neq 1, & \text{otherwise} \end{cases}$$

and recalling the zero-one decision variables of the MMPSP ($x_{jmt} = 1$ if activity j is scheduled in mode m to finish at the end of period t and 0 otherwise) the PSPST can be modelled as follows:

$$\text{minimise } \phi_{PSPST} = \sum_{t=EFT_J}^{LFT_J} t\, x_{J1t} \tag{2.26}$$

s.t.

$$\sum_{m=1}^{M_j} \sum_{t=EFT_j}^{LFT_j} x_{jmt} = 1 \qquad\qquad j=1,...,J \tag{2.27}$$

$$\sum_{m=1}^{M_i} \sum_{t=EFT_i}^{LFT_i} t\, x_{imt} \leq \sum_{m=1}^{M_j} \sum_{t=EFT_j}^{LFT_j} (t - d_{jm})\, x_{jmt} \qquad j=2,...,J, i \in P_j \tag{2.28}$$

$$\sum_{j=1}^{J} \sum_{m=1}^{M_j} k_{jr} \sum_{\tau=t}^{t+d_{jm}-1} x_{jmt} \leq K_r \qquad\qquad r \in R \cup R^S,\ t=1,...,T \qquad (2.29)$$

$$k_{jru}\, x_{j1(t+d_{j1})} \leq y_{rut} \qquad\qquad j=1,...,J,\ r \in R^S,\ u=1,...,U_r,\ t=0,...,T \qquad (2.30)$$

$$y_{rut} \leq y_{ru(t-1)} + \sum_{j=1}^{J} k_{jru}\, x_{j2(t+d_{j2})} \qquad r \in R^S,\ u=1,...,U_r,\ t=0,...,T \qquad (2.31)$$

$$\sum_{\substack{s=1 \\ s \neq u}}^{U_r} y_{rst} + \sum_{j=1}^{J} k_{jru}\, x_{j2(t+d_{j2})} \leq 1 \qquad r \in R^S,\ u=1,...,U_r,\ t=0,...,T \qquad (2.32)$$

$$x_{jmt} \in \{0,1\} \qquad\qquad j=1,...,J,\ m=1,...,M_j,\ t=EFT_j,...,LFT_j \qquad (2.33)$$

$$0 \leq y_{rut} \leq 1 \qquad\qquad r \in R^S,\ u=1,...,U_r,\ t=0,...,T \qquad (2.34)$$

The objective function (2.26) and constraint sets (2.27) to (2.29) are as presented for the MMPSP. Note that the constraints (2.29) hold for all types of renewable resources, i.e. for standard renewable resources as well as for setup-resources. Management of setup-states and the choice of modes is controlled by constraint sets (2.30) to (2.32). More precisely, (2.30) ensures that activity j, $1 < j < J$, in mode $m=1$, i.e. without setup, can be started in period t and finished in period $t+d_{j1}$ only if the required setup-resource r is in the appropriate setup-state in period t. Otherwise, (2.30) together with (2.27) causes that mode $m=2$, i.e. setup *and* processing, has to be performed.

Constraint set (2.31) represents the dynamic setup-state balance equation for each setup-resource, respectively. It has to be recalled that the objective function is seeking the shortest makespan and hence (generally) tries to schedule activities in the shortest mode. This forces setup-resources to be in the appropriate setup-state whenever possible, i.e. $y_{rut}=1$, $r \in R^S$, $u=1,...,U_r$, $t=0,...,T$. Thus, the setup-state u of setup-resource r at the end of period t is $y_{rut}=1$ if the setup-state at the end of the (prior) period $t-1$ equals 1 or an activity j, $1 < j < J$, in mode $m=2$ with $k_{jru}=1$ is scheduled to begin in t and to end in $t+d_{j2}$, i.e. a setup u takes place in t.

Finally, the constraints (2.32) guarantee that if the start of an activity j, $1 < j < J$, in mode $m=2$ implies a setup u on setup-resource r in period t, any former setup-state $s \neq u$ of setup-resource r at the end of period t is cancelled.

It should be quite clear that the PSPST as a generalisation of the SMPSP belongs to the class of *NP*-hard problems.

Solving (2.26) to (2.34) for the instance depicted in Table 2.11 with LINDO to optimality yields the solution presented in Tables 2.12 and 2.13, which is illustrated in Figure 2.7.

j	1	2	3	4	5	6	7
$\mu(j)$	1	2	2	2	1	1	1
FT_j	0	4	5	3	6	6	6

Table 2.12: Optimal Schedule for the PSPST Example

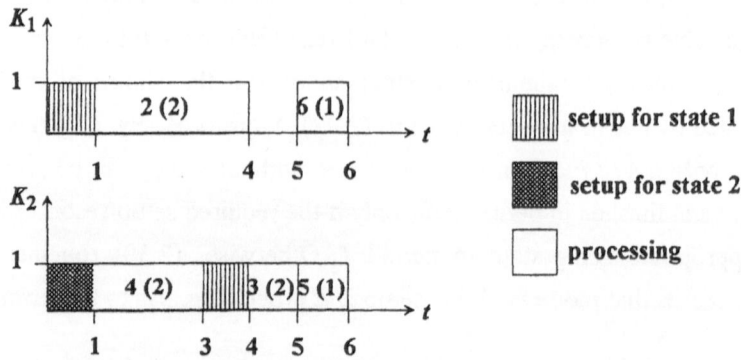

Figure 2.7: Optimal Solution of the PSPST Example

t	0	1	2	3	4	5	6
y_{11t}	0	1	1	1	1	1	1
y_{21t}	0	0	0	0	1	1	1
y_{22t}	0	1	1	1	0	0	0

Table 2.13: Setup-States of the Optimal Schedule for the PSPST Example

Four comments on the model seem to be in place:

(*i*) Note that the difference between the period index of (2.29) and the other constraint sets results from the different definitions of periods for resources and setup-states: While resources are managed within periods, setup-states are accounted for at the end of periods.

(*ii*) If PSPST is used within a rolling planning environment, the setup-states at the end of period "0" have to be initialised appropriately.

(*iii*) The complexity of the PSPST (in terms of the number of required binary variables) increases only by introducing a second mode for those activities which require a setup-resource and not by the introduction of the continuous setup-state variable y_{rut}.

(*iv*) By using the setup-state variable y_{rut}, idle periods do not alter the setup-state. E.g., in the solution provided above the setup-resource $r=1$ is put into setup-state 1 by activity 2 at the end of period 1. This setup-state is maintained even after activity 2 is finished at the end of period 4 and the setup-resource is idle in period 5. Thus, no setup is necessary to process activity 6 in period 6.

Of course the model presented can be generalised to the (real) multi-mode version. Considering setup times doubles the number of operating modes for each activity requiring a setup, respectively.

Chapter 3

Classification of Schedules

Based on the notion of a schedule introduced in Chapter 2, this chapter presents a classification of schedules for project scheduling problems. While classification of schedules has been undertaken for the job shop problem (JSP) (cf. Baker (1974)), no systematic efforts are reported for project scheduling problems. Hence, based on the (informal) definitions given by Baker (1974) for the JSP, more precise and formal definitions are derived for the SMPSP and thus for the JSP, too. It has to be stressed that the schedule classification for the SMPSP covers multi-mode project scheduling problems (like the MMPSP and the PSPDL) as well since a solution of the latter is made of a mode-assignment M and a schedule S (cf. Section 2.1.4). Thus, it is sufficient to classify S. Furthermore, note that for the SMPSP start and finish times are functionally dependent as follows: $ST_j=FT_j-d_j$, $1 \leq j \leq J$. Hence the definitions supplied can be easily adapted to start times.

Chapter 3 is organised as follows (cf. Sprecher et al. (1994)): Section 3.1 stresses the necessity of a precise schedule classification by providing a brief review of the relevant literature. Section 3.2 gives formal definitions for schedules of the SMPSP. Finally, Section 3.3 supplies examples in order to illustrate these definitions.

3.1 Introduction

Classifying schedules is the basic work to be done before attacking scheduling problems. For the case of the JSP thorough studies have been performed (cf. Conway et al. (1967), Baker (1974), Rinnooy Kan (1976), and French (1982)). Schedules for the JSP are classified as feasible, semi-active, active, and non-delay schedules. Procedures minimising a regular performance measure are usually enumerating semi-active or active schedules (cf. Rinnooy Kan (1976)). The latter are known to constitute the smallest dominant set of schedules (cf. French (1982) and Rinnooy Kan (1976)).

For the single-mode project scheduling problem (SMPSP) as a generalisation of the JSP the majority of researchers did not make use of any schedule classification (cf. e.g. Davis / Heidorn (1971), Stinson et al. (1978), Talbot / Patterson (1978), Talbot (1982), and Patterson et al. (1989)). Some researchers just defined the type of schedule needed. Accordingly, different definitions were proposed for the same type of schedules and identical definitions were used for different kinds of schedules. E.g., Elmaghraby (1977, p. 205) defines an *eligible schedule* as a schedule where no activity can be started earlier without changing the start times of any other activity and still maintain feasibility. In Schrage (1970) the same type of schedule is called to be an *active schedule*.

Wiest (1964) defines a *left-justified schedule* as a "feasible schedule in which ... no job can be started at an earlier date by local left-shifting of that job alone", whereas Gonguet (1969) calls a schedule left-justified if "each job is scheduled as early as possible".

Finally, other researchers just took over the schedule classification of the JSP without modifications (cf. Radermacher (1985 / 86), Demeulemeester / Herroelen (1992a), and Herroelen / Demeulemeester (1992)). This is somewhat reasoned by the way schedule classification is presented in the textbooks for the JSP most oftenly cited (cf. Baker (1974) and French (1982)). There, the definitions are more illustrative than formal and thus bear ambiguity in the case of the more general SMPSP.

In order to present a general and precise schedule classification the proceeding is as follows: Using the schedule classification for the JSP proposed by Baker (1974) as a stepping stone, more formal and general definitions are developed for the SMPSP. That is, it is discriminated between semi-active, active, and non-delay schedules. Naturally this classification holds for the JSP as well. Moreover, the (dominance) relations between the different sets of schedules - as known from the JSP - are preserved. This helps to classify procedures for the SMPSP based on the schedules they examine.

3.2 Types of Schedules

At the beginning, recall the JSP as stated in Section 2.2.2 where a number of A jobs have to be processed on B different machines and job a, $1 \leq a \leq A$, on machine b, $1 \leq b \leq B$, is referred to as operation (a,b). As shown in Section 2.2.2, the JSP is a special case of the SMPSP with $|R| = B$ renewable resources, each of which with an availability of one unit per period. For the JSP context, Baker defines a schedule to be a feasible resolution of resource and logical constraints (cf. Baker (1974, p. 179)). More precisely, the following is defined:

Definition 3.1: For a given schedule S and a period t, $1 \leq t \leq T$, the set of **activities being in progress in period t** is $A_t(S) = \{j | 1 \leq j \leq J, FT_j - d_j + 1 \leq t \leq FT_j\}$.

Definition 3.2: A **schedule** S is called **feasible** if the precedence relations are maintained, i.e. $FT_i \leq FT_j - d_j$, $j=2,...,J$, $i \in P_j$, and the resource constraints are met, i.e. $\sum_{j \in A_t(S)} k_{jr} \leq K_r$, $r \in R$, $t=1,...,T$.

For a given schedule S of the JSP the local or limited left-shift is defined as follows (cf. Baker (1974, p. 181)): A local or limited left-shift is "moving an operation block to the left on the Gantt-chart while preserving the operation sequences". Since the term "operation sequence" is not interpretable within the project scheduling context, the following is defined:

Definition 3.3 (cf. Wiest (1964)): A **left-shift** of activity j, $1 \leq j \leq J$, is an operation on a feasible schedule S, which derives a feasible schedule S', such that $FT'_j < FT_j$ and $FT'_i = FT_i$ for i, $1 \leq i \leq J$, $i \neq j$.

Remark 3.1 (cf. Definition 2.5): If a regular performance measure ϕ is considered and a schedule S' is obtainable from S by a left-shift of activity j, $1 \leq j \leq J$, then S is dominated by S' w.r.t. ϕ.

Definition 3.4: A left-shift of activity j, $1 \leq j \leq J$, is called a **one-period left-shift** iff $FT_j\text{-}FT'_j = 1$.

Definition 3.5: A **local left-shift** of activity j, $1 \leq j \leq J$, is a left-shift of activity j which is obtainable by one or more successively applied one-period left-shifts of activity j.

Remark 3.2: Within a local left-shift each intermediate derived schedule is feasible by definition.

Regarding a schedule where no further local left-shifts are possible, Baker defines a global left-shift, as to start an operation earlier without delaying any other operation (cf. Baker (1974, p. 183)). Instead, it is stated:

Definition 3.6: A **global left-shift** of activity j, $1 \leq j \leq J$, is a left-shift of activity j, which is not obtainable by a local left-shift.

Remark 3.3: A global left-shift of activity j, $1 \leq j \leq J$, implies $FT_j\text{-}FT'_j > 1$.

Remark 3.4: If a feasible schedule S' is derived from the feasible schedule S by a global left-shift, then S' is not obtainable from S by a series of local left-shifts since at least one intermediate schedule is not feasible with respect to the resource constraints.

Based on the notion of a local left-shift, Baker defines the set of semi-active schedules to be those schedules in which no local left-shifts are possible (cf. Baker (1974, p. 181)). By employing Definition 3.5 it is defined:

Definition 3.7: A **semi-active schedule** is a feasible schedule, where none of

Remark 3.5: A feasible schedule can be transformed into a semi-active schedule by a series of local left-shifts. Note that - in general - the derived semi-active schedule is not unique.

Obviously, Definition 3.7 coincides with the definition given by Baker. The remark "In a semi-active schedule the start time of a particular operation is constrained by the processing of a different job on the same machine or by the processing of the directly preceding operation on a different machine" (cf. Baker (1974, p. 183)) has to be generalised in the following way:

Remark 3.6: In a semi-active schedule S the finish time FT_j of any activity j, $1 \leq j \leq J$, cannot be reduced by one period, because there is at least one (renewable) resource r, $r \in R$, for which the left-over capacity in period FT_j-d_j-1 is exceeded by the requirements of activity j or at least one predecessor of activity j is not finished up to the end of period FT_j-d_j-1.

For the JSP the set of active schedules is defined as "the set of all schedules in which no global left-shift can be made" (cf. Baker (1974, p. 183)). For the SMPSP the following generalisation is used:

Definition 3.8: An **active schedule** is a feasible schedule, where none of the activities j, $1 \leq j \leq J$, can be locally or globally left-shifted.

Finally, in the JSP context (cf. Baker (1974, p. 185)) a non-delay schedule is a schedule where "no machine is kept idle at a time when it could begin processing some operation". Employing Remark 3.7, the more general Definition 3.9 of a non-delay schedule can be given.

Remark 3.7: Each SMPSP can be uniquely transformed into a unit-time-duration SMPSP (PSPUTD) where each activity j, $1 < j < J$, is split into d_j activities, each of which with duration one (cf. Davis / Heidorn (1971) and Demeulemeester / Herroelen (1992c)). Thus, a feasible schedule S of the SMPSP uniquely corresponds to a feasible schedule S_{UTD} of the PSPUTD.

Definition 3.9: A feasible schedule S for the SMPSP is called a **non-delay schedule** if the corresponding schedule S_{UTD} is active.

By definition, the following theorem can be stated:

Theorem 3.1: Let S denote the set of schedules, FS the set of feasible schedules, SAS the set of semi-active schedules, AS the set of active schedules, and NDS the set of non-delay schedules, then the following holds: $NDS \subseteq AS \subseteq SAS \subseteq FS \subseteq S$.

3.3 Examples and Illustrations

In order to illustrate the above definitions, Figure 3.1 provides an example where $|R|=1$.

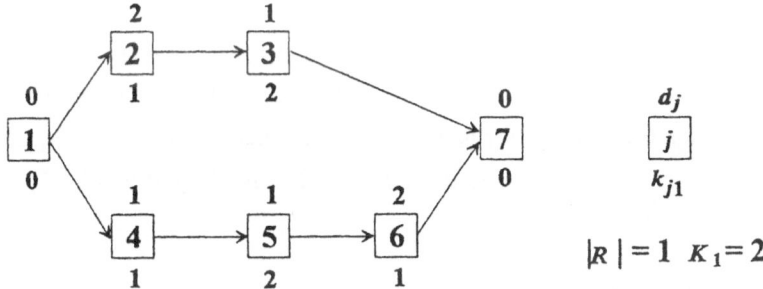

Figure 3.1: An Example for the SMPSP

A feasible schedule $S=(0,5,6,1,2,9,9)$ of the above problem is depicted in Figure 3.2.

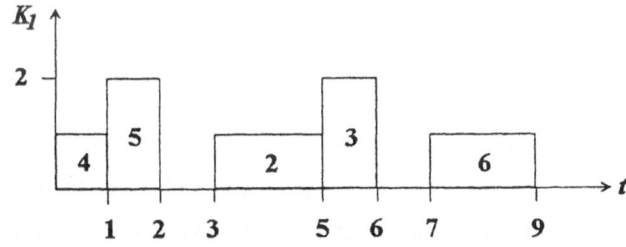

Figure 3.2: Feasible Schedule for the Example Problem

By performing a local left-shift (consisting of a one-period left-shift) of activities 2 and 3, respectively, and a local left-shift (consisting of two one-period left-shifts) of activity 6 the semi-active schedule $S=(0,4,5,1,2,7,7)$ displayed in Figure 3.3 is derived. Note that the intermediate schedule $S'=(0,4,5,1,2,8,8)$ which is derived after the first one-period left-shift of activity 6 is feasible.

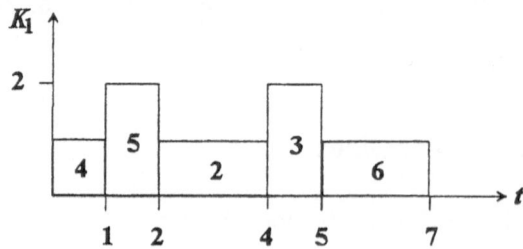

Figure 3.3: Semi-Active Schedule for the Example Problem

Regarding the semi-active schedule $S=(0,4,5,1,2,7,7)$ depicted in Figure 3.3, clearly none of the activities can be locally left-shifted anymore. Nevertheless, activity 6 can be globally left-shifted by performing a three-period left-shift. Doing so, one obtains the active schedule $S=(0,4,5,1,2,4,5)$ displayed in Figure 3.4.

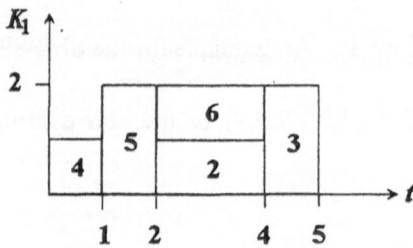

Figure 3.4: Active (and Unique Optimal) Schedule for the Example Problem

Again, note that the two intermediate schedules $S'=(0,4,5,1,2,6,6)$ and $S''=(0,4,5,1,2,5,5)$ are not feasible. Hence, a local left-shift has not been performed, respectively. Since none of the activities can be locally or globally left-shifted, the schedule is active. Furthermore, the schedule is the unique optimal schedule of the example problem. Optimality can easily be verified by applying the resource-based lower bound (cf. Section 5.1.1), while the uniqueness can be shown by performing an explicit enumeration with one of the schemes presented in Stinson et al. (1978) or Demeulemeester / Herroelen (1992a). Both procedures will be sketched out in Section 5.1.1.

In order to see whether the optimal solution is a non-delay schedule or not, the example problem is transformed into the corresponding PSPUTD where each activity j, $1 \leq j \leq J$, of the SMPSP is transformed into the activities $j1,...,jd_j$, respectively (cf. Figure 3.5).

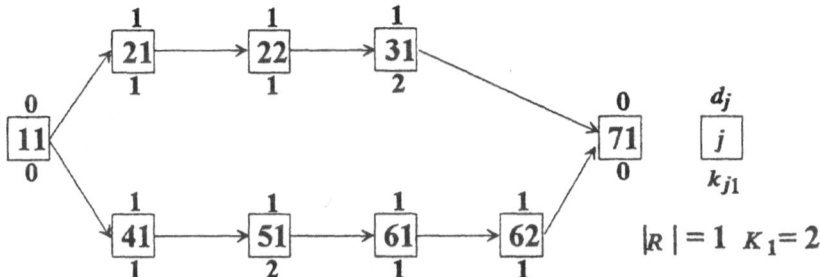

Figure 3.5: Corresponding PSPUTD

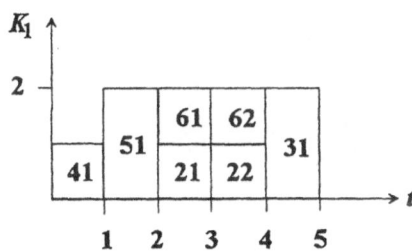

Figure 3.6: Solution for the PSPUTD

The solution S_{UTD}=(0,3,4,5,1,2,3,4,5) is displayed in Figure 3.6. Within this schedule activity 21 can be globally left-shifted (FT_{21}=3 $\rightarrow$ FT'_{21}=1). Therefore, the schedule for the SMPSP does not belong to the set of non-delay schedules. Since the optimal schedule is unique the following can be stated:

Remark 3.8: When considering a regular performance measure the set of non-delay schedules does not necessarily contain an optimal schedule.

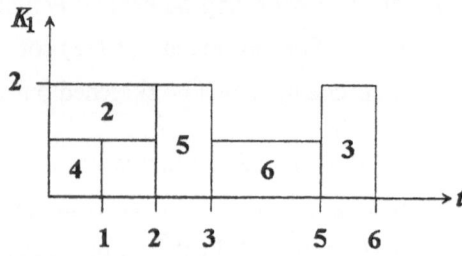

Figure 3.7: Non-Delay Schedule for the Example Problem

The schedule $S=(0,2,6,1,3,5,6)$ presented in Figure 3.7 is obtained by assigning to activity 2 the finish time of 2 which in turn alters the finish times of the activities 3, 5, and 6, respectively. Again, by applying Definition 3.9 it can be shown that this is a non-delay schedule. Note that since the optimal solution is unique and not a non-delay schedule there is an empty intersection between the set of optimal solutions and the set of non-delay schedules for the example problem.

Chapter 4

Characterisation and Generation of Instances

Chapter 4 is concerned with a discussion of problem parameters to characterise project scheduling problems (PSP). Based on the derived parameters a framework to generate benchmark instances for several problem classes of the PSP is developed which essentially relies on three concepts: a network construction procedure which is based on the definition of a network, the resource factor as a measure of the density of the coefficient matrix, and the resource strength expressing the degree of availability of the resources. The implemented project generator (ProGen) is employed in Chapters 5 - 8 to derive problem instances for the SMPSP, the MMPSP, the PSPDL, and the PSPST, respectively.

The Chapter is organised as follows: Section 4.1 provides a review of the literature and summarises that there is no generally applicable instance generator for PSP's available today. In Sections 4.2 to 4.4 problem parameters and methodologies for the generation of the base-data, the precedence relations as well as the resource demand and availability are introduced, respectively.

4.1 Introduction

From the beginning of resource-constrained project scheduling research rapid progress regarding models and methods has been documented in the literature (cf. Pritsker et al. (1969), Stinson et al. (1978), Talbot (1982), Patterson et al. (1989) and (1990) as well as Demeulemeester / Herroelen (1992a)). But at the same time very little research concerned with the systematic generation of benchmark instances has been published. The only paper dealing explicitly with an instance generator for project scheduling problems has been presented by Demeulemeester et al. (1993a). There, a generator for the random generation of activity-on-arc (AOA) networks has been presented. Two disadvantages should be mentioned: (*i*) Except of the number of nodes and arcs, respectively, no further network characteristics can be specified. Hence, special network structures cannot be generated. (*ii*) The resource demand and availability generation (cf. Section 4.4) is only performed in accordance with general distributions without making use of a specified set of characteristics.

Except of Demeulemeester et al. (1993a), numerous authors have documented their way of obtaining instances as a vehicle for their numerical experiments (cf. Alvarez-Valdes / Tamarit (1989a), Patterson (1984), and Patterson et al. (1990)). Thereby, different project characteristics have been suggested. Worth mentioning are the papers of Pascoe (1966), Kurtulus / Davis (1982), and Cooper (1976). But as will be discussed in Section 4.4.2, all of them encountered difficulties with the important measure of resource scarceness.

Today, only a few commonly used benchmark instances are available. Patterson (1984) compared four exact procedures for the single-mode project scheduling problem (SMPSP) on 110 instances. Amongst others, these instances were used by Bell / Han (1991), Demeulemeester / Herroelen (1992a), and Sampson / Weiss (1993). Therefore, they became a quasi-standard. Nevertheless, there are some points of attack left: (*i*) Being a collection of problems from different sources, the instances are not generated by using a controlled design of specified problem parameters. (*ii*) Only the single-mode case together with makespan minimisation is taken into consideration. (*iii*) Recent advances (cf. Demeulemeester / Herroelen (1992a)) in the development of exact single-mode procedures demonstrated that the Patterson-set is solvable within an average CPU-time of less than a second on a personal computer. Since there are instances (with the same number of activities) which are much more difficult to solve, the Patterson-instances can no longer be considered as a benchmark anymore. On account of these three points the necessity arises to develop an instance generator which overcomes the outlined deficiencies in order to generate well controlled problem instances for the SMPSP, the MMPSP, the PSPDL, and the PSPST, respectively.

Four functions which are applied within ProGen are shortly introduced: The function ROUND rounds a real argument to an integer while the function TRUNC truncates the decimal fraction of a given real. Furthermore, the random function RAND (<u>RAND</u>) is defined by drawing a uniformly distributed integer (real) from a specified interval. The (pseudo) random numbers are constructed by transforming [0,1[uniformly distributed random numbers which are calculated with the generator proposed by Schrage (1979).

4.2 Base-Data Generation

The input of the base-data generation is displayed in Table 4.1.

Symbol	Definition
J^{min} (J^{max})	minimal (maximal) number of non-dummy activities
M^{min} (M^{max})	minimal (maximal) number of modes per activity
d^{min} (d^{max})	minimal (maximal) duration of an activity-mode tuple
δ_{fac}	deadline factor $\in [0,1]$

Table 4.1: Input Base-Data Generation

The generation of the base-data follows formulas (4.1) - (4.5). It has to be recalled that EFT_J denotes the earliest finish time of the dummy sink calculated by forward recursion (cf. Sections 2.2.1 and 2.3.1) and that modes are labelled w.r.t. non-decreasing duration (cf. Section 2.1.2).

$$J = \text{RAND}[J^{min}, J^{max}] + 2 \qquad (4.1)$$

$$M_j=\text{RAND}[M^{min},M^{max}] \qquad\qquad 1<j<J, (M_1=M_J=1) \qquad (4.2)$$

$$d_{jm}=\text{RAND}[d^{min},d^{max}] \qquad 1<j<J, 1\le m\le M_j, (d_{11}=d_{J1}=0) \qquad (4.3)$$

$$T=\sum_{j=1}^{J} d_{jM_j} \qquad\qquad (4.4)$$

$$DL=\text{TRUNC}(EFT_J+\delta_{fac}(T-EFT_J)) \qquad\qquad (4.5)$$

4.3 Network Generation

In Section 2.1.3 the precedence relations of a project have been depicted as an acyclic AON graph. Thus, it is a quite natural approach to construct the network by using a simple implication of the definition of a network:

Remark 4.1 (cf. Neumann (1975, p. 33): Let $G=(V,A)$ be a **network** with node set V and arc set A. Then, for every node $v \in V$ there is a directed path from the single source to v and a directed path from v to the single sink.

That is, every node except of the sink (source) has at least one successor (predecessor). Therefore, the basic idea is as follows: First, determine one predecessor for each node, second, determine one successor for each node and then add further arcs. When adding further arcs, it has to be assured that arcs do not become redundant (cf. Definition 2.1). Recalling P_j (S_j) to be the set of the immediate predecessors (successors) and $\bar{P}_j$ ($\bar{S}_j$) to be the set of all predecessors (successors) of activity j, $1 \le j \le J$, Figure 4.1 shows the four cases of redundancy which have to be considered.

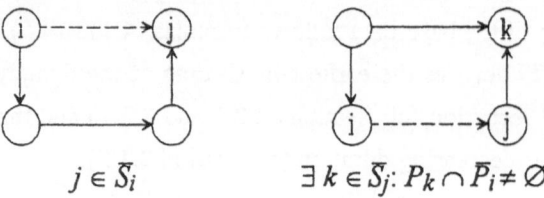

$$j \in \bar{S}_i \qquad\qquad \exists\, k \in \bar{S}_j\colon P_k \cap \bar{P}_i \ne \varnothing$$

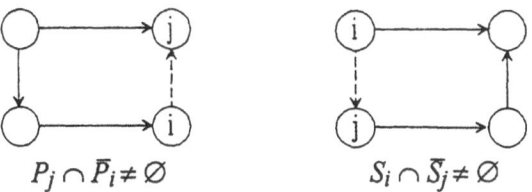

Figure 4.1: Four Cases of Redundancy

For a given cardinality of the set of nodes the minimal and maximal number of non-redundant arcs of a network are given in the following theorem and illustrated in Figure 4.2.

Theorem 4.1: Let $G=(V,A)$ be a network with $|V|=n$. Since a network is connected the minimal number of non-redundant arcs A^{min} is $A^{min}=n-1$. The maximal number of non-redundant arcs A^{max} in a network with $n \geq 6$ is given by $A^{max}=n-2+\frac{1}{4}(n-2)^2$ if n is even and $A^{max}=n-2+\frac{1}{4}(n-1)(n-3)$ if n is odd.

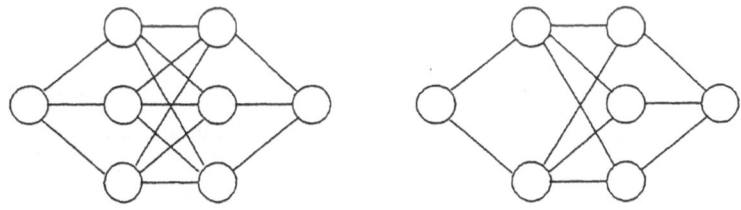

Figure 4.2: Maximal Number of Non-Redundant Arcs

For the characterisation of the network the following input data are employed: the minimal (maximal) number of start activities S_1^{min} (S_1^{max}), the minimal (maximal) number of finish activities P_J^{min} (P_J^{max}) as well as the maximal number of successor (predecessor) activities S_j^{max} (P_j^{max}) an activity j, $1 < j < J$, may have. Moreover, the network complexity (NC), i.e. the average number of non-redundant arcs per node (including the super-source and -sink) and the tolerated network complexity deviation ε_{NET} is used. The network complexity has been introduced by Pascoe (1966) for AOA networks and adopted by Davis (1975) for the AON representation.

The construction of the network is performed in the following four steps (cf. Figure 4.3): In step (1) the numbers of start- and finish-activities are drawn randomly from the interval $[S_1^{min}, S_1^{max}]$ and $[P_J^{min}, P_J^{max}]$, respectively. Then, the arcs which connect the dummy source with the start activities and the finish activities with the dummy sink are added to the network. In step (2), beginning with the lowest-indexed non-start activity, to each activity a predecessor activity is assigned at random. Similar it is proceeded in step (3) where to each activity which has no successor one successor (cf. arcs (3,6) and (6,9) in Figure 4.3) is assigned. In both steps the activities are considered in the order of increasing activity number. Finally, in step (4) further arcs are added until the network complexity is reached.

During the whole procedure one has to take into account: (*i*) To avoid redundancy there must be no precedence relations within the start activities and within the finish activities, respectively. (*ii*) Adding arcs in step (3), e.g. arc (6,8), or in step (4), e.g. arc (3,5), must not produce redundant precedence relations. (*iii*) Further, one has to take into account the limitation given by the maximal number of successors (predecessors) as well as the number of start and finish activities. E.g., arc (4,6) in step (4) cannot be incorporated if at most two predecessors are allowed.

In the following cases the generation procedure has to be restarted: (*i*) If the required network complexity is low, i.e. $NC \approx 1$, it might happen that after step (3) the number of arcs integrated into the network (*ActArcs*) is too high, i.e. $ActArcs > J \cdot NC \cdot (1 + \varepsilon_{NET})$. (*ii*) If in step (3) due to the limited number of predecessors there is no successor of an activity j available. (*iii*) If in step (3) for an activity j there are only successors available which lead to redundant precedence relations. (*iv*) If the required network complexity is not obtainable in step (4). That is, within a limited number of trials of randomly selecting a node and calculating possible successors there are no further arcs addable to obtain $ActArcs \geq J \cdot NC \cdot (1 - \varepsilon_{NET})$. By an appropriate reduction of the set of choosable predecessors and successors in the steps previously described a numerically labelled network is realised.

By adjusting the input parameters special network structures, e.g. serial, general, and parallel structures as well as the network shapes described in Kurtulus / Davis (1982), Kurtulus / Narula (1985), and Smith-Daniels / Smith-Daniels (1987), can be obtained.

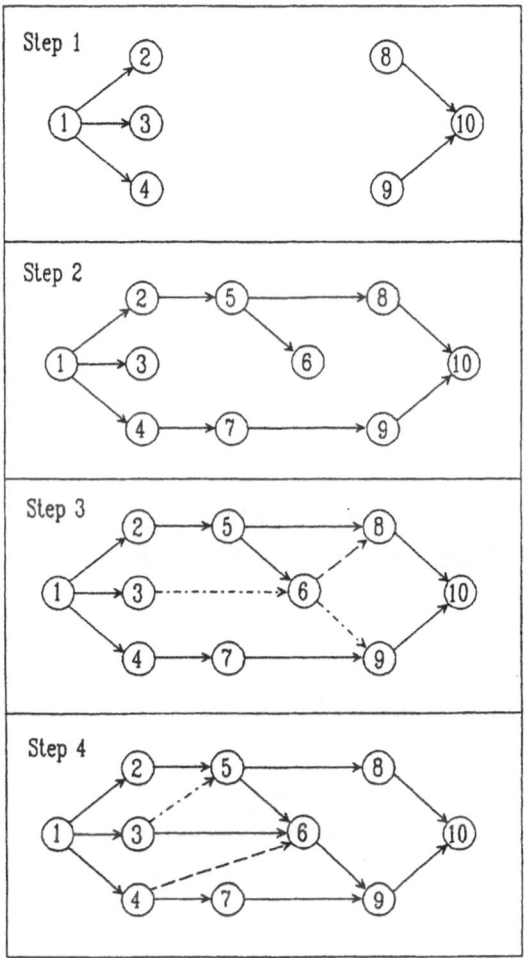

Figure 4.3: Network Generation

4.4 Resource Demand and Availability Generation

4.4.1 Resource Demand Generation

The resource demand generation compromises two decisions to be made. First, the resources used or consumed by the activity-mode tuple $[j,m]$, $1 < j < J$, $1 \leq m \leq M_j$, have to be determined. Second, if an activity-mode tuple uses or consumes a resource, the number of units used or consumed has to be calculated. The first step it is referred to as *request generation* (cf. Subsection I) while the latter is termed *generation of demand-level* (cf. Subsection II). The number of resources of category τ, $\tau \in \{R,N\}$, is determined by randomly drawing $|\tau|$ from the interval $[\tau^{min}, \tau^{max}]$.

I. Requested Resources

For characterisational purposes a generalisation of the resource factor (RF) which was introduced by Pascoe (1966) for the SMPSP and later was utilised in studies by Cooper (1976) and Alvarez-Valdes / Tamarit (1989a) is calculated as follows:

$$RF = \frac{1}{J-2} \frac{1}{|R|} \sum_{j=1}^{J} \sum_{r \in R} \begin{cases} 1, \text{ if } k_{jr} > 0 \\ 0, \text{ otherwise} \end{cases} \tag{4.6}$$

The resource factor reflects the average portion of resources requested per activity. It is a measure of the density of the array k_{jr}, $1 < j < J$, $r \in R$. If $RF = 1$, then each activity requests all resources while $RF = 0$ indicates that no activity requests any resource; thus the resource-unconstrained CPM-case (cf. Section 2.2.2) is obtained. In order to use RF for the multi-mode case as well it is generalised straightforwardly to a category-dependent resource factor $RF(\tau)$, $\tau \in \{R,N\}$:

$$RF(\tau) = \frac{1}{J-2} \frac{1}{|\tau|} \sum_{j=2}^{J-2} \frac{1}{|M_j|} \sum_{m=1}^{M_j} \sum_{r \in \tau} \begin{cases} 1, \text{ if } k_{jmr} > 0 \\ 0, \text{ otherwise} \end{cases} \tag{4.7}$$

Again, $RF(\tau)$ is normalised to the interval $[0,1]$ with the interpretation very close to the one of the original RF: It reflects the average portion of resources out of category τ, $\tau \in \{R,N\}$, requested by each activity-mode tuple $[j,m]$, $1 < j < J$, $1 \leq m \leq M_j$, and it measures the density of the three dimensional array k_{jmr}, $1 < j < J$, $1 \leq m \leq M_j$, $r \in \tau$. Of course, $RF(\tau)$ equals the one proposed by Pascoe (1966) for the case $N=\varnothing$ and $M_j=1$, $1 \leq j \leq J$. Table 4.2 shows all input parameters employed for the resource demand generation.

Symbol	Definition
$|\tau^{min}|$ $(|\tau^{max}|)$	minimal (maximal) number of resources of category τ
$Q_\tau^{min}(Q_\tau^{max})$	minimal (maximal) number of resources of category τ used by an activity-mode tuple $[j,m]$
$U_\tau^{min}(U_\tau^{max})$	minimal (maximal) demand for a resource of category τ
$RF(\tau)$	resource factor of category τ
$RS(\tau)$	resource strength of category τ
ε_{RF}	tolerated resource factor deviation

Table 4.2: Input Demand Generation

For the generation of the resource request, the following internal variables and data structures are used: First, the information whether an activity-mode tuple $[j,m]$ requests resource r is represented by a three-dimensional array $Rq[j,m,r]$ of binary digits. $Rq[j,m,r]$ is initialised with zeros and is set equal to one iff $[j,m]$ requests resource r. The actual resource factor (ARF) is then calculated as follows:

$$ARF(\tau) = \frac{1}{J-2} \frac{1}{|\tau|} \sum_{j=2}^{J-2} \frac{1}{|M_j|} \sum_{m=1}^{M_j} \sum_{r \in \tau} Rq[j,m,r] \tag{4.8}$$

$Q[j,m]$, the current number of resources requested by $[j,m]$, is obtained from

$$Q[j,m] = \sum_{r \in \tau} Rq[j,m,r] \tag{4.9}$$

Finally, CT is the set of currently choosable triplets:

$$CT = \{[j,m,r] \mid Rq[j,m,r]=0, Q[j,m] < Q_\tau^{max}\} \tag{4.10}$$

CT is the set of activity-mode-resource tuples $[j,m,r]$ which are further-more choosable ($Rq[j,m,r]=0$) without $Q[j,m]$ exceeding Q_τ^{max}. During the two steps which are outlined in the sequel the internal variables $Rq[j,m,r]$, $ARF(\tau)$, $Q[j,m]$, and CT are continuously updated.

In step (1) for each activity-mode tuple $[j,m]$ - as far as Q_τ^{min} the minimal number of requested resources is not reached - additional resources are se-lected randomly. As long as in step (2) the actual resource factor is less than the asserted one and in addition there are choosable triplets in CT, i.e. $CT \neq \varnothing$, the actual resource factor is incremented by randomly drawing a triplet from CT while taking into account Q_τ^{max}. If after step (2) the actual resource factor declines more then tolerated, i.e. $ARF(\tau) \notin [RF(\tau)\cdot(1-\varepsilon_{RF(\tau)}), RF(\tau)\cdot(1+\varepsilon_{RF(\tau)})]$, a warning message is given.

II. Level of Demand

If there is $Rq[j,m,r]=1$, then a positive demand of the activity-mode tuple $[j,m]$ for resource r has to be generated. The interrelation between the dura-tions of the modes and the demand for resource r is reflected by two types of functions: (*i*) duration-independent and (*ii*) time-resource tradeoff (cf. Sec-tion 2.1.2). For each resource $r \in \tau$ the function is determined in accordance with category dependent probabilities. If a duration-independent level is ob-tained then for each activity the demand U' is randomly drawn from the inte-ger interval $[U_\tau^{min}, U_\tau^{max}]$ and is then assigned to all modes which request the resource under consideration. For the time-resource tradeoff case for each activity j, $1 < j < J$, two levels are drawn randomly from the parameter specified interval. The lower one defines U^{low} and the higher one U^{high}. Let M_j be the number of modes of activity j, $1 < j < J$, with different durations requesting resource r. Calculating

$$\Delta = \frac{U^{high} - U^{low}}{M_j} \tag{4.11}$$

one can obtain M_j intervals I_k, $1 \le k \le M_j$, as follows:

$$I_k = [\text{ROUND}(U^{high} - \Delta \cdot k), \text{ROUND}(U^{high} - \Delta \cdot (k-1))] \tag{4.12}$$

Since the modes are ordered by non-decreasing durations the demand can be randomly drawn from the intervals corresponding to the durations.

Remark 4.2: If for m, m', $1 \le m$, $m' \le M_j$, $m \ne m'$, it is $d_{jm} = d_{jm'}$ and $Rq[j,m,r] = 1 = Rq[j,m',r]$ holds, then the demand is generated randomly from the same interval.

Due to the construction, inefficiency, which is defined in the following, may occur:

Definition 4.1: An activity j, $1 < j < J$, has **inefficient modes** if there are modes m and m' with $d_{jm} \le d_{jm'}$ and $k_{jmr} \le k_{jm'r}$ for all $r \in R \cup N$.

If inefficient modes occur for activity j then Q_j, the number of resources requested by activity j, is calculated as follows:

$$Q_j = \sum_{m=1}^{M_j} \sum_{r \in \tau} Rq[j,m,r] \tag{4.13}$$

and the request and demand generation is restarted with the additional constraint

$$Q_j = \sum_{m=1}^{M_j} Q[j,m] \tag{4.14}$$

If efficiency is not reached within a pre-specified maximal number of trials the generation is interrupted; then the parameters have to be adjusted. Finally, note that the outlined methodology does not only generate the time-resource tradeoff but the resource-resource tradeoff case (cf. Section 2.1.2) as well.

4.4.2 Resource Availability Generation

In order to express the relationship between the resource demand of the activities and the resource availability, Cooper (1976) introduced the resource strength (RS) which is calculated as follows:

$$RS(R) = \frac{K_r}{\frac{1}{J-2}\sum_{j=2}^{J-1} k_{jr}} \qquad r \in R \tag{4.15}$$

Later, the RS was utilised by Alvarez-Valdes / Tamarit (1989a). There are three drawbacks of the proposed measure: (i) The RS is not normalised to the interval [0,1]. (ii) A rather small RS does not guarantee a feasible solution. E.g., for three activities with k_{jr}=1, 1 and 10, respectively, one has to adjust the resource strength to $RS(R) \geq 2.5$ in order to achieve a feasible solution. (iii) Most important, regard the myopic fashion in which the scarcity of resources is calculated. This is depicted with the following simple example: Consider two projects, with exactly the same data except the precedence relations. Project 1 has a parallel structure where each activity is immediate successor of the dummy source and immediate predecessors of the dummy sink. Project 2 has a serial structure where each activity has exactly one predecessor and one successor. Furthermore, assume that the resource availability is large enough in order to assure feasibility of both problems. Then, the RS for both projects is exactly the same. But the serially structured project represents the CPM-case and is quite easy to solve while the parallel structured project is - dependent on the amount of resource availability - rather difficult.

In order to overcome these disadvantages the following measure of resource scarceness which is applicable to all categories of resources is introduced. A minimal demand K_r^{min} as well as a maximal demand K_r^{max} are determined and the resource availability is calculated as a convex combination of the two with $RS(\tau)$ as a scaling parameter:

$$K_r = K_r^{min} + \text{ROUND}(RS(\tau) \cdot (K_r^{max} - K_r^{min})) \qquad r \in \tau \tag{4.16}$$

Thus, with respect to one resource the smallest feasible resource-availability-level is obtained for $RS(\tau)=0$. For $RS(\tau)=1$ the amount of resources is approximately large enough to achieve the CPM-case.

For each nonrenewable resource r, $r \in N$, the minimal and maximal availabilities (K_r^{min} and K_r^{max}) to complete the project are calculated as follows:

$$K_r^{min}= \sum_{j=2}^{J-2} \min\{k_{jmr}|\ 1 \le m \le M_j\} \qquad\qquad r \in N \qquad (4.17)$$

$$K_r^{max}= \sum_{j=2}^{J-2} \max\{k_{jmr}|\ 1 \le m \le M_j\} \qquad\qquad r \in N \qquad (4.18)$$

Formulas (4.17) and (4.18) represent the sum of the minimal and maximal consumption of the activities, respectively. If the considered resource is renewable the minimal demand is

$$K_r^{min}= \max_{j=2}^{J-1}\{\min\{k_{jmr}|\ 1 \le m \le M_j\}\} \qquad\qquad r \in R \qquad (4.19)$$

The maximal demand is calculated as the peak demand of the earliest finish schedule which is defined as follows:

Definition 4.2: An **earliest finish schedule** S_{EFT} is a schedule S where the finish time FT_j of each activity j, $1 \le j \le J$, equals the earliest finish time EFT_j, as calculated by the forward recursion (cf. Section 2.2.1).

Thus, each activity is performed in the lowest-indexed mode employing maximal per-period demand w.r.t. the resource under consideration. That is, the maximal per-period demand of activity j regarding resource r is calculated as follows:

$$k^*_{jr}= \max\{k_{jmr}|\ 1 \le m \le M_j\} \qquad\qquad r \in R \qquad (4.20)$$

and the corresponding mode with shortest duration is then:

$$\mu_r(j) = \min_{m=1}^{M_j} \{m \mid k_{jmr} = k^*_{jr}\} \qquad\qquad r \in R \qquad (4.21)$$

Given the mode-assignment $M(r) = (\mu_r(1),...,\mu_r(J))$, the earliest finish schedule S_{EFT} is obtained by applying the forward recursion as described in Section 2.2.1. The peak period demand w.r.t. resource r is

$$K_r^{max} = \max\{ \sum_{j \in A_t(S_{EFT})} k_{j\mu_r(j)r} \mid 1 \le t \le T \} \qquad\qquad r \in R \qquad (4.22)$$

By construction the following can be stated:

Remark 4.3: If $\tau = 1$ and $RS(\tau) = 0$, then the lowest resource-feasible level w.r.t. resource type τ is generated.

Remark 4.4: If $RS(\tau) \ll 1$ and $\exists j,\ 1 < j < J: M_j > 1$, feasibility of the problem can not be assured because of mode-coupling via resource-constraints.

The outlined procedures were coded in PASCAL. The microcomputer implementation generates projects with up to thirty activities within a few seconds. If difficult network structures (i.e. with very low or high network complexity) have to be generated the effort increases slightly. Note that the description of this chapter was restricted to the single-project case but the generation of multi-project instances can be treated analogously (cf. Kolisch et al. (1995)).

Chapter 5

The Single-Mode Project Scheduling Problem

Chapter 5 deals with the single-mode project scheduling problem (SMPSP). An outline of the problem and a 0-1 programming formulation have been provided in Section 2.2. The relevant literature is reviewed in Section 5.1. Section 5.2 is devoted to a precise description of the two basic elements of single-pass priority-rule-based scheduling procedures: scheduling schemes and priority rules. Additionally, a thorough investigation of a specific priority rule leads to new rules. Section 5.3 shows alternative ways of how the single-pass heuristics can be improved by multi-pass (biased random sampling) approaches. Section 5.4 is concerned with an in-depth computational study which gives insight into the performance of scheduling schemes, priority rules, and ways of sampling w.r.t. different problem parameters. The conclusions of the experimental investigation are then exploited in order to devise a new (hybrid) solution procedure which is improved by lower bounding schemes. Finally, the new heuristic is compared to other heuristics which have been recently proposed for the SMPSP.

5.1 Literature Review

A review of solution methods for the SMPSP can be found in Davis (1966), Herroelen (1972), Davis (1973), and Domschke / Drexl (1991b). In the sequel, an outline of optimal procedures is given in Section 5.1.1 while a survey of heuristic algorithms is provided in Section 5.1.2.

5.1.1 Optimal Procedures

In addition to the references already cited, an overview covering only optimal solution procedures is presented in Patterson (1984) and very recently
in Demeulemeester (1992) as well as in Herroelen / Demeulemeester (1992).
The methods so far applied to solve the SMPSP exactly are dynamic programming (for details cf. Carruthers / Battersby (1966)), zero-one programming, and implicit enumeration with branch and bound.

I. Zero-One Programming

Amongst others, zero-one programming formulations for the SMPSP have
been presented by Bowman (1959), Pritsker et al. (1969), Patterson / Huber
(1974), and Patterson / Roth (1976). With their "horizon-varying" approach,
Patterson and Huber presented an elaborate way of solving (2.4)-(2.8) with
zero-one programming. They take advantage of the fact that objective functions of the SMPSP are always integer. They do not solve the original problem to optimality. Instead, they employ a lower bound (*LB*) of the SMPSP
and set up the zero-one-program (2.4)-(2.8) with *T=LB*. If the program is
not feasible then *LB* is increased by one time period and the process is repeated until feasibility is reached. Thus, the final *LB* equals the optimal solution. Besides this lower bound strategy Patterson and Huber proposed an upper bound and a binary search strategy, respectively. In the upper bound
strategy one starts with a heuristically determined upper bound (*UB*) and the
zero-one-program for the SMPSP is set up with *T= UB*-1. Afterwards, the
resulting problem is checked for feasibility. As long as feasibility can be
assured *T* is decreased by one time period and the procedure is reiterated. As
soon as one reaches the first infeasible problem the optimal objective
function value equals *T*+1. In the binary search strategy the search is performed in the interval [*LB,UB*[.[1]

---

[1] Where the interval [*LB,UB*[equals {*LB,...,UB*-1}.

The bound for the lower bound strategy is calculated as follows:

$$LB = \max \{ EFT_J, RLB \} \tag{5.1}$$

with

$$RLB = \max \{ \lceil \sum_{j=1}^{J} d_j \, k_{jr} \, / \, K_r \rceil \mid r \in R \} \tag{5.2}$$

$f = \lceil u \rceil$ denotes the unique integer in the interval $[u, u+1[$. LB is the maximum of the precedence-based lower bound (the resource-unconstrained CPM-makespan) and the resource-based lower bound (RLB) which equals the integer number of days needed to work off the whole work content with respect to each resource, respectively. Both bounds are well-known and have been presented e.g. in Johnson (1967), Müller-Merbach (1967), and Schrage (1970).

II. Implicit Enumeration with Branch and Bound

The majority of exact approaches utilise implicit enumeration with branch and bound. Enumeration schemes for special types of the SMPSP have been proposed by Johnson (1967), Müller-Merbach (1967), and Schrage (1970), whereas schemes for the general SMPSP are reported by Balas (1971), Davis / Heidorn (1971), Hastings (1972), Radermacher (1985 / 86), Stinson et al. (1978), Talbot / Patterson (1978), Christofides et al. (1987), Bell / Park (1990), Carlier / Latapie (1991), and Demeulemeester / Herroelen (1992a).

In the following, two of the procedures, i.e. those of Stinson et al. (1978) and Demeulemeester / Herroelen (1992a) will be presented in more detail. This is due to several reasons: First, they seem to be the most powerful procedures available today (cf. Patterson (1984) and Demeulemeester / Herroelen (1992a)) and thus benchmark solutions for the SMPSP were derived with the algorithm by Demeulemeester / Herroelen (1992a). Second, w.r.t. the enumeration tree there are analogies between the exact algorithms and the heuristics which will be described later. Finally, bounds employed within the exact schemes are made applicable to new heuristics which which will be proposed.

The algorithm of **Stinson** (cf. Stinson (1976) and Stinson et al. (1978)) is a best-first branch and bound approach based on the enumeration tree originally developed by Johnson (1967) for the single-resource SMPSP. Associated with each node is a schedule time and an exclusive division of all activities into four disjoint subsets: Activities which are completed up to the schedule time are in the *complete set*. Activities which are already scheduled but at the schedule time still active are in the *active set*. Activities which are available for scheduling w.r.t. the precedence constraints but yet unscheduled are in the *decision set*. Finally, all other activities are in the *remaining set*.

Definition 5.1 (cf. Schrage (1970)): Let X be the set of the activities $1,...,J$. A **partial schedule** PS is a schedule S where finish times are assigned to only a (not necessarily proper) subset of X.

Employing Definition 5.1 it can be further stated that each intermediate node represents a feasible partial schedule (consisting of the activities in the complete and active set) and each terminal node represents a unique and feasible schedule. The schedule time associated with a node measures the time elapsed in completing the (partial) schedule.

It has been proven by Johnson (1967) that the schedule time of a node equals the earliest finish time of activities in the active set of its ancestral node. Thus, the offsprings of a node are created by enumerating all feasible combinations of not yet scheduled, precedence-feasible activities, i.e. activities in the decision set which can be jointly started at the schedule time without violating the resource constraints. In the case where activities which have been started at ancestral nodes are still in process at the schedule time, one additional descendant node is generated which contains the empty set. Thus, moving from a node to any of the descendants the schedule time as well as the total number of activities in the partial schedule is non-decreasing.

The selection of nodes is done by utilising a set of six lexicographically ordered priority rules. Whenever a node is encountered with an *LB* greater than the *LB* of any other node, a depth-first routine is started in order to seek an improved upper bound.

To prune the solution tree, Stinson used two dominance rules: The stronger one is due to Schrage (1970). It states that a node associated with a partial schedule *PS* can be pruned if there exists another node with a partial schedule *PS'* which can be derived from *PS* by a left-shift. This coincides with Remark 3.1 provided in Section 3.2.

The lower bounds utilised are the precedence-based and the resource-based lower bound as already presented. In addition, based on the work of Wiest (1964) a critical-sequence-based lower bound is employed which jointly takes into account precedence and resource constraints.

The algorithm presented by **Demeulemeester and Herroelen** (cf. Demeulemeester (1992) and Demeulemeester / Herroelen (1992a)) is an extension of the depth-first branch and bound approach proposed by Christofides et al. (1987). The main difference to Stinson's procedure w.r.t. the enumeration tree is in the fact that new nodes are not created by considering sets of activities which are scheduled, but by considering sets of activities which are delayed. To be more precise, the descendants of a node are created in two steps: First, all activities in the decision set are temporarily put into progress at the schedule time determined by the ancestral node. Second, a descendant node for each undominated subset of activities which have to be delayed due to resource constraints, the set of so-called "minimal delaying alternatives", is created. Thus, activities which have already been scheduled at an ancestral node are removed from the partial schedule if they become member of a delaying set. This is an important difference to the Stinson procedure where activities are only scheduled once.

Two dominance rules are used to prune the enumeration tree. The first one is a variation of the left-shift dominance rule. The second one makes use of a so-called "cutset", i.e. unscheduled activities for which all predecessors belong to the partial schedule. Bounding is performed with the precedence-based and the critical-sequence-based lower bound already used by Stinson.

In case of branching, the node associated with the smallest critical-sequence-based lower bound is chosen. Ties are resolved arbitrarily. If a final node is reached, the algorithm backtracks to the highest level in the enumeration tree which contains unpruned node(s). Termination occurs when there are no more unpruned portions of the enumeration tree.

5.1.2 Heuristic Procedures

An overview of heuristic approaches to solve the SMPSP can be found in Davis (1966), Herroelen (1972) and Davis (1973).

Heuristic approaches for the SMPSP basically involve four different solution methodologies: single- and multi-pass priority-rule-based scheduling, truncated branch and bound procedures, disjunctive arc concepts, and local search techniques.

I. Priority-Rule-Based Scheduling

The first attempts to solve the SMPSP heuristically were done by using priority rules to decide the order in which activities are considered for the allocation of scarce resources.

Priority-rule-based scheduling is made up of two components: a schedule generation scheme and a priority rule. Two different schemes for the generation of feasible schedules can be distinguished: the so-called serial and the parallel method, respectively. Both generate a feasible schedule by extending a partial schedule in a stage-wise fashion. In each stage the generation scheme forms the set of all schedulable activities, the so-called decision set. A specific priority rule is then employed in order to choose one or more activities from the decision set which will be scheduled.

W.r.t. the number of feasible schedules generated, single- and multi-pass priority-rule-based scheduling can be discriminated. Single-pass procedures make use of one single pass and one priority rule in order to create one feasible solution. Multi-pass procedures perform Z single passes and are thereby generating a sample of less than or equal Z unique feasible solutions. In order to obtain different solutions for each single pass, either a different priority rule is employed or the selection of activities from the decision set is biased by using a random device.

The **serial method** was proposed by Kelley (1963). It consists of exactly J stages, in each of which one activity is selected and scheduled. Associated with each stage is a partition of all activities into three disjoint subsets: Activities which have already been scheduled and thus belong to the partial schedule are in the *complete set*. Unscheduled activities with every predecessor being in the complete set are in the *decision set*. Finally, all remaining activities are in the *remaining set*. In each stage one activity from the decision set is selected with a priority rule and scheduled at its earliest precedence- and resource-feasible start time. Afterwards, the selected activity is removed from the decision set and put into the complete set. This in turn may free a number of activities currently being in the remaining set to be placed into the decision set since all their predecessors are now completed. The algorithm terminates at stage number J when all activities are in the partial schedule, i.e. the complete set.

Utilising the serial method in a single-pass environment, results were published by Pascoe (1966), Müller-Merbach (1967), Gonguet (1969), Fehler (1969), Cooper (1976) and (1977),[2] Boctor (1990), and Valls et al. (1992). The experimental investigation which seems to be the most sound is from Boctor who performed a computational study on the basis of 36 small instances from literature. For both of the two best priority rules employed, he

---

[2] Misleadingly, Cooper terms his scheduling scheme parallel (serial) when using priority rules in a dynamic (static) fashion. But as already pointed out by Valls et al. (1992), he clearly employed a serial scheduling scheme.

reported an average deviation of 9.13% above the optimal objective function value.

Multi-pass applications of the serial method are documented by Cooper (1976), Boctor (1990), and Li / Willis (1992).

Kelley (1963) presented also a second scheduling scheme, the so-called **parallel method**. In the same year an unpublished paper of Brooks (cf. Bedworth / Bailey (1982)) proposed another heuristic for the SMPSP, the so-called "Brooks algorithm" (BAG) which equals the parallel method presented by Kelley except of one subtle difference. Whereas some work publicised later on explicitly referred to Brooks algorithm,[3] the majority of researchers cited the work of Kelley and / or classified the scheduling scheme employed to be parallel.[4] But a closer look reveals that mostly the BAG was utilised.[5] As a consequence, two different versions of the parallel scheduling scheme are available today.

Like in the majority of publications, the scheduling scheme as proposed by Brooks is used and henceforth referred to as parallel method. Consequently, this variety of the parallel scheduling scheme is described in the sequel. For the purpose of clarification, the difference of the version due to Kelley is pointed out thereafter.

---

[3] Cf. Moder / Phillips (1964), Bedworth (1973), Whitehouse / Brown (1979), and Elsayed (1982).

[4] Cf. Pascoe (1966), Patterson (1973), Davies (1973), Davis / Patterson (1975), Patterson (1976), Thesen (1976), Whitehouse / Brown (1979), Elsayed (1982), Lawrence (1985), Ulusoy / Özdamar (1989), Alvarez-Valdes / Tamarit (1989a), Alvarez-Valdes / Tamarit (1989b), Boctor (1990), and Valls et al. (1992).

[5] Pascoe (1966), Davies (1973), Thesen (1976), Lawrence (1985), Ulusoy / Özdamar (1989), Alvarez-Valdes / Tamarit (1989a), and Alvarez-Valdes / Tamarit (1989b) provide a description of BAG. Davis / Patterson (1975) and Boctor (1990) do not give a description of the method but confer to Kelley. Patterson (1973) and Patterson (1976) neither provide a description nor confer to Kelley or Brooks. Finally, Valls et al. (1992) confer to Kelley but describe BAG.

The parallel method consists of at most J stages in each of which a set of activities (which might be empty) is scheduled. Associated with each stage is a schedule time and an exclusive partition of all activities into four disjoint sets: Activities which are completed up to the schedule time are in the *complete set*. Activities which have already been scheduled but are still active during the schedule time are in the *active set*. Activities which are available for scheduling w.r.t. precedence and resource constraints but yet unscheduled are in the *decision set*. Finally, all remaining activities are in the *remaining set*. It has to be noted that in contrast to the decision set as defined in the procedure of Stinson, activities in the decision set of the parallel method have to be additionally resource-feasible. Hence, the decision set of the parallel method is a subset of the decision set in the Stinson procedure.

The partial schedule of each stage is made up of the activities in the complete set and the active set. The schedule time of a stage equals the earliest completion time of activities in the active set of the ancestral stage. Each stage consists of two steps: First, activities with a finish time equal to the (new) schedule time are removed from the active set and put into the complete set. This in turn may free a number of activities currently in the remaining set to be put into the decision set. Second, one activity from the decision set is selected with a priority rule and scheduled, respectively started, at the current schedule time. Afterwards, the chosen activity is removed from the decision set and put into the active set. Step 2 is repeated until the decision set is empty, i.e. activities have been scheduled or are not longer available for scheduling w.r.t. resource constraints. The parallel method terminates when all activities are in the partial schedule, i.e. the complete or active set.

The parallel method (due to Brooks) and the enumeration procedure of Stinson are sharing some common components. E.g., each activity is only scheduled once and each solution of the parallel method is associated with a unique path from the root to a final node in Stinson's enumeration tree. Thereby, only those nodes are visited which represent maximal active sets, i.e. sets which are not a subset of any active set associated with a node sharing the same ancestor.

The parallel method of Kelley differs from the one of Brooks w.r.t. the first step of each stage: Activities in the active set which are not finished at the new schedule time are (temporarily) removed from the active set and put in the decision set. Formerly active activities which are selected (again) remain in the active set while the unselected ones are removed from the active set. Hence, the latter activities are scheduled more than once.

The parallel method due to Kelley shares common components with the enumeration tree of Demeulemeester and Herroelen. E.g., an activity might be scheduled more than once and each solution of the parallel method due to Kelley is associated with a unique path from the root to a final node in the enumeration tree.

Computational experiments conducted with the single-pass version of the parallel method are more frequent than those with the serial method and are reported by each paper mentioned above. Additionally, Arora / Sachdeva (1989) report an implementation of the parallel method on parallel processors.

The two most profound experimental investigations seem to be the ones by Davis / Patterson (1975) and Alvarez-Valdes / Tamarit (1989a). Davis and Patterson used 83 of the 110 problem instances assembled by Patterson (1984) in order to test 8 different priority rules. They report an average deviation from the optimal objective function value of 5.6% and 6.7% for the two best priority rules, respectively. Alvarez-Valdes and Tamarit, utilising a problem set consisting of 48 instances with 27 activities, came up with an average deviation of 2.89% for the first ranked and 3.09% for the second and third ranked priority rule, respectively.

Multi-pass efforts on the basis of the parallel method are reported by Wiest (1967),[6] Lawrence (1985), Alvarez-Valdes / Tamarit (1989b), Ulusoy / Özdamar (1989), and Boctor (1990). Alvarez-Valdes / Tamarit compared a single- and a multi-pass approach on a set of 48 instances with 103 activities each. The multi-pass approach generated for each instance 100 solutions with one priority rule biased by a random device. For the best (second best) priority rule an average increase above the optimal objective function value of 3.23% (3.45%) when used in the single-pass procedure and 2.31% (1.65%) when used in the multi-pass procedure is reported.

II. Truncated Branch and Bound

A truncated branch and bound approach was proposed by Alvarez-Valdes / Tamarit (1989a). It makes use of the enumeration tree as presented in Christofides et al. (1987). Essentially, it is the same enumeration tree as employed in the procedure of Demeulemeester / Herroelen (1992a). Consequently, the offsprings of each node are associated with activities in the active and the decision set which have to be delayed. Delaying is achieved in Christofides et al. and Alvarez-Valdes / Tamarit through the introduction of additional arcs. Instead of enumerating all offspring nodes, the heuristic implicitly or explicitly chooses one node. Implicit selection is achieved by repeatedly choosing a temporarily scheduled activity for delaying until the remaining activities are resource-feasible. The choice is based on the latest start time (LST) priority rule, i.e. the activity with the maximum LST is selected. Explicit selection is performed by choosing the node with the smallest upper bound where the bound is calculated by employing the implicit selection strategy. On a set of 84 instances similar to the ones used by Davis / Patterson (1975), the upper bound rule performed best with an average deviation from the optimal objective function of 1.21%.[7]

---

[6] Wiest proposed a scheme slightly different which produces exactly the same results.

[7] On the set of 48 instances used to benchmark the priority-rule-based single- and multi-pass approach, the upper bound rule revealed an average increase above the optimum of

III. Disjunctive-Arc-Based Heuristics

Based on the methodology of disjunctive arcs developed by Balas (1969) for solving the job shop problem (JSP), heuristic solution methods for the SMPSP were proposed by Shaffer et al. (1965), Alvarez-Valdes / Tamarit (1989a) and Bell / Han (1991).

Definition 5.2 (cf. Radermacher (1985/86, p. 229)): A **forbidden set** F is a subset of X such that activities are technologically independent, i.e. for each pair of activities (i, j), $1 \leq i, j \leq J$ and $i \neq j$, there is $i \notin \{\overline{P}_j \cup \overline{S}_j\}$ and $j \notin \{\overline{P}_i \cup \overline{S}_i\}$, and such that activities are not allowed to be in progress at the same time due to resource constraints. A forbidden set is called a **minimal forbidden set** MF, if none of its proper subsets is a forbidden set. F denotes the set of all forbidden sets and MF denotes the set of all minimal forbidden sets.

Employing Definitions 4.2 and 5.2, the basic idea of the disjunctive-arc-based approaches is to extend the precedence relations (the set of so-called conjunctive arcs) by adding additional arcs (the so-called disjunctive arcs) such that the minimal forbidden sets are destroyed and thus the earliest finish schedule is feasible w.r.t. (precedence and) resource constraints. Hence, the main problem is to add the disjunctive arcs in a manner that the earliest finish time of the unique dummy sink (and thus the makespan) is minimised. It has to be pointed out that additional arcs might cause redundant arcs or even cycles of positive length. While the former do not pose any problems, the latter lead to infeasibility because the earliest finish schedule cannot be calculated anymore.

Although never calling it a disjunctive arc approach, **Shaffer et al.** were the first who designed an algorithm with this concept for solving the SMPSP. Within their "resource scheduling method" (RSM) the scope is restricted

---

2.0%, 0.77%, and 0.49% for an imposed time limit of 72, 180, and 360 seconds, respectively.

solely to those forbidden sets for which all activities in the earliest finish schedule are processed at the same time. Starting with the forbidden set associated with the earliest period t, the disjunctive arc which produces the smallest increase in the earliest finish time of the unique sink is introduced and the earliest finish schedule is recalculated. The algorithm terminates as soon as a (precedence- and) resource-feasible earliest finish schedule is found. Shaffer et al. do not report on computational results. Nevertheless, their approach is almost identical to the first part of the algorithm presented by Bell / Han which is introduced in the sequel. Consequently, it can be concluded that on the basis of the instance set assembled by Patterson (1984) the average increase above the optimal objective function value is approximately 5%.

Alvarez-Valdes / Tamarit proposed four different ways of destroying the minimal forbidden sets. The best results were achieved by applying the following strategy: Beginning with the minimal forbidden sets of lowest cardinality, one set is arbitrarily chosen and destroyed by adding the disjunctive arc for which the earliest finish time of the unique dummy sink is minimal (no advice is given in the case of ties). The procedure terminates when all forbidden sets are destroyed. On their set of 84 instances (cf. Subsection II) this rule achieved an average increase above the optimal objective function value of 1.41%.

Bell / Han presented a two-phase algorithm. The first phase is very similar to the approach of Shaffer et al. In contrast to the latter, Bell and Han employ a tie-breaking rule which in case of ties selects the disjunctive arc (i, j) associated with the earliest start time of activity i. Phase 2 tries to improve the feasible solution obtained by phase one: After removing redundant arcs, each disjunctive arc being part of the critical path(s) is temporarily cancelled and the phase 1 procedure is applied again. If a better solution is found, the latter replaces the incumbent best solution. Bell and Han tested both phases on the instances of Patterson (1984) and came up with an average increase above the optimal objective function value of 4.8% and 2.6% for the first as well as the first and the second phase, respectively.

IV. Local Search Techniques

So far, **Sampson / Weiss** (1993) are the only ones who tried their hand on local search techniques in order to solve the SMPSP heuristically. Basically, their procedure consists of three components: the representation of a solution, the neighbourhood structure, and the way in which the neighbourhood is searched (cf. Papadimitriou / Steiglitz (1982, p. 469)). A *solution* is represented by a so-called shift vector V, a $1 \times J$ array with integer elements $V[j] \geq 0$ for all j, $1 \leq j \leq J$. A schedule S is then defined as a mapping $\phi : V \rightarrow S$ in the following manner: The start time of each activity j, $1 \leq j \leq J$, equals the maximum finish time of its predecessors plus $V[j]$. The resulting schedule is feasible w.r.t. precedence constraints only. Infeasibility w.r.t. resource constraints is handled by penalising the objective function with a measure taking into account the number of renewable resources used in excess of the period limit. The *neighbourhood structure* of vector V w.r.t. activity j is made of all vectors V' with $V'[j] \neq V[j]$ and $V'[i] = V[i]$ for $i \neq j$ for which the makespan of the corresponding schedule S' does not exceed a prescribed upper bound. A thus defined entire neighbourhood is searched for the best V' and a new intermediate solution is stored if the objective function associated with the best V' is a certain amount better than the one of V. Regarding activity j, the *search procedure* initialises element $V'[j]$ as $V'[j] = 0$ and considers it contiguously, i.e. $V'[j] = 1, 2, \dots,$. When terminating the neighbourhood search of activity j, V is set to V'. It has to be noted that this is not the best shift vector of the neighbourhood search but the last shift vector which has been evaluated. An intermediate solution which is feasible w.r.t. resource constraints and better than the so far best solution replaces the latter. One iteration of the local search algorithm consists of performing a neighbourhood search for each activity j in a contiguous fashion. The solution process is distorted by differently weighting the penalising functions every four iterations. Termination of the algorithm occurs when a maximal number of iterations is reached. A computational study performed on the basis of the instances by Patterson (1984) with 10 iterations per problem revealed an average increase above the optimal objective function value of 1.98%.

5.2 Single-Pass Priority-Rule-Based Scheduling

Section 5.2.1 presents the already introduced priority-rule-based scheduling schemes more formally. In addition, theorems are proposed, stating the class of schedules on which the generation is performed. This provides valuable information regarding the capability of generating good and / or optimal solutions. As already pointed out in Section 5.1, the focus is on the serial method and on the parallel method due to Brooks. Section 5.2.2 provides an overview of traditional priority rules proposed in the literature. Furthermore, it presents two new priority rules which are based on a thorough description of the RSM priority rule. As indicated by the name, the latter stems from the "resource scheduling method" proposed by Shaffer et. al. (1965), which has been reviewed in Section 5.1.2.

5.2.1 Schedule Generation Schemes

I. The Serial Scheduling Scheme

To give a formal description of the serial scheduling scheme some additional notation has to be introduced. At stage $n = 1,...,J$ let

C_n be the complete set,

D_n be the decision set,

R_n be the remaining set,

PS_n be the partial schedule, and

πK_{rt} be the left-over capacity of the renewable resource r in period t.

Furthermore, recall that X denotes the set of all activities and that $A_t(PS_n)$ denotes the set of activities of the partial schedule PS_n which are in progress in period t. Then, for a given complete set C_n, the decision set D_n, the remaining set R_n, the partial schedule PS_n, and the left-over capacity πK_{rt} are defined as follows:

$$D_n = \{ j \mid j \notin C_n, P_j \subseteq C_n \}$$
$$R_n = X \setminus \{ C_n \cup D_n \}$$
$$PS_n = \{ C_n \}$$
$$\pi K_{rt} = K_r - \sum_{j \in A_t(PS_n)} k_{jr}$$

Finally, let denote PST_j the precedence-feasible start time and - as outlined in Section 5.2.2 - let denote $v(j)$ a priority value of activity $j, j \in D_n$. The serial scheduling scheme (SSS) can then be described formally as follows:

$$\boxed{\text{SSS}}$$

Initialisation: $n := 1$; $C_n = PS_n := \varnothing$;

WHILE $|PS_n| < J$ DO **Stage n**
BEGIN
   UPDATE D_n, R_n, and πK_{rt}, $t=1,...,T$, $r \in R$;
   $j^* := \min_{j \in D_n} \{ j \mid v(j) = \text{extremum}_{i \in D_n} v(i) \}$;
   $PST_{j^*} := \max \{ FT_i \mid i \in P_{j^*} \}$;
   $ST_{j^*} := \min \{ t \mid PST_{j^*} \leq t \leq LST_{j^*}, k_{j^*r} \leq \pi K_{r\tau}, \tau = t+1,...,t+d_{j^*}, r \in R \}$;
   $FT_{j^*} := ST_{j^*} + d_{j^*}$;
   $C_{n+1} := PS_{n+1} := C_n \cup \{ j^* \}$;
   $n := n+1$;
END;

Stop: A feasible schedule $S = (FT_1,...,FT_J)$ has been generated;

***

In order to illustrate the serial scheduling scheme, consider the project illustrated by Figure 5.1 as well as the associated priority values which are presented in Table 5.1.[8]

---

[8] The values have been derived by backward recursion with $T=EFT_J=6$.

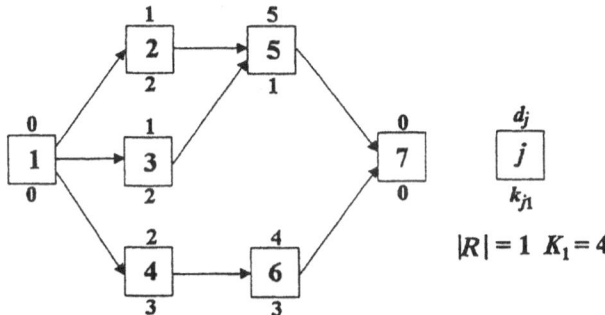

Figure 5.1: Example Project

j	1	2	3	4	5	6	7
$v(j)$	0	1	1	2	6	6	6

Table 5.1: Priority Values for the Example Project

The report of the serial scheduling scheme is provided in Table 5.2 and the derived schedule $S = (0,1,1,3,6,7,7)$ is displayed in Figure 5.2. Since its makespan equals the resource-based lower bound (cf. formula 5.2), the solution is optimal.

n	$\pi K_{1t},\ 1 \le t \le 8$	$C_n = PS_n$	D_n	R_n	$v(j)$	j^*	FT_{j^*}
1	(4,4,4,4,4,4,4,4)	$\emptyset$	1	2,...,7	0	1	0
2	(4,4,4,4,4,4,4,4)	1	2,...4	5,...,7	1,1,2	2	1
3	(2,4,4,4,4,4,4,4)	1,2	3,4	5,...,7	1,2	3	1
4	(0,4,4,4,4,4,4,4)	1,...,3	4,5	6,7	2,6	4	3
5	(0,1,1,4,4,4,4,4)	1,...,4	5,6	7	6,6	5	6
6	(0,0,0,3,3,3,4,4)	1,...,5	6	7	6	6	7
7	(0,0,0,0,0,0,1,4)	1,...,6	7	$\emptyset$	6	7	7

Table 5.2: Report of the Serial Scheduling Scheme

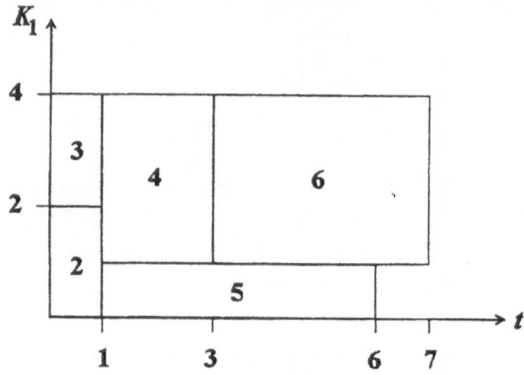

Figure 5.2: Optimal Solution of the Example Project

Three important questions associated with each heuristic are: (*i*) Is a feasible solution always granted, (*ii*) on what kind of solution space does the heuristic operate, i.e. is the heuristic generally capable to produce optimal solutions, and (*iii*) does the heuristic produce optimal solutions if the problem is not longer *NP*-hard? In the sequel all three questions are answered for the serial scheduling scheme. This provides deeper insight into this well-known heuristic.

Theorem 5.1: For any (feasible) instance of the SMPSP the serial scheduling scheme always generates a feasible schedule.

Proof: Recalling Definition 3.2, a schedule S if feasible if the precedence and resource constraints are maintained. While line 3 within stage n of the serial scheduling scheme meets the former prerequisite, the latter is preserved by line 4 of stage n for each activity j, $1 \leq j \leq J$. Thus, the resulting schedule is feasible. ■

Theorem 5.2: A schedule S generated with the serial scheduling scheme and any priority rule belongs to the set of active schedules AS.

Proof: To prove that S belongs to AS it must be shown that no activity can be locally or globally left shifted (cf. Definition 3.8). Consider activity j to be selected at stage n. Then, its time window of precedence-feasible start times is restricted from the latest finish times of all its immediate predecessors to its latest start time. Afterwards, activity j is scheduled at the earliest contiguous resource-feasible interval of d_j units length in the precedence-feasible time window. A left shift of activity j is therefore not possible and thus the schedule S is at least active. Furthermore, it has to be proven that S is not in the set of non-delay schedules NDS. This can be achieved by showing that in the corresponding unit-time-duration schedule S_{UTD} at least one of the unit-time-duration activities can be locally or globally left shifted (cf. Definitions 3.5 and 3.6). Again, consider that activity j with a duration of $d_j > 1$ is selected at stage n and, additionally, that there are two contiguous resource-feasible intervals in the precedence-feasible time window of activity j: the "earlier" one with less than d_j and the "latter" one with d_j units in length. Activity j is then scheduled at the earliest contiguous resource-feasible interval of d_j units length in the precedence-feasible time window. Hence, within the corresponding unit-time-duration schedule at least $j1$, the first unit-time-duration activity emanating from activity j, can be globally left-shifted. Therefore S is not in NDS.   ■

Theorem 5.3: For any instance of the SMPSP with $RS(R)=1$, i.e. the resource-unconstrained case, the serial scheduling scheme always derives the optimal solution.

Proof: For the resource-unconstrained case there exists exactly one active schedule which at the same time is the earliest finish schedule (cf. Definition 4.2). Since within the latter EFT_J, the finish time of the unique sink, is a lower bound for the SMPSP (cf. formula 5.1) the solution is optimal.   ■

II. The Parallel Scheduling Scheme

To give a formal description of the parallel scheduling scheme some additional notation has to be introduced. At stage n, $1 \le n \le J$, let

t_n be the schedule time,

A_n be the active set, and

πK_r be the left-over period capacity of the renewable resource r at the schedule time.

For a given schedule time t_n and a given complete set C_n, the active set A_n, the left-over capacity πK_r, the decision set D_n, the remaining set R_n, and the partial schedule PS_n are defined as follows:

$A_n = \{ j \mid ST_j \leq t_n < FT_j \}$

$\pi K_r = K_r - \sum_{j \in A_n} k_{jr}$

$D_n = \{ j \mid j \notin \{ C_n \cup A_n \}, P_j \subseteq C_n, k_{jr} \leq \pi K_r \ \forall \, r \in R \}$

$R_n = X \setminus \{ C_n \cup A_n \cup D_n \}$

$PS_n = \{ C_n \cup A_n \}$

Now, the parallel scheduling scheme (PSS) can be described as follows:

$$\boxed{\text{PSS}}$$

Initialisation: $n := 1; \ t_n := 0; \ D_n := \{1\}; \ A_n = C_n := \varnothing; \ \pi K_r := K_r \ \forall \, r \in R;$
GOTO Step (2);

WHILE $|PS_n| < J$ DO **Stage n**
BEGIN
  (1) $t_n := \min \{ FT_j \mid j \in A_{n-1} \};$
      $A_n := A_{n-1} \setminus \{ j \mid j \in A_{n-1}, FT_j = t_n \};$
      $C_n := C_{n-1} \cup \{ j \mid j \in A_{n-1}, FT_j = t_n \};$
      UPDATE $\pi K_r \ \forall \, r \in R, D_n$, and R_n;
  (2) $j^* := \min_{j \in D_n} \{ j \mid v(j) = \text{extremum}_{i \in D_n} v(i) \};$
      $ST_{j^*} := t_n;$
      $FT_{j^*} := ST_{j^*} + d_{j^*};$
      $A_n := A_n \cup \{ j^* \};$
      UPDATE $\pi K_r \ \forall \, r \in R, PS_n, D_n$, and R_n;
      IF $D_n \neq \varnothing$ THEN GOTO Step (2), ELSE DO
      BEGIN
          $PS_{n+1} := PS_n, \ n := n+1;$
      END;
END;

Stop: A feasible schedule $S = (FT_1, ..., FT_J)$ has been generated;

$$* * *$$

In order to illustrate the parallel scheduling scheme, the problem depicted in Figure 5.1 was solved by employing the same priority values as for the serial scheme (cf. Table 5.1). The solution derived is identical to the one created by the serial scheduling scheme (cf. Figure 5.2). Table 5.3 provides a report of the solution procedure.

A slightly different parallel scheduling scheme has been proposed by Thesen (1976) and for the multi-project SMPSP by Patterson (1973). Instead of repeating step (2) until the decision set is empty, they select the activities to be scheduled in a single step. This is achieved by setting up a zero-one integer program which maximises the priority values of all activities in the decision set subject to the left-over period capacity.[9]

n	t_n	πK_1	A_n	C_n	PS_n	D_n	R_n	$v(j)$	j^*	FT_{j^*}
1	0	4	∅	∅	∅	1	2,...,7	0	1	0
2	0	4	∅	1	1	2,...,4	5,...,7	1,1,2	2	1
		2	2	1	1,2	3	4,...,7	1	3	1
		0	2,3	1	1,2	∅	4,...,7			
3	1	4	∅	1,...,3	1,...,3	4,5	6,7	2,6	4	3
		1	4	1,...,3	1,...,4	5	6,7	6	5	6
		0	4,5	1,...,3	1,...,5	∅	6,7			
4	3	3	5	1,...,4	1,...,5	6	7	6	6	7
		0	5,6	1,...,4	1,...,6	∅	7			
5	6	1	6	1,...,5	1,...,6	∅	7			
6	7	4	∅	1,...,6	1,...,6	7	∅	6	7	7

Table 5.3: Report of the Parallel Scheduling Scheme

The following three theorems can be stated for the parallel scheduling scheme:

---

[9] Note that this results in solving a (multi-period) knapsack problem for the single (multiple) resource-constrained SMPSP.

Theorem 5.4: For any (feasible) instance of the SMPSP the parallel scheduling scheme generates always a feasible schedule.

Proof: Recalling Definition 3.2, for a schedule S the precedence constraints and the resource constraints have to be met in order to be feasible. Both constraints are met by definition of the decision set. Hence, each scheduled activity and thus the resulting schedule is feasible.   ■

Theorem 5.5: A schedule S generated with the parallel scheduling scheme and any priority rule belongs to the set of non-delay schedules NDS.

Proof: To prove that S belongs to NDS it must be shown that in the corresponding unit-time-duration schedule S_{UTD} none of the unit-time-duration activities can be locally or globally left-shifted (cf. Definitions 3.5 and 3.6, respectively).

Assume that in the unit-time-duration schedule the first activity $j1$ emanating from activity j can be globally or locally left-shifted to period t_n. Hence, at stage n of the parallel scheduling scheme, activity j has been in the decision set because as a prerequisite to left-shift $j1$ all predecessors of j were finished and each resource provided enough left-over capacity, respectively. In addition, stage n was finished without scheduling activity j, leaving enough left-over capacity in period t_n to accommodate the unit-time-duration activity $j1$. Therefore, activity j still has been in the decision set when stage n was finished. But this is not possible because the algorithm terminates a stage only when the decision set is empty. This assures that activity $j1$ cannot be left-shifted at all which causes the resulting schedule S to be in NDS.   ■

At this juncture, Remark 3.8 has to be recalled which states that the set of non-delay schedules might not contain a schedule which optimises a regular measure of performance. On this account, it has to be noted that the parallel scheduling scheme has the severe drawback of searching in a solution space which might not contain the optimal solution.

Theorem 5.6: For any instance of the SMPSP with $RS(R)=1$, i.e. the re-source-unconstrained case, the parallel scheduling scheme always derives the optimal solution.

Proof: For the resource-unconstrained case there is only one non-delay schedule which at the same time is the earliest finish schedule. Since within the latter EFT_J, the finish time of the unique sink, is a lower bound for the SMPSP (cf. formula 5.1) the solution is optimal. ∎

5.2.2 Priority Rules

I. Classical Priority Rules

The number of priority rules proposed in the scheduling literature is abundant. Other terms such as scheduling rule or dispatching rule are often used synonymously. The majority of rules stems from the static and dynamic JSP, respectively.[10] A survey of priority rules for the JSP can be found in Conway et al. (1967), Panwalkar / Iskander (1977), and Haupt (1989). A review of priority rules for the SMPSP solely is provided in Lawrence (1985) and Alvarez-Valdes / Tamarit (1989a).

Regarding resource-constrained project scheduling, priority rules were stated and investigated for single- and multiple-project problems. Whereas publications dealing with priority rules for the single-project case were already introduced in Section 5.1.2, work on the multiple-project case can be found in Pritsker et al. (1969), Patterson (1973), Patterson (1976), Kurtulus / Davis (1982), Kurtulus / Narula (1985), Norbis / Smith (1986), Mohanty / Siddiq (1989), Bock / Patterson (1990), Tsubakitani / Deckro (1990), Kim / Leachman (1993), and Lawrence / Morton (1993).

Generally, a priority rule is made up by (*i*) a mapping

---

[10] Where the latter is characterised by random job arrival times and / or random processing times (cf. Conway et al. (1967)).

$$v : j \in D_n \rightarrow R_{\geq 0} \tag{5.3}$$

which assigns to each activity j in the decision set D_n a priority value $v(j)$ and (*ii*) the way the extremum of the priority values is determined. That is, the decision whether the activity with the minimum (extremum = min) or maximum (extremum = max) priority value is selected. Ties can be resolved by choosing the activity with the minimum activity number. In that case any priority rule can be written formally as follows:

$$j^* = \min_{j \in D_n} \{ j \mid v(j) = \text{extremum}_{i \in D_n} v(i) \} \tag{5.4}$$

Henceforth each priority rule is labelled with the most frequent used acronym and for ease of notation described by the tuple (v, extremum). E.g., the SPT rule is denoted as:

Shortest processing time (SPT)

$$v(j) = d_j, \qquad\qquad\qquad \text{extremum} = \min \tag{5.5}$$

Priority rules can be classified according to different criteria. It should be mentioned that the classes provided by these criteria are neither exhaustive nor exclusive and are just one way of characterising the abundance of rules presented.

A straightforward discrimination w.r.t. the information processed is to classify priority rules into **network-**, **time-**, and **resource-**based priority rules (cf. Lawrence (1985) and Alvarez-Valdes / Tamarit (1989a)).[11] An example for each class is "the most immediate successors" , the "latest start time", and the "greatest (renewable) resource demand" rule, respectively (cf. Alvarez-Valdes / Tamarit (1989a)):

---

[11] Alvarez-Valdes / Tamarit propose a slightly different discrimination

Most immediate successors (MIS)

$$v(j) = |S_j|, \qquad\qquad \text{extremum} = \text{max} \qquad (5.6)$$

Latest start time (LST)

$$v(j) = LST_j, \qquad\qquad \text{extremum} = \text{min} \qquad (5.7)$$

Greatest resource demand (GRD)

$$v(j) = d_j \sum_{r \in R} k_{jr}, \qquad\qquad \text{extremum} = \text{max} \qquad (5.8)$$

Priority rules which return the same priority value for a certain activity - regardless of the stage they are performed in - are called **static**, whereas priority rules which may produce different values are called **dynamic**. E.g., clearly MIS and GRD are static whereas the "minimum slack" rule (cf. Davis/ Patterson (1975)) is dynamic:

Minimum slack (MSLK)

$$v(j) = LST_j - EST'_j, \qquad\qquad \text{extremum} = \text{min} \qquad (5.9)$$

EST'_j denotes the earliest precedence- and resource-feasible start time of activity j.[12]

Another distinction of priority rules is due to the amount of information processed: Rules which employ a small amount of input, usually w.r.t. the activity under consideration only, are regarded to be **local** or myopic while rules which make use of a large amount of information are called **global**. Surely, SPT is a local rule whereas the "greatest rank positional weight" rule (cf. Alvarez-Valdes / Tamarit (1989a)) is one global rule.

---

[12] Note that in the parallel scheduling scheme EST'_j equals t_n for $j \in D_n$ and thus MSLK and LST derive identical priority values which was first proven by Davis / Patterson (1975).

Greatest rank positional weight (GRPW)

$$v(j) = d_j + \sum_{i \in S_j} d_i, \qquad\qquad \text{extremum = max} \qquad (5.10)$$

Further to mention is the differentiation in **single** and **composite priority rules**. Let a priority value $v(j)$ be defined as the weighted sum of L different priority values $v_l(j)$, $l=1,...,L$, i.e.

$$v(j) = \sum_{l=1}^{L} w_l \, v_l(j) \qquad 0 \leq w_l \leq 1, \ \sum_{l=1}^{L} w_l = 1 \qquad (5.11)$$

where v_l and w_l denote the priority value and the weight associated with the l-th priority rule, respectively. Then we have a single priority rule for $L=1$ and a composite priority rule for $L > 1$. An example for a composite priority rule is the "weighted resource utilisation ratio and precedence" rule (WRUP) proposed by Ulusoy / Özdamar (1989). It is a combination of the MIS rule and the "relative resource usage" priority rule.

Weighted resource utilisation ratio and precedence (WRUP)

$$v(j) = w_1 \, |S_j| + w_2 \sum_{r \in R} \frac{k_{jr}}{K_r}, \qquad\qquad \text{extremum = max} \qquad (5.12)$$

An important issue regarding composite rules is the imbalance of scales between the priority values of employed rules. Imbalance of scales can be considered in two ways: implicitly by properly adjusting the weighting vector or explicitly by scaling the priority values (cf. Whitehouse / Brown (1979)). Amongst others, composite rules for the SMPSP were proposed by Elsayed (1982), Whithouse / Brown (1979), and Ulusoy / Özdamar (1989).

Finally, priority rules can be classified into rules where the priority value is a **lower bound** or makes use of a lower bound on the one side and rules where no lower bound is part of the priority value on the other side. The "latest finish time" rule (cf. Davis / Patterson (1975)) is a priority rule which uses the well-known precedence-based lower bound (cf. Section 5.1.1) while the "most total successors" rule (cf. Alvarez-Valdes / Tamarit (1989a)) does not employ any lower bounds.

Latest finish time (LFT)

$$v(j) = LFT_j, \qquad\qquad\qquad \text{extremum} = \min \qquad (5.13)$$

Most total successors (MTS)

$$v(j) = |\bar{S}_j|, \qquad\qquad\qquad \text{extremum} = \max \qquad (5.14)$$

Table 5.4 gives an overview of the (alphabetically ordered) priority rules presented so far as well as their characterisation via the bold capital letters.

	Network-, Time-, Resource-based	Static, Dynamic	Local, Global	Single, Composite	Lower Bound
GRD	- / - / R	S	L	S	-
GRPW	N / - / -	S	G	C	-
LFT	N / T / -	S	G	S	LB
LST	N / T / -	S	G	S	LB
MIS	N / - / -	S	L	S	-
MSLK	N / T / -	D	G	S	LB
MTS	N / - / -	S	G	S	-
SPT	- / T / -	S	L	S	-
WRUP	N / - / R	S	G	C	-

Table 5.4: Characterisation of Classical Priority Rules

In order to select the best traditional priority rules, the most profound computational studies w.r.t. single-pass priority rules were consulted.[13] Table 5.5 lists the ranking of the three best priority rules in all 4 publications, respectively. $a \succ b$ states that priority rule a outperformed priority rule b within the paper under consideration It has to be pointed out that only the

---

[13] Cf. Davis / Patterson (1975), Alvarez-Valdes / Tamarit (1989a), Valls et al. (1992), and Boctor (1990).

studies by Boctor (1990) and Valls et al. (1992) employed (the parallel and) the serial scheduling scheme and that none of the three best rules was applied in the serial scheduling scheme. Note that LST and MSLK are listed separately because the priority rules were employed in both schemes and that the RSM rule will be presented in the following section.

Literature	Ranking of Priority Rules
Davis / Patterson (1975)	MSLK $\succ$ LFT $\succ$ RSM
Boctor (1990)	MSLK $\succ$ LFT $\succ$ RSM
Alvarez / Tamarit (1989a)	GRPW $\succ$ LFT $\succ$ MTS
Valls et al. (1992)	MSLK $\succ$ GRPW $\succ$ MTS

Table 5.5: Ranking of Priority Rules in the Literature

II. Two New Priority Rules

Stepping stone for two new priority rules is the so-called RSM rule. As indicated by the name, the fundamental idea of this classical priority rule stems from the disjunctive-arc-based heuristic proposed in Shaffer et al. (1965) which has been introduced in Section 5.1.2. The RSM rule is applicable to the parallel scheduling scheme only and has been considered in studies undertaken by Davis / Patterson (1975), Alvarez-Valdes / Tamarit (1989a), Boctor (1990), Ulusoy / Özdamar (1989), and Valls et al. (1992).

The idea of the RSM rule is as follows: For each pair of activities i and j in the decision set, it is calculated how many periods activity i is delayed beyond its (precedence-based) latest start time if scheduled after activity j. The activity j which induces the smallest delay of every other activity in the decision set is scheduled. In order to write the RSM rule formally we denote by AP_n the set of all activity pairs in the decision set at stage n, i.e. $AP_n = \{ (i,j) \mid i, j \in D_n, i \neq j \}$.

Resource scheduling method (RSM)

$$v(j) = \max \{0, t_n + d_j - LST_i \mid (i,j) \in AP_n \}, \qquad \text{extremum} = \min \qquad (5.15)$$

Stated this way, the RSM priority rule implicitly makes use of the following assumption: For each pair of activities i and j one activity has always to be delayed until the end of the other activity. This assumption does not hold in general and hence might produce poor results when applying the RSM priority rule. This is demonstrated with the following two examples: Consider the project displayed in Figure 5.3 where there are 6 activities and $|R|=1$ resource with a period availability of $K_1=4$. The associated latest start times derived by backward recursion (with a latest project finish time $T=EFT_6=5$) are given in Table 5.6.

j	1	2	3	4	5	6
LST_j	0	3	1	2	0	5

Table 5.6: Latest Start Times for the Example Project

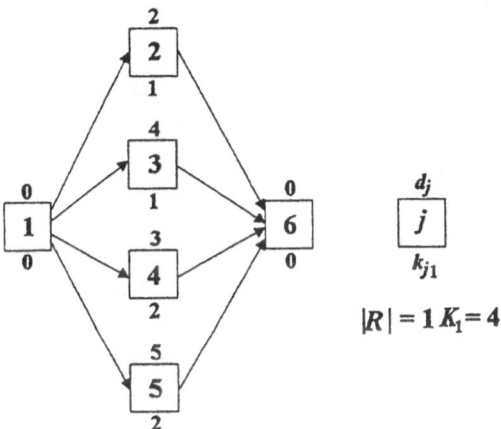

Figure 5.3: Example Project

At stage $n=2$ the following situation arises: $t_n=0$, $\pi K_1=4$, $C_n=\{1\}$, $A_n=\emptyset$, $D_n=\{2,3,4,5\}$, and $AP_n= \{(2,3),(2,4),(2,5),(3,4),(3,5),(4,5)\}$. The RSM priority value for activity 2 is calculated to $v(2) = \max \{0, t_2+d_2-LST_3, t_2+d_2-$

$LST_4, t_2+d_2-LST_5\} = \max \{0, 0+2-1, 0+2-2, 0+2-0\} = \max \{0,1,0,2\} = 2$. Presuming that the above stated assumption holds, scheduling activity 2 would induce a delay of two periods for the latest start time of activity 5. Obviously, this is not the case since each of the activity pairs containing activity 2, i.e. (2,3), (2,4), and (2,5), can be started simultaneously at the schedule time.

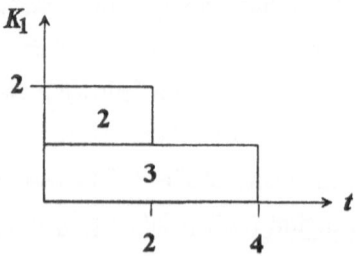

Figure 5.4: Partial Schedule of the Example Project

Consider now that activity 2 and 3 have been scheduled and consequently at stage $n=2$ the partial schedule is as shown by Figure 5.4, i.e. $t_n=0$, $\pi K_1=2$, $C_n=\{1\}$, $A_n=\{2,3\}$, $D_n=\{4,5\}$, and $AP_n=\{(4,5)\}$. Actually, at this stage the activities of the pair (4,5) in the decision set cannot be started jointly. The RSM priority values turn out to be $v(4)=\max \{0, t_2+d_4-LST_5\} = \max \{0, 0+3-0\} = 3$ and $v(5)=\max \{0, t_2+d_5-LST_4\} = \max \{0, 0+5-2\} = 3$. A look at Figure 5.5 reveals that scheduling activity 4 indeed forces activity 5 to be delayed until the end of activity 4, i.e. three periods beyond its latest start time as indicated by $v(4)$.

But as can be seen in Figure 5.6, if activity 5 is scheduled, activity 4 is only postponed two periods beyond its latest start time. Hence, the assumption implicitly stated by the RSM priority rule is associated with severe drawbacks. Consequently, the priority rule cannot suggest properly which activity has to be scheduled first.

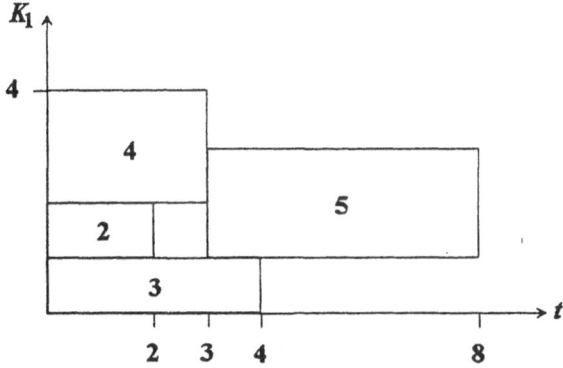

Figure 5.5: Feasible Solution of the Example Project

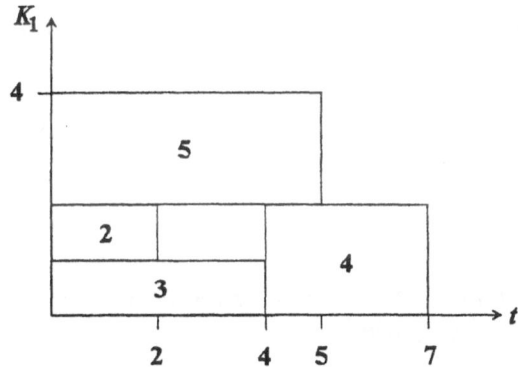

Figure 5.6: Optimal Solution of the Example Project

The RSM priority rule is now refined as follows: The set of activity pairs AP_n is divided into three disjoint subsets: The set of generally forbidden pairs (GFP_n) contains activity pairs which - due to resource constraints - can never be scheduled simultaneously, the set of temporarily forbidden pairs (TFP_n) contains pairs of activities which in general can be scheduled simultaneously but - due to limited left-over capacity - cannot be scheduled simultaneously at the schedule time. Finally, the set of currently schedulable pairs (CSP_n) contains the activity pairs which can be scheduled simultaneously at the current schedule time. More formally:

$$GFP_n = \{ (i,j) \mid (i,j) \in AP_n, \exists\, r \in R : k_{ir} + k_{jr} > K_r \} \qquad (5.16)$$

$$TFP_n = \{ (i,j) \mid (i,j) \in AP_n, (i,j) \notin GFP_n, \exists\, r \in R : k_{ir} + k_{jr} > \pi K_r \} \quad (5.17)$$

$$CSP_n = \{ (i,j) \mid (i,j) \in AP_n, \forall\, r \in R : k_{ir} + k_{jr} \leq \pi K_r \} \qquad (5.18)$$

Since there are three disjoint subsets, $AP_n = GFP_n \cup TFP_n \cup CSP_n$ holds. Consider the example above: At the beginning of stage $n{=}2$ there are $GFP_n{=}$ $TFP_n{=}\emptyset$ and $CSP_n{=}AP_n{=}\{(2,3), (2,4), (2,5), (3,4), (3,5), (4,5)\}$. After activities 2 and 3 have been scheduled there are $GFP_n = \emptyset$, $TFP_n = AP_n = \{(4,5)\}$, and $CSP_n{=}\emptyset$.

Obviously, the earliest time two activities of an activity pair can be started simultaneously is the schedule time if $(i,j) \in CSP_n$ and ∞ if $(i,j) \in GFP_n$. The question is at what period the two activities of a pair can be scheduled simultaneously if they belong to the set TFP_n. Let us make the following considerations: At stage n, $\Pi'_{(i,j)}$, the earliest time the temporarily forbidden activity pair (i,j) can be processed simultaneously w.r.t. resource type r only, is given by

$$\Pi^r_{(i,j)} = \min \{ \tau \mid \sum_{h \in An \mid FTh \leq \tau} k_{hr} + \pi K_r \geq k_{ir} + k_{jr},\ \tau = t_n,...,T \} \qquad (5.19)$$

with $(i, j) \in TFP_n$. Then, $\Pi_{(i,j)}$, the earliest time to process two activities (i,j) of a temporarily forbidden activity pair simultaneously w.r.t. to all resource types, is

$$\Pi_{(i,j)} = \max \{ \Pi^r_{(i,j)} \mid r \in R \} \qquad\qquad (i,j) \in TFP_n \qquad (5.20)$$

Now, $\overline{\Pi}_{(i,j)}$, the earliest time for any pair (i,j) of activities to be scheduled simultaneously, can be defined as

$$\overline{\Pi}_{(i,j)} = \begin{cases} \infty, & \text{if } (i,j) \in GFP \\ \Pi_{(i,j)}, & \text{if } (i,j) \in TFP \\ t_n, & \text{if } (i,j) \in CSP \end{cases} \qquad (i,j) \in AP_n \qquad (5.21)$$

Consequently, for the activity pair (i,j), $E_{(j,i)}$, the earliest time to schedule activity i if activity j is started at the schedule time t_n, is given by

$$E_{(j,i)} = \min \{\, t_n + d_j,\ \overline{\Pi}_{(i,j)} \mid (i,j) \in AP_n \,\} \tag{5.22}$$

and $E_{(i,j)}$, the earliest time to schedule activity j if activity i is started at the schedule time t_n, is given by

$$E_{(i,j)} = \min \{\, t_n + d_i,\ \overline{\Pi}_{(i,j)} \mid (i,j) \in AP_n \,\} \tag{5.23}$$

Now, an improved <u>RSM</u> priority rule (IRSM) can be stated as follows: Schedule the activity j which induces the smallest increase of the precedence-based lower bound for the activities in the decision set which have not been chosen.

Improved RSM priority rule (IRSM)

$$v(j) = \max \{0,\ E_{(j,i)} - LST_i \mid (i,j) \in AP_n \},\qquad \text{extremum} = \min \tag{5.24}$$

The activity with the minimum value is selected. Note that we start activity j, $j \in D_n$, at the current schedule time and hence calculate $E_{(j,i)}$ for all activities i, $i \in D_n$ and $i \neq j$.

Utilising $E_{(i,j)}$ and combining it with the notion of slack another new priority rule can be formulated as follows: Schedule the activity j which - if not chosen - has the worst case slack.

<u>W</u>orst <u>c</u>ase <u>s</u>lack priority rule (WCS)

$$v(j) = LST_j - \max \{\, E_{(i,j)} \mid (i,j) \in AP_n \,\},\qquad \text{extremum} = \min \tag{5.25}$$

The two new priority rules are demonstrated by applying them to the example project of this section. Consider stage $n=2$ of the partial schedule depicted in Figure 5.4 with $t_n=0$, $\pi K_1=2$, $A_n=\{2,3\}$, $D_n=\{4,5\}$. The set of the temporarily forbidden pairs is $TFP_n = AP_n = \{(4,5)\}$, i.e., activities 4 and 5 cannot be started jointly at the current schedule time t_n. Consequently, the set of general forbidden pairs and the set of currently schedulable pairs are empty, i.e., $GFP_n = CSP_n = \varnothing$. Now, the earliest time to process activities 4 and 5 simultaneously is $\overline{\Pi}_{45} = \overline{\Pi}_{54} = 4$. Then, the earliest time to start activity

5, if activity 4 is scheduled at t_2, is $E_{(4,5)} = \min\{t_2+d_4, \overline{\Pi}_{54}\} = \min\{0+3,4\} =$ 3. Correspondingly, the earliest time to start activity 4 if activity 5 is scheduled at t_2 is $E_{(5,4)} = \min\{t_2+d_5, \overline{\Pi}_{45}\} = \min\{0+5,4\} = 4$.

Hence, the values for the IRSM rule are $v(4) = \max\{0, E_{(4,5)}\text{-}LST_5\} =$ $\max\{0,3\text{-}0\} = 3$ and $v(5) = \max\{0,4\text{-}2\} = 2$, respectively. I.e., scheduling activity 4 (5) increases the precedence-based lower makespan bound by 3 (2) periods. The IRSM rule chooses activity 5 to be started, which leads to the optimal solution as depicted in Figure 4.

Applying the WCS priority rule, the following priority values are calculated: $v(4) = LST_4\text{-}\max\{E_{(5,4)}\} = 2\text{-}4 = \text{-}2$ and $v(5) = 0\text{-}3 = \text{-}3$. That is, if activity 4 (5) is not scheduled at t_2 it has a negative slack of 2 (3) periods. Hence, the WCS priority rule also chooses activity 5 and thus derives the optimal solution.

Table 5.7 provides an overview of the classical RSM rule and the two new priority rules presented in this section.

	Network, Time, Resource-based	Static, Dynamic	Local, Global	Single, Composite	Lower Bound
RSM	N / T / -	D	G	S	LB
IRSM	N / T / R	D	G	S	LB
WCS	N / T / R	D	G	S	LB

Table 5.7: Characterisation of RSM-Based Priority Rules

5.3 Multi-Pass Priority-Rule-Based Scheduling

The fact that priority-rule-based single-pass approaches are very modest w.r.t. the computational effort, has brought up the idea of performing several passes (cf. Baker (1974, pp. 202 and 279) and French (1982, p. 165)). In order to benefit from multiple passes the selection of activities via priority rules has to be altered between two adjacent passes. W.r.t. the number of schedules inspected, multi-pass procedures can be viewed as a solution method in-between single-pass and enumeration procedures (cf. Baker (1974, p. 71)). Whilst single-pass procedures generate just one schedule and enumeration procedures have to inspect at least implicitly all schedules of a specific set, multi-pass procedures inspect only a subset of the schedules. Generally, two different approaches of multi-pass procedures have been proposed in the literature (cf. Baker (1974, p. 202)): The first one, entitled as **multi-priority rule approach**, employs one scheduling scheme and different priority rules while the second one makes use of one scheduling scheme and one priority rule only. For the latter, different schedules are obtained by biasing the selection of the priority rule through a random device. This solution methodology is commonly known as **sampling**. Another scheme which can be classified somewhere in-between multi-priority rule and sampling approaches was proposed by Fisher / Thompson (1963) and Storer et al. (1992). They choose different priority rules in a randomised fashion and apply them for a number of stages less than the number needed for a single pass.

5.3.1 Multi-Priority Rule Procedures

Multi-priority rule procedures were suggested by Baker (1974, p. 202), Fisher / Thompson (1963), and Storer et al. (1992) for solving the JSP and by Lawrence (1985), Ulusoy / Özdamar (1989), Boctor (1990), and Li / Willis (1992) for solving the SMPSP.

Lawrence (1985) employs - beyond other rules - a priority rule which takes into consideration the static slack (calculated by forward and backward recursion with $T=EFT_J$) and the duration of activities. He then performs Z single passes of the parallel scheduling scheme where after each pass the duration of activities is modified by taking into account the time they spent in the decision set without being selected. Consequently, although employing one priority rule only, different priority values and hence different schedules are generated. Out of the Z generated schedules, the one with the lowest makespan is chosen.

Ulusoy / Özdamar (1989) use their composite priority rule WRUP (cf. Section 5.2.2.) and perform 11 passes. In the first pass they start with the weights set to $w_1=0$ and $w_2=1$. In the following passes 2 through 11 they increase for every pass the weight w_1 by 0.1 until they end with $w_1=1$ and $w_2=0$ for the final pass.

On the basis of a computational study, **Boctor** (1990) orders Z priority rules w.r.t. a performance measure in a non-increasing order. A particular instance is then tackled by performing Z single passes, where pass z, $1 \leq z \leq Z$, employs the z-th priority rule on the list. The best current solution is replaced in pass z as soon as the application of the z-th priority rule revealed a better solution than the priority rules $1,...,z-1$.

Li / Willis (1992) propose a hill-climbing approach which iteratively performs serial forward and backward scheduling.[14] Forward scheduling chooses the activity associated with the minimum start time of the immediate preceding (backward-) schedule. Backward scheduling selects the activity associated with the minimum finish time of the previous (forward-) schedule. The procedure terminates as soon as the incumbent best solution cannot be improved further.

5.3.2 Sampling Procedures

I. Introduction

Sampling is a quite oftenly proposed solution methodology for the JSP[15] which was applied to the (multi-project) SMPSP by Levy et al. (1962), Wiest (1967), Cooper, (1976), and very recently by Alvarez-Valdes / Tamarit

---

[14] Where serial forward scheduling corresponds to the serial scheduling scheme as introduced in Section 5.2.1. Serial backward scheduling does exactly the same but with the reversed network. I.e., the scheduling scheme starts with activity J.

[15] Cf. Giffler / Thompson (1960), Heller / Logemann (1962), Fisher / Thompson (1963), Giffler et al. (1963), Conway et al. (1967, pp. 124-129) as well as Baker (1974, pp. 71-75 and pp. 200-205).

(1989b). The essence of sampling procedures is easy to describe (cf. Baker (1974, p.71)): Using some random device, construct and evaluate Z schedules and identify the best schedule in the sample. The key questions thereby arising are: What sample size should be chosen (cf. Baker (1974, p. 74)), which population should be sampled from, and finally how should a random device be used in order to select activities probabilistically?

The question of the sample size is clearly a function of the computational effort which is undertaken. With an ascending number of generated schedules, the probability of finding a better solution than the incumbent best one increases.

The decision on the sample space depends on the scheduling scheme employed. The serial method provides the set of active schedules as population while the parallel method restricts the sample space to the set of non-delay schedules.

The use of a random device can be interpreted as a mapping

$$\psi : j \in D_n \to [0,1] \tag{5.26}$$

which at stage n assigns to each activity in the decision set D_n a probability $\psi(j)$ of being selected.[16] Three different methods can be pointed out: random sampling, biased random sampling, and regret-based biased random sampling. All three techniques are introduced in the subsequent sections.

The first method assigns to each activity in the decision set the same probability and is referred to as **random sampling**. The second method biases the probabilities depending on the priority values of the activities to favour those activities which seem to be a more sensible choice. This scheme is therefore called **biased random sampling** (cf. Baker (1974, p. 72)). In the JSP context it is usually referred to as probabilistic dispatching (cf. Conway

---

[16] Of course, $\sum_{j \in D_n} \psi(j) = 1$ holds.

et al. (1967, p. 124) and Baker (1974, pp. 202-206)). A special case of biased random sampling is the utilisation of regret measures for determining the selection probabilities. It was introduced by Drexl (1991) and Drexl / Grünewald (1993) and is referred to as **regret-based biased random sampling**.

II. Random Sampling

Random sampling assigns to each activity in the decision set the same probability. Hence, at stage n the probability of activity j to be selected is

$$\psi(j) = \frac{1}{|D_n|} \qquad\qquad (5.27)$$

III. Biased Random Sampling

Cooper (1976) proposed the following probability mapping:

$$\psi(j) = \frac{v(j)}{\sum_{i \in D_n} v(i)} \qquad \text{if extremum=max} \qquad (5.28)$$

$$\psi(j) = \frac{\frac{1}{v(j)}}{\sum_{i \in D_n} \frac{1}{v(i)}} \qquad \text{if extremum=min and } v(j) \neq 0 \qquad (5.29)$$

Two disadvantages connected with this probability mapping have to be pointed out. To wit: The mapping is applicable to priority values with $v(j) > 0 \ \forall j \in D_n$ only. Additionally, for (equally) large $v(j)$ random sampling is performed regardless of the priority rule.

Alvarez-Valdes / Tamarit (1989b) proposed the same probability mapping as Cooper for extremum = max (cf. formula 5.29). In the case of extremum = min their probability mapping becomes:

$$\psi(j) = \frac{T\text{-}v(j)}{\sum\limits_{i \in D_n} (T\text{-}v(i))} \quad \text{if extremum} = \min \tag{5.30}$$

An exception to the probability mapping stated in (5.30) is used for the RSM priority rule. When used within biased random sampling, Alvarez-Valdes / Tamarit calculate the priority value $v(j)$ differently than in the single-pass procedures.[17]

Before presenting the parameterised probability mapping due to Wiest (1967) and Baker (1974, p. 72) the notion of a priority list has to be introduced. A priority list λ is a mapping

$$\lambda : j \in D_n \to [1, |D_n|] \tag{5.31}$$

which based on a priority rule assigns to each activity in the decision set j, $j \in D_n$, a unique ordinal position $\lambda(j)$. Hence, λ maps the cardinal order of the activities in D_n into an ordinal one.

Wiest (1967) assigns to the activity j, $j \in D_n$, with $\lambda(j)=1$, i.e. the first activity on the priority list, the probability of α_w, $0 < \alpha_w \le 1$. If the activity is not selected then the second activity on the list is considered with probability α_w and so forth. Hence, at stage n activity j with $\lambda(j)=2$ has a selection probability of $(1-\alpha_w)\alpha_w$. If the list is scanned completely without having selected any activity, the first activity on the list is reconsidered etc. Thus, by varying the parameter α_w, the biased random sampling approach can be adjusted anywhere between random sampling ($\alpha_w \to 0$) and deterministic selection w.r.t. the priority rule employed ($\alpha_w = 1$).

Baker (1974, p. 72) suggests the following parameterised probability mapping:

---

[17] Specifically, $v(j)$ is set equal to the number of times the disjunctive arc (j, i), with $i \in D_n \setminus j$, produces a smaller delay of the precedence-based lower bound than the disjunctive arc (i, j).

$$\psi(j) = \frac{\alpha_b^{\lambda(j)}}{\sum_{i \in D_n} \alpha_b^{\lambda(i)}} \tag{5.32}$$

with the parameter α_b, $0 < \alpha_b \leq 1$. Adjusting α_b to 1 gives way to random sampling whereas an arbitrary small α_b causes deterministic activity selection.[18]

Both parameterised probability mappings are functionally dependent as follows:

$$\alpha_b + \alpha_w \approx 1 \qquad 0 < \alpha_b, \alpha_w \leq 1, \tag{5.33}$$

Once more it has to be stressed that the mappings transfer the cardinal order of activities into an ordinal one whereby (valuable) information is lost.

IV. Regret-Based Biased Random Sampling

Drexl introduced the notion of regrets for the probability mapping (cf. Drexl (1991) and Drexl / Grünewald (1993)). The regret ρ_j compares the priority value of activity j with the worst consequence in the decision set as follows:

$$\rho_j = \begin{cases} \max_{i \in D_n} v(i) - v(j), & \text{if extremum} = \min \\ v(j) - \min_{i \in D_n} v(i), & \text{if extremum} = \max \end{cases} \tag{5.34}$$

Now, the parameterised probability mapping is defined as

$$\psi(j) = \frac{(\rho_j + 1)^\alpha}{\sum_{i \in D_n} (\rho_i + 1)^\alpha} \tag{5.35}$$

---

[18] Baker (1974, p. 73) incorrectly states that random sampling is performed for a small value of α_b while a large α_b gives way to deterministic selection.

Adding the constant "1" to the regret value ρ_j assures that the selection probability for each activity in the decision set is greater than zero and thus every schedule of the population may be generated. With the choice of the parameter α the amount of bias can be controlled. Associated with an arbitrarily large α is no bias and thus deterministic activity selection on the basis of the employed priority rule (with random selection as a tie breaker) while an α of 0 gives way to the maximum bias and hence to random activity selection.

5.4 Computational Results

In order to measure the quality of heuristics the following methods have been proposed in the literature (cf. Ball / Magazine (1981)): worst case analysis (cf. Fisher (1980)), probabilistic analysis (cf. Pearl (1984) and Weber (1990)), statistical analysis and experimental analysis (cf. Golden / Steward (1985)).[19] The latter seems to be the most widely used and trusted form of analysis (cf. Ball / Magazine (1981)). Jackson et al. (1991) and Crowder et al. (1979) provide extensive guidelines for computational experiments. Of importance are the choice of the *test problems*, the *experimental design*, and the *performance indicators*.

Test problems should be systematically generated with a well defined parameter driven problem generator. This demand is met by employing ProGen (cf. Chapter 4) in order to create an experimental design with full factorial layout. *Performance indicators* should reflect the average proximity of heuristic solutions to the optimum solution as well as the computational effort which has to be undertaken. For the former the percentage deviation from the optimal solution (cf. Badiru (1988)), denoted as *DEV*, for the latter the CPU-time in seconds, denoted as *CPU*, is used in this study. Finally, the *experimental design* is the full factorial layout as described in Section 5.4.1.

---

[19] Golden / Steward (1985) speak of empirical analysis which they define as "mean analysis originating in or based on computational *experiments*". Based on this definition it is rather referred to *experimental analysis*.

Most of the analysis is carried out by simply comparing means, where a mean of a parameter level o lower than a mean of a parameter level p is denoted as $o \succ p$. Additionally, statistical tests are applied. Only for the results of the latter it is spoken of "significant" better performance, denoted as $o \succ\succ p$. Since it is not confirmed that DEV is normally distributed, only nonparametric tests are employed (cf. Alvarez-Valdes / Tamarit (1989a) and Golden / Steward (1985)). Namely, these are the Wilcoxon signed rank test and the Friedman test.[20] All tests are carried out with the 1% level of confidence.

With the Wilcoxon signed rank test two levels o and p of one factor are compared w.r.t. the mean π of the population. Let E[] denote the expected value, than the null hypothesis is $E[\pi_o] = E[\pi_p]$ and the alternate hypothesis is $E[\pi_o] \neq E[\pi_p]$.

Dealing with more than two levels, the Friedman test is applied. It is the nonparametric equivalent to the analysis of variance (ANOVA) and thus used to test the null hypothesis $E[\pi_1] = E[\pi_2] = ... = E[\pi_u]$. The alternate hypothesis is $E[\pi_o] \neq E[\pi_p]$ for at least two levels $o, p, o \neq p, o, p \in \{1,...,u\}$.

All programs were coded in PASCAL and implemented on an IBM compatible personal computer with 80386dx processor and 40 MHz clockpulse at the computer laboratory of the Christian-Albrechts-Universität zu Kiel. Random numbers were drawn with the generator proposed by Schrage (1979).

5.4.1 Single-Pass Analysis

The purpose of the computational study in this section is threefold: First, it is investigated whether one of the scheduling schemes presented is more

---

[20] All tests are carried out on the one-way layout without replications which is derived by simply averaging over all factors except the one under consideration (cf. Kurtulus / Davis (1982)).

suited for embedding single-pass priority rules than the others. Second, the performance of traditional priority rules is tested. Third, we are interested in the performance of heuristics w.r.t. the problem parameters. Finally, the new rules proposed in Section 5.2.2 are compared with the traditional rules.

I. Statistical Model

For the SMPSP-instances under full factorial design the following statistical model with five factors can be stated (cf. Kurtulus / Davis (1982) and Kurtulus / Narula (1985)):

$$DEV_{klmno} = \delta\,(PR_k,\,SS_l,\,NC_m,\,RF(R)_n,\,RS(R)_o) + \varepsilon_{klmno} \qquad (5.36)$$

$$CPU_{klmno} = \theta\,(PR_k,\,SS_l,\,NC_m,\,RF(R)_n,\,RS(R)_o) + \varepsilon_{klmno} \qquad (5.37)$$

where DEV_{klmno} (CPU_{klmno}) denotes the percentage deviation from the optimal objective function value (the average running time in CPU seconds) when the instances with the m-th, n-th, and o-th level of the problem parameters NC, $RF(R)$, and $RS(R)$, respectively, are solved with priority rule k (PR_k) applied within scheduling scheme l (SS_l). For the errors ε it is assumed that they are mutually independent and that each ε is drawn from the same continuous distribution. The levels of the *procedure parameters* are as follows:

$$PR_k \in \{LST,\,LFT,\,MTS,\,MSLK,\,GRPW,\,WRUP\}^{21} \qquad (5.38)$$

$$SS_l \in \{PSS,\,SSS\}^{22} \qquad (5.39)$$

---

[21] The classical priority rules were chosen w.r.t. the review of literature presented in Section 5.2.2 and summed up in Table 5.5. Additionally the combined priority rule WRUP with weights w_1=0.7 and w_2=0.3 was included. Since every rule is applied within both scheduling schemes, the LST as well as the MSLK priority rule (which produce for the parallel scheduling scheme identical schedules) were selected and the RSM priority rule (which can only be applied to the parallel scheduling scheme) was discarded.

while the levels of the *problem parameters* are:

$$NC_m \in \{1.5, 1.8, 2.1\} \tag{5.40}$$

$$RF(R)_n \in \{0.25, 0.5, 0.75, 1\} \tag{5.41}$$

$$RS(R)_o \in \{0.2, 0.5, 0.7\} \tag{5.42}$$

In order to generate problems with these problems parameters, ProGen (cf. Chapter 4) was employed as follows: Additionally to the levels of the variable parameters given in formulas (5.40) - (5.42), the levels for the constant parameter were adjusted according to Table 5.8 and all tolerances were set to 0.05. Generating 10 instances for each combination of NC, $RF(R)$, and $RS(R)$, a total of $3 \cdot 4 \cdot 3 \cdot 10 = 360$ problems emerged. Imposing a time limit of 3600 CPU-seconds, for 308 instances the optimal solution was obtained with the exact procedure of Demeulemeester / Herroelen (1992a).[23] Hence, each of these 308 problems was treated by every level combination of the procedure parameters.

	J	M_j	d_j	$|R|$	U_R	Q_R	S_1	S_j	P_j	P_J
min	30	1	1	4	1	1	3	1	1	3
max	30	1	10	4	10	4	3	3	3	3

Table 5.8: Constant Parameter Levels for the SMPSP Instances

II. Evaluation of Procedure Parameters

Table 5.9 gives a comparison of the priority rules. The Friedman test revealed a significant different performance w.r.t. the average deviation from the optimal solution ($s=0.0000$). By pairwise application of the Wilcoxon test

---

[22] Where PSS denotes the parallel scheduling scheme (of Brooks) and SSS denotes the serial scheduling scheme. As already stated in Section 5.2, the parallel scheduling scheme of Kelley is not dealt with in here since preliminary computational results revealed a rather poor performance (cf. Figge (1992)).

[23] For details of this study refer to Kolisch et al. (1992).

the following ranking has been observed: LST $\succ$ LFT $\succ\succ$ MTS $\succ$ MSLK $\succ\succ$ GRPW. Four groups can be distinguished significantly ($s\le0.0051$): The lower-bound-based rules LST and LFT which perform quite good, MTS and MSLK ranging in the middle, GRPW, and finally WRUP. The two latter reveal a rather poor performance. The computational effort for all rules was very modest. Within both scheduling schemes the rule MTS required slightly more CPU-time, whereas the MSLK rule demanded only within the serial scheduling scheme more CPU-time. This is due to the fact that the earliest precedence- and resource-feasible start time has to be determined for every activity in the decision set, respectively.

PR_k	LST	LFT	MTS	MSLK	GRPW	WRUP
DEV_k	5.06	5.32	6.65	7.53	10.78	11.66
CPU_k	.02	.02	.03	.03	.02	.03

Table 5.9: Performance of Priority Rules

Table 5.10 summarises the performance of the scheduling schemes. The ranking reveals to be PSS$\succ\succ$SSS and hence confirms the conjecture that the parallel scheduling scheme is significantly ($s=0.0000$) superior to the serial one when used for single-pass priority rules (cf. Alvarez-Valdes / Tamarit (1989a)). Each priority rule performs better w.r.t. the quality of solutions when applied in the parallel scheme. Even more, every priority rule with the exception of the lower-bound-based rules LST and LFT performs significantly better within the parallel scheduling scheme ($s\le0.0013$). Nevertheless, since LST and LFT belong to the best rules in both schemes, the serial scheduling scheme cannot be excluded a priori. This conclusion has already been drawn in the study by Valls et al. (1992).

SS_l	PSS	SSS
DEV_l	6.46	9.21
CPU_l	.02	.03

Table 5.10: Performance of Scheduling Schemes

The running time of the parallel scheduling scheme is slightly shorter than the one of the serial scheme. Whereas the parallel scheme uses most of the time to update the decision set, the serial scheme requires the majority of the CPU-time for setting up and managing the array πK_{rt}, $r \in R$, $t=1,...,T$, which is (especially in the case of a poor upper bound for the makespan T) very time-consuming.

III. Evaluation of Problem Parameters

Tables 5.11 to 5.13 demonstrate the effect of the problem parameters network complexity NC, resource factor $RF(R)$, and resource strength $RS(R)$, respectively. Most noteworthy is the fact that the ranking of priority rules and scheduling schemes is not significantly influenced by any of the problem parameters. Regarding priority rules, this outcome confirms the conclusion made in the studies by Cooper (1976) and Alvarez-Valdes / Tamarit (1989a).

NC_m	1.5	1.8	2.1
DEV_m	8.46	7.23	7.84
CPU_m	.023	.023	.024

Table 5.11: Effect of the Network Complexity on the Performance

The Friedman test has not revealed a significant influence of NC ($s=0.2929$). Nevertheless, the following can be observed (cf. Table 5.11): Increasing the network complexity from 1.5 to 1.8 and 2.1, the performance first inclines and then declines again.[24]

---

[24] The latter deterioration was not observed in the experiments conducted by Alvarez-Valdes / Tamarit (1989a).

$RF(R)_n$	0.25	0.5	0.75	1.0
DEV_n	4.99	9.43	8.53	8.91
CPU_n	.023	.23	.024	.025

Table 5.12: Effect of the Resource Factor on the Performance

The effect of the resource factor (cf. Table 5.12) is highly significant ($s=0.0000$): Increasing the resource factor from 0.25 results in a sharp deterioration of the solution quality. As pointed out by Alvarez-Valdes / Tamarit (1989a), the priority rules show a better performance for projects with a (high) resource factor of 1 than for projects with a medium resource factor of 0.5. However, Alvarez-Valdes and Tamarit observed a far greater performance sensitivity w.r.t. the resource factor.

$RS(R)_o$	0.2	0.5	0.7
DEV_o	12.10	8.20	4.85
CPU_o	.024	.023	.023

Table 5.13: Effect of the Resource Strength on the Performance

The influence of the resource strength is also highly significant ($s=0.0000$). In addition, it shows the most appealing effect: Increasing the resource strength results in an monotonically increasing performance.[25]

Thus, it can be concluded that for single-pass scheduling schemes the influence of the problem parameters on the performance is similar as for optimal procedures (cf. Kolisch et al. (1995)). Generally, a high resource factor and a low resource strength induce a poor performance.[26] The computational effort is not influenced by any of the problem parameters.

---

[25] Recall that for the highest resource strength, i.e. $RS(R)_o=1$, Theorems 5.3 and 5.6 state: $DEV_o=0$.

[26] Precisely, for an ascending resource factor, the performance of optimal procedures is monotonically decreasing, whereas the single-pass priority-rule-based heuristics reveal the lowest performance for an $RF(R)$ of 0.5.

IV. Evaluation of New Priority Rules

In order to investigate the performance of the (new) priority rules solely amenable within the parallel scheduling scheme, the set of priority rules was enlarged to the best classical as well as the new rules, i.e. $PR_k=\{$LFT, MTS, MSLK, GRPW, WRUP, RSM, IRSM, WCS$\}$ and the scheduling scheme was restricted to the parallel algorithm only, i.e. $SS_l=\{$PSS$\}$.[27] Table 5.14 compares the (for parallel scheduling) best classical rule LFT with the RSM priority rule and the two new rules IRSM and WCS, respectively. Both new rules outperform the LFT rule w.r.t. the solution quality while being slightly inferior w.r.t. the running-time. WCS is significantly better than all other rules ($s \le 0.0061$). IRSM is significantly better than RSM, MTS, WRUP and GRPW ($s=0.0000$). The RSM rule ranges in the middle and is only significantly better than the two worst rules WRUP and GRPW ($s=0.0000$).

PR_k	WCS	IRSM	LFT	RSM
DEV_k	4.27	4.77	4.83	5.67
CPU_k	.02	.02	.01	.02

Table 5.14: Comparison of Classical and New Priority Rules

5.4.2 Sampling Analysis

In the following it is investigated whether the conclusions which have been drawn for the single-pass case are still valid in the case of sampling. CPU-times are not provided any more because - as has been shown in Section 5.4.2 - they are not influenced by any of the parameters. The proceeding is as follows: In order to run the experiment with one probability mapping only, Subsection I is concerned with the evaluation of the best probability mapping and the best mapping parameter, respectively. Subsections II and III report on the influence of the procedure and problem parameters, respectively, on the performance.

---

[27] This time LST was not considered since it shows exactly the same results as MSLK.

I. Evaluation of Probability Mappings

In order to first determine suited mapping parameters for the two parameterised probability mappings of Baker (1974) and Drexl (1991), the following statistical model is employed:

$$DEV_{klmnopqr} = \delta(PR_k, SS_l, NC_m, RF(R)_n, RS(R)_o, PM_p, MP_q, Z_r) + \varepsilon_{klmnopqr} \quad (5.43)$$

where PM_p and MP_q denote the probability mapping and the mapping parameter, respectively, while Z_r represents the sample size. The levels of the parameters introduced for the single-pass analysis remain as defined in formulas (5.38) to (5.42), while the additional (procedure) parameters are as follows:[28]

$$PM_p \in \{BAK, DRE\}^{[29]} \quad (5.44)$$

$$MP_q \in \{0\%, 25\%, 50\%, 75\%, 100\%\} \quad (5.45)$$

$$Z_r \in \{10, 40, 70, 100\} \quad (5.46)$$

The levels of the probability mapping parameter MP_q reflect the amount of bias. Table 5.15 presents the resulting values for the probability mappings.[30]

MP_q	0%	25%	50%	75%	100%
BAK	<<1	.25	.5	.75	1
DRE	∞	3	2	1	0

Table 5.15: Levels of the Probability Mapping Parameter

---

[28] The parameterised probability mapping of Wiest (1967) was not considered since - as outlined in Section 5.3.2 - it is functionally dependent on the mapping of Baker (1974) and hence generates the same results.

[29] Where BAK refers to the probability mapping due to Baker (1974) and DRE to the one by Drexl (1991).

[30] Due to limitations in the representation of large real numbers on a computer, for the regret-based probability mapping the deterministic case was defined to be $\alpha = 4$. Hence,

As can be seen in Table 5.16, the mapping parameter MP_q has a significant influence ($s=0.0000$) for both probability mappings. No bias (i.e. deterministic scheduling) and total bias (i.e. random sampling) are clearly inferior than any of the intermediate biases. The best adjustment of the mapping parameter is found to be 50% and 75% for the probability mappings due to Baker and Drexl, respectively.

MP_q	0%	25%	50%	75%	100%
BAK	7.83	3.24	*2.76*	2.95	3.48
DRE	7.83	3.26	2.94	*2.73*	3.48

Table 5.16: Performance of the Mapping Parameter

In the second step, the different probability mappings are compared. Hence, (5.44) is altered to $PM_p=\{$ALV, BAK, COP, DRE$\}$.[31] Since the parameterised probability mappings are used with their best mapping parameter, respectively, MP_q was omitted. Table 5.17 shows the performance of the different probability mappings.

PM_p	DRE	BAK	ALV	COP
DEV_p	2.73	2.76	2.91	3.21

Table 5.17: Performance of the Probability Mappings

The (not significant ($s=0.0595$)) ranking obtained is DRE ≻ BAK ≻ ALV ≻ COP. On that account, it can be concluded that parameterised biased random sampling performs best, followed by biased random sampling while - as already displayed in Table 5.16 - pure random sampling reveals the poorest results. Of the parameterised sampling procedures, the regret-based approach shows the best performance. Not fully apparent from Table 5.17, this

---

for the latter adjustment a single-pass employing the deterministic priority rule under consideration was performed.

[31] Where ALV refers to the probability mapping due to Alvarez-Valdes / Tamarit (1989b) and COP to the one proposed by Cooper (1976).

becomes clearly evident by looking at Table 5.18. It displays the frequency distribution of the best 3% for the 192 tested heuristics.[32] The frequency of the regret-based probability mapping doubles the one of the straightly parameterised mapping.

PM_p	DRE	BAK	ALV	COP
#	4	2	0	0

Table 5.18: Frequency Distribution of Probability Mappings for the Best 3%

II. Evaluation of Procedure Parameters

As a result of the observations made so far, hereafter only the probability mapping of Drexl is considered, i.e. PM_p is set to DRE and can therefore be omitted. The statistical model then reduces to:

$$DEV_{klmnor} = \delta\,(PR_k,\,SS_l,\,NC_m,\,RF(R)_n,\,RS(R)_o,\,Z_r) + \varepsilon_{klmnor} \qquad (5.47)$$

with the procedure and problem parameters as defined in (5.38) - (5.42) and (5.46), respectively.

Table 5.19 reveals the performance of the priority rules. As for the single-pass case, a significant difference between rules can be detected (s=0.0024). The lower-bound-based rules LST and LFT perform best, MTS and MSLK range in the middle while WRUP and GRPW have the worst performance.[33]

---

[32] Where heuristic is defined as each procedure-tuple $(PR_k,\,SS_l,\,PM_p,\,Z_r)$, which equals $6 \cdot 2 \cdot 4 \cdot 4 = 192$ different tuples.

[33] The results of MSLK have to be interpreted with caution because - like for the single-pass approach - it shows a quite different performance within each of the two scheduling schemes, respectively: For the parallel scheme it performs like the "good" LST rule, within the serial scheme MSLK gives rather poor results.

PR_k	LFT	LST	MTS	MSLK	WRUP	GRPW
DEV_k	2.08	2.11	2.48	2.56	3.36	3.79

Table 5.19: Performance of Traditional Priority Rules for Sampling

By comparing the ranking (LFT ≻ LST ≻≻ MTS ≻ MSLK ≻≻ WRUP ≻≻ GRPW) with the one of the single-pass approach the following can be stated:

(*i*) With two exceptions (LST and LFT as well as WRUP and GRPW) the ranking obtained is the same as for the single-pass case.

(*ii*) While the difference between groups (i.e. LFT, LST vs. MTS, MSLK vs. WRUP vs. GRPW) has about the same level of significance ($s \leq 0.0036$), the difference between rules is slightly less significant.[34] Thus, it can be stated that, in general, priority rules which perform good for single-pass approaches perform good for biased random sampling approaches and vice versa.

Although not explicitly pointed out, Alvarez-Valdes / Tamarit (1989b) obtained similar results in their study.[35] The contrary observation of Cooper (1976) is a direct consequence of the drawbacks associated with his probability mapping, as already mentioned in Section 5.3.2.

With Table 5.20 some insight into the performance w.r.t. the sample size is given. As expected, it demonstrates that increasing the sample size continuously produces better solutions. Depending on the sample size, the average performance of the single-pass approach is thus improved between 50% (Z_r=10) and 73% (Z_r=100). This is up to ten times more than observed by Cooper (1976). Hence, it can be stated that sampling significantly outper-

---

[34] Of course, the interrelation between single-pass and sampling heuristics depends on the amount of bias: Whereas with 0% bias the significance equals the one of the (deterministic) single-pass case, a bias of 100% (i.e. random sampling) results in no (significant) difference between the priority rules.

[35] With the exception of one priority rule, the same ranking was obtained for single-pass scheduling and biased random sampling, respectively.

forms the single-pass approach (s=0.0000).[36] But it has to be noted that the marginal improvement diminishes. This implies a growing computational effort in order to produce better solutions.

Z_r	10	40	70	100
DEV_r	3.92	2.61	2.28	2.11

Table 5.20: Performance as a Function of the Sample Size

Finally, Table 5.21 demonstrates the effect of the scheduling schemes w.r.t. the sample size Z_r. The overall performance (AVG) of both schemes is almost identical, but a second glance reveals a (not significant ($s \geq 0.1994$)) different performance w.r.t. the sample size. While the parallel scheme is clearly superior for small sample sizes (i.e. less than 40 generated schedules), the serial scheme shows better results for large samples. Consequently, for sampling procedures solving the SMPSP, the general superiority of non-delay schedules as announced in Conway et al. (1967, pp. 121-124) for the JSP with minimum average flow time objective does not hold true. The rationale of the observation is as follows: For small sample sizes the superiority of the parallel scheme w.r.t. the single-pass approach is dominant. With increasing sample size, this effect diminishes and at the same time the parallel scheme suffers from the fact that the sample space is the set of non-delay schedules which not necessarily contains the optimal solution.

Z_r	10	40	70	100	AVG
SS_F=PSS	3.58	2.67	2.43	2.32	2.75
SS_F=SSS	4.26	2.55	2.13	1.89	2.71

Table 5.21: Performance of Scheduling Schemes

---

[36] This contradicts the conclusions drawn by Conway et al. (1967, p. 128) for the JSP, stating that sampling reveals only modest improvement over single-pass procedures.

III. Evaluation of Problem Parameters

The effect of the three problem parameters network complexity, resource factor, and resource strength is analysed in Tables 5.22 to 5.24. As for the single-pass case, no significant influence can be observed for the network complexity ($s=0.6485$), while resource strength and resource factor, in this order, turn out to be highly significant ($s=0.0000$). The ranking of the priority rules is not significantly affected by the problem parameters, but resource factor and resource strength influence the ranking of scheduling schemes significantly.

NC_m	1.5	1.8	2.1
DEV_m	2.94	2.56	2.77

Table 5.22: Effect of the Network Complexity on the Performance

Table 5.22 shows that the network complexity affects the performance in the same way as already observed for the single-pass procedure. The serial scheduling scheme slightly outperforms the parallel scheduling scheme for each measure of network complexity.

$RF(R)_n$	0.25	0.5	0.75	1.0
SS_f=PSS	1.90	3.30	*3.93*	*3.25*
SS_f=SSS	*0.80*	*3.15*	3.40	4.07

Table 5.23: Effect of the Resource Factor on the Performance

Regarding the parameter resource factor, a difference between the scheduling schemes can be recognised from Table 5.23: While parallel scheduling shows the same tendency for the multi-pass and for the single-pass case, serial scheduling acts for the multi-pass case like exact algorithms: With an increasing resource factor the performance decreases. This makes parallel scheduling significantly superior to serial scheduling ($s \leq 0.0061$) for problems with a high resource factor, i.e. $RF(R) \geq 0.75$.

$RS(R)_o$	0.2	0.5	0.7
SS_F=PSS	*4.58*	*2.85*	1.65
SS_F=SSS	4.62	3.14	*1.12*

Table 5.24: Effect of the Resource Strength on the Performance

The effect of the resource strength is reported in Table 5.24. The parallel scheme performs slightly better in the case of scarce resources, while for $RS(R) = 0.7$ the serial scheme clearly produces significant better results (s=0.0070).

Thus, it can be concluded that the performance of scheduling schemes for single and multiple passes are affected in almost the same way by the problem parameters. An exception has to be stated for the serial scheme which shows a decreasing performance for high levels of the resource factor.

Finally, it can be stated that when used within sampling procedures the parallel scheme produces better results for hard problems (i.e. a large resource factor and a low resource strength).

5.4.3 Summary

The results of the experimental investigation undertaken in Section 5.4 can be summarised as follows:

(*i*) Single-pass scheduling

- Three groups of priority rules can be distinguished significantly: These are in the order of declining performance: The lower-bound-based rules LST and LFT, MTS and MSLK, and finally GRPW and WRUP.

- W.r.t. the solution quality, the parallel scheduling scheme is significantly superior to serial scheduling. Within the parallel scheduling scheme, the new priority rule WCS outperforms all other tested rules significantly.

- The ranking of priority rules and scheduling schemes as well as the CPU-times are not influenced by any of the problem parameters while the impact on the performance is significant for the resource factor and the resource strength.

(*ii*) Sampling

- With increasing bias the difference between priority rules as observed for the single-pass case is diminishing. For the bias employed (i.e. 75%), approximately the same ranking as for the single-pass case was obtained while the difference between priority rules was slightly less significant. Thus, priority rules which perform good for single-pass approaches do so for biased random sampling approaches and vice versa.

- Sampling significantly outperforms the single-pass approach. The ranking of sampling schemes is (in the order of decreasing performance): Regret-based biased random sampling, parameterised biased random sampling, biased random sampling, and at last, random sampling.

- The parallel scheduling scheme is superior for small sample sizes (i.e. less than 40 generated schedules) while the serial scheduling scheme becomes the better scheme for large samples.[37]

- The influence of the problem parameters is the same as for the single-pass approach with the only exception that for a high resource factor the performance of the serial scheduling scheme declines significantly. Hence, for this case the parallel scheduling scheme is superior regardless of the sample size.

Finally, both single-pass and sampling heuristics, show the worst performance on the problems which are the hardest for optimal procedures.

---

[37] It is conjectured that this "critical sample size", i.e. 40 for the instances tested, increases when the problem size - expressed in the number of activities - is enlarged.

5.5 A Hybrid Solution Procedure

The insight gained from the results of the computational study of Section 5.4 will now be exploited in order to derive a hybrid solution approach. In addition, the procedure is speeded up by the utilisation of lower bound techniques. A comparison with so far presented heuristics for solving the SMPSP demonstrates that this approach is a highly competitive one.

5.5.1 A Hybrid Sampling Procedure

As shown in Section 5.4, no scheduling scheme is totally dominated by the other one because of the partial superiority w.r.t. certain levels of problem parameters and sample sizes. Hence, a quite straightforward way to design an improved heuristic is to combine the advantages of both schemes in a hybrid solution procedure.

In distinction to the work presented by Kurtulus / Davis (1982) and Patterson (1976) this approach is not concerned with the determination of the best priority rule for a certain problem class by classifying the instance w.r.t. problem parameters. Rather - on the basis of the robust ranking of priority rules - the best rule is employed in each scheduling scheme, respectively.

PR_k	LFT	LST
DEV_k	1.74	1.81

Table 5.25: The Two Best Rules of the Serial Scheme

PR_k	WCS	IRSM
DEV_k	2.33	2.38

Table 5.26: The Two Best Rules of the Parallel Scheme

Tables 5.25 and 5.26 show the performance of the two best rules within the serial and the parallel scheduling scheme, respectively. Notwithstanding the fact that both first ranked rules are not significantly superior to the other one, they were chosen. Table 5.27 shows the derived assignment of priority rules to scheduling schemes.

SS_l	PSS	SSS
PR_k	WCS	LFT

Table 5.27: Assignment of Priority Rules to Scheduling Schemes

Two general conclusions drawn in Section 5.4.3 were that (*i*) the performance increases with growing sample size and that (*ii*) a bias of 75% (i.e. α=1) revealed the overall best results for regret-based biased random sampling. A question still open is if there exists a dependency between bias and sample size when seeking for the best performance. In order to get more insight, the statistical model (5.43) was applied with problem parameters (5.40) - (5.42) and procedure parameters as follows: $SS_l \in$ {PSS, SSS}, PR_k as defined in Table 5.27, PM_p=DRE, $MP_q \in$ {0%, 25%, 75%, 100%}, and $Z_r \in$ {1, 5, 10, 40, 70, 100}.

MP_q	0%	25%	50%	75%	100%
Z_r=1	*5.042*	6.23	6.48	7.65	12.97
Z_r=5	5.042	*3.41*	3.46	3.68	7.25
Z_r=10	5.042	3.04	*2.83*	3.02	5.12
Z_r=40	5.042	2.20	2.03	*1.89*	3.36
Z_r=70	5.042	2.06	1.79	*1.65*	2.89
Z_r=100	5.042	1.93	1.69	*1.57*	2.57

Table 5.28: Performance of the Mapping Parameter and the Sample Size

Table 5.28 demonstrates that there is a quite strong relation between the sample size and the bias with the best performance. As the former is increased the latter has to be enlarged too. For a sample size greater than 10, the bias with the highest performance remains at the overall best value of 75%. On account of these results, the mapping parameter α is adjusted depending on the number of the actual sample size z as follows (cf. Table 5.29):[38]

z	1	]1,5]	]5,10]	> 10
$\alpha=\varphi(z)$	∞	3	2	1

Table 5.29: Adjustment of the Mapping Parameter

In the next step the partial dominance of the scheduling schemes w.r.t. the problem parameters and the sample size, respectively, was investigated for the already determined priority rules and mapping parameters. Regarding the influence of the network complexity the general results of Section 5.4.3 could be confirmed. Concerning the resource factor and the resource strength, deviating from the general findings of Section 5.4.3, the tandem "parallel scheduling scheme / WCS" has been superior for $RF(R) > 0.75$ and sample sizes $Z \le 5$ only.[39] Based on these observations the scheduling scheme (and hence the priority rule) is determined as shown in Table 5.30.

$RF(R)$	≤ 0.75	> 0.75
$Z \le 5$	PSS / WCS	PSS / WCS
$Z > 5$	SSS / LFT	PSS / WCS

Table 5.30: Choice of the Scheduling Scheme

---

[38] Note that there is a remarkable difference between the actual sample size z and the sample size Z. That is, when the z-th schedule is generated, z-1 schedules have already been evaluated and Z-z more schedules will be constructed in order to obtain a sample size of Z. E.g., for a sample size of Z=15, the first schedule is generated with $\alpha=\infty$, the second to the fifth schedule with $\alpha=3$, the sixth to the tenth schedule with $\alpha=2$, and finally the remaining five schedules with $\alpha=1$.

[39] The difference between the general and the special case is reasoned by the extraordinary good performance of the lower-bound-based LFT priority rule within the serial scheduling scheme, which has been pointed out in Section 5.4.2.

Due to Tables 5.27, 5.29, and 5.30, the only parameter left to be defined in the final single-mode heuristic (SMH) is the sample size Z. Hence, SMH/Z refers to the different versions of SMH. Introducing $\underline{S}=(\underline{FT}_1,...,\underline{FT}_J)$ as the best schedule found so far and recalling BR to be the backward recursion from T, the upper bound of the project's makespan (cf. Section 2.2.1), SMH can be formally described as follows:

$$\boxed{\text{SMH}}$$

Initialisation: READ Problem Data and Sample Size Z; CALCULATE $RF(R)$;
CALCULATE T; PERFORM BR on the basis of T;
ASSIGN $\underline{FT}_j:=LFT_j$, $1 \le j \le J$;

FOR $z = 1$ TO Z DO **Pass z**
BEGIN
  $\alpha := \varphi(z)$;
  IF $(Z \ge 5$ AND $RF(R) \le 0.75)$ THEN PERFORM SSS (α, LFT)
  ELSE PERFORM PSS (α, WCS);
  IF $\phi_{SMPSP}(S) < \phi_{SMPSP}(\underline{S})$ THEN $\underline{S}:=S$;
END;

Stop: A feasible schedule $S=(\underline{FT}_1,...,\underline{FT}_J)$ has been generated;

***

5.5.2 Lower Bounding Techniques

As already pointed out (cf. Section 5.3) multi-pass procedures are a solution method between single-pass heuristics and enumeration procedures. Therefore, it almost suggests itself to borrow from central concepts of the latter, namely bounding and dominance rules, in order to prune the enumeration tree. Without presenting specific bounds or computational results this idea has already been suggested by Cooper (1976).

Two well-known bounds are the precedence- and the resource-based lower bounds (cf. Section 5.1.1) which will be employed in the SMH. The precedence-based lower bound is computed by assuming adherence only to precedence constraints while the resource-based lower bound does only take the resource constraints into consideration. Although both bounds belong to the oldest which were suggested for the SMPSP, especially the first one still pertains to the most powerful bounds available today (cf. Demeulemeester / Herroelen (1992a) and Stinson (1976)). Additionally, each bound is cheap in terms of the computational effort. More elaborated bounds like the skyline bound (cf. Baker (1974, p. 276)), the critical sequence bound (cf. Stinson (1976) and Stinson et al. (1978)), as well as the extended critical sequence bound (cf. Demeulemeester (1992)) do not seem useful for heuristic multi-pass approaches since the computational effort quickly exceeds the quite modest CPU-time of a single pass.

The general precedence bound (GPB) and the general resource bound (GRB) can be used independently of the scheduling scheme, respectively. Hence the label general. Whenever GPB or GRB is met at the final stage of pass z, $1 \leq z < Z$, a solution with the optimal makespan has been generated and the multi-pass procedure is finished prematurely.

$$\text{GPB:} \quad FT_J = EFT_J \tag{5.48}$$

$$\text{GRB:} \quad FT_J = \max_{r \in R} \left\lceil \frac{\sum_{j=1}^{J} d_j k_{jr}}{K_r} \right\rceil \tag{5.49}$$

PPB and PRB are the acronyms for the precedence- and resource-based bound, respectively, when employed in the parallel scheduling scheme. Both bounds are used to discard the schedule currently generated during stage n, $1 \leq n < J$ of pass z, $1 < z \leq Z$. Note that in contrast to GPB and GRB the sampling procedure is continued afterwards with pass $z+1$.

$$\text{PPB:} \quad t_n \geq \min \{ LST_j \,|\, j \in D_n \cup R_n \} - (LFT_J - \underline{FT_J}) \tag{5.50}$$

$$\text{PRB:} \quad t_n \geq \underline{FT_J} - \begin{array}{c} \max \\ r \in R \end{array} \left[\frac{\sum\limits_{j \in D_n \cup R_n} d_j k_{jr} + \sum\limits_{j \in A_n} (FT_j - t_n) k_{jr}}{K_r} \right] \qquad (5.51)$$

Recalling $\underline{S} = (\underline{FT_1},...,\underline{FT_J})$ to be the incumbent best solution, PPB states that schedule S cannot be better than the so far best schedule $\underline{S}$, if the actual schedule time t_n equals or exceeds the minimum latest start time of the un-scheduled activities when calculated by backward recursion with the currently best makespan, i.e. $T=\underline{FT_J}$ (cf. Section 2.2.1). Since the latest start times have been derived with the first upper bound amenable, they are updated by subtracting the difference between the first upper bound LFT_J and the incumbent best makespan $\underline{FT_J}$.

PRB states that schedule S cannot overcome the incumbent best solution $\underline{S}$ if the actual schedule time t_n plus the minimum time for scheduling not yet finished activities w.r.t. resource constraints only is equal or is exceeding the so far lowest makespan $\underline{FT_J}$.

Both bounds are calculated at the end of step (1) and thus exactly once during each stage n, $1 \leq n < J$, of the parallel scheduling scheme.

In order to clarify the calculation of each bound, respectively, Figure 5.7 and Table 5.31 recall the example project and the associated report of the parallel scheduling scheme originally depicted in Figure 5.1 and Table 5.3, respectively.

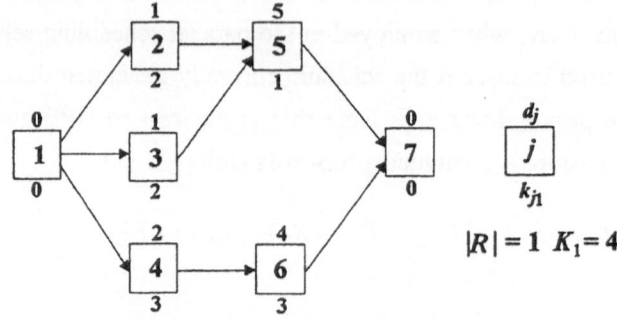

Figure 5.7: Example Project

n	t_n	πK_1	A_n	C_n	PS_n	D_n	R_n	$v(j)$	j^*	FT_{j^*}
1	0	4	∅	∅	∅	1	2,...,7	0	1	0
2	0	4	∅	1	1	2,...,4	5,...,7	1,1,2	2	1
		2	2	1	1,2	3	4,...,7	1	3	1
		0	2,3	1	1,2	∅	4,...,7			
3	1	4	∅	1,...,3	1,...,3	4,5	6,7	2,6	4	3
		1	4	1,...,3	1,...,4	5	6,7	6	5	6
		0	4,5	1,...,3	1,...,5	∅	6,7			
4	3	3	5	1,...,4	1,...,5	6	7	6	6	7
		0	5,6	1,...,4	1,...,6	∅	7			
5	6	1	6	1,...,5	1,...,6	∅	7			
6	7	4	∅	1,...,6	1,...,6	7	∅	6	7	7

Table 5.31: Report of the Parallel Scheduling Scheme

Additionally, Table 5.32 lists the latest start times derived by backward recursion with $T=13$.

j	1	2	3	4	5	6	7
LST_j	7	7	7	7	8	9	13

Table 5.32: Latest Start Times for the Example Project

Now, consider a solution with $\underline{FT}_J = 7$ has been found in pass z-1. For a new pass z the following state arises at the end of step (1) in stage $n=2$ (cf. Table 5.31 line 2): $t_2=0$, $\pi K_1=4$, $D_2=\{2,3,4\}$, and $R_2=\{5,6,7\}$. Then, PPB is calculated as follows: $t_2 \geq \min \{LST_2, LST_3, LST_4, LST_5, LST_6, LST_7\}$ - $(LFT_7-\underline{FT}_7) \Leftrightarrow 0 \geq \min \{7, 7, 7, 8, 9, 13\} - (13-7) \Leftrightarrow 0 \geq 7-6 \Leftrightarrow 0 \geq 1$. Since PPB is met, pass z is finished prematurely.

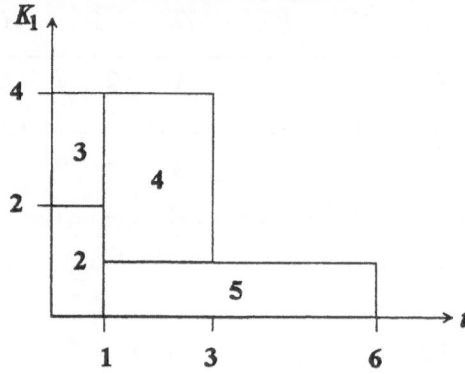

Figure 5.8: Partial Schedule of the Example Project

In order to depict PRB, consider the state arising at the end of step (1) in stage $n=4$ (cf. Table 5.31 line 8): $t_4=3$, $\pi K_1=3$, $A_4=\{5\}$, $D_4=\{6\}$, and $R_4=\{7\}$. The corresponding partial schedule is displayed in Figure 5.8. Now, PRB is calculated to $t_4 \geq FT_7$ - max $\lceil (d_6\ k_{61}+(FT_5-t_4)\ k_{51})/K_1 \rceil$ $\Leftrightarrow$ $3 \geq 7-\lceil(4\cdot3+(6-3)\cdot1)/4\rceil \Leftrightarrow 3 \geq 7-\lceil 15/4 \rceil \Leftrightarrow 3 \geq 7-4 \Leftrightarrow 3 \geq 3$. Again, pass z is finished prematurely because this time PRB is met.

SPB is the precedence-based lower bound when applied in the serial scheduling scheme to discard the currently generated schedule during stage n, $1 \leq n < J$ of pass z, $1 < z \leq Z$. Whenever j^* the scheduled activity has a start time which equals or exceeds the updated latest start time, pass z is finished prematurely. As for PPB, the sampling procedure is afterwards continued with pass $z+1$.

$$\text{SPB:} \qquad ST_{j^*} \geq LST_{j^*} - (LFT_J - FT_J) \qquad\qquad (5.52)$$

Operationally, SPB is applied after the earliest precedence- and resource-feasible start time ST_{j^*} for the selected activity j^* has been calculated (cf. line 4 of stage n within the formal description of the serial scheduling scheme in

Section 5.2.1). This is the case exactly once during each stage n of the serial scheduling scheme.[40]

SPB is clarified once more with the example project depicted in Figure 5.7, the latest finish times provided by Table 5.32, and the associated report of the serial scheduling scheme which is recalled in Table 5.33. The partial schedule at stage $n=4$ is depicted in Figure 5.9.

n	$\pi K_{1t},\ 1 \le t \le 8$	$C_n = PS_n$	D_n	R_n	$v(j)$	j^*	FT_{j*}
1	(4,4,4,4,4,4,4,4)	∅	1	2,...,7	0	1	0
2	(4,4,4,4,4,4,4,4)	1	2,...4	5,...,7	1,1,2	2	1
3	(2,4,4,4,4,4,4,4)	1,2	3,4	5,...,7	1,2	3	1
4	(0,4,4,4,4,4,4,4)	1,...,3	4,5	6,7	2,6	4	3
5	(0,1,1,4,4,4,4,4)	1,...,4	5,6	7	6,6	5	6
6	(0,0,0,3,3,3,4,4)	1,...,5	6	7	6	6	7
7	(0,0,0,0,0,1,4)	1,...,6	7	∅	6	7	7

Table 5.33: Report of the Serial Scheduling Scheme

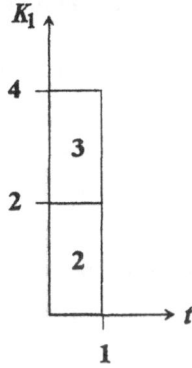

Figure 5.9: Partial Schedule of the Example Project

[40] In the basic serial scheduling scheme the computation of the precedence- and resource-feasible earliest start time ST_j is rather costly in terms of the computational effort and has to be only performed for the chosen activity j^*. An exception holds when the MSLK priority rule is applied and EST'_j has to be computed for all activities in D_n (cf. formula 5.9).

As is evident by the report of the serial scheduling scheme, activity $j^*=4$ with an earliest precedence- and resource-feasible start time of $ST_4=1$ is chosen. Now, SPB is calculated to $ST_4 \geq LST_4 - (LFT_7-\underline{FT_7}) \Leftrightarrow 1 \geq 7-(13-7)$ $\Leftrightarrow 1 \geq 7-6 \Leftrightarrow 1 \geq 1$ and consequently pass z is finished prematurely because SPB is met.

A resource-based bound for the serial scheduling scheme has not been considered since preliminary tests revealed that the computational effort exceeds the computational saving by far.

In order to test the bounds presented, the instances used so far were solved with SMH as described in Section 5.5.1 whereby a sample size of $Z=100$ was chosen. Table 5.34 shows the average CPU-time when using the parallel scheduling scheme and the WCS priority rule with each of the bounding rules applicable. "–" indicates that no bound was employed. Whereas the precedence-based bounds reduce the computational effort, the general resource bound does not reveal any influence. The parallel resource bound even increases the CPU-time. Jointly applying the three bounds GPB, GRB, and PPB almost cuts down the computational time by half.

Bounds	–	GPB	GRB	PPB	PRB	GPB,GRB,PPB
CPU	2.42	1.97	2.42	1.36	3.06	1.29

Table 5.34: Performance of Bounds for the Tandem PSS / WCS

Table 5.35 reveals the reduction of the CPU-time when applying the bounds for the serial scheme in conjunction with the LFT priority rule. Again, the two precedence-based bounds lower the computational effort while the general resource bound does not affect the CPU-time. The overall reduction when jointly using GPB, GRB, and SPB is about 50%.

Bounds	–	GPB	GRB	SPB	GPB, GRB, SPB
CPU	4.72	3.42	4.72	2.26	2.24

Table 5.35: Performance of Bounds for the Tandem SSS / LFT

It has to be noted that the poor performance of the (general) resource bound is due to the fact that only instances with $RS(R) \leq 0.7$ were used. Nevertheless, it is conjectured that for (some) practical problems the resource strength is rather high and thus the general resource bounds reduces the computational effort drastically. Therefore, for SMH both general bounds as well as the special bounds PPB and SPB are employed. Table 5.36 demonstrates the performance of the fully-fledged SMH for sample sizes up to Z=500.

	SMH/1	SMH/10	SMH/100	SMH/500
DEV	4.27	2.96	1.17	0.69
CPU	.03	0.26	2.01	9.42

Table 5.36: Performance of SMH/Z

5.5.3 Computational Comparison with other Procedures

For a comparison of SMH with other recently proposed heuristics, the ProGen-instances could not be utilised since the source code of most procedures was not available.[41] Hence, the 110 test problems assembled by Patterson (1984) were used as benchmark problems. Table 5.37 shows the performance of SMH on these instances.

	SMH/1	SMH/10	SMH/100	SMH/500
DEV	3.71	1.75	0.83	0.43
CPU	0.02	0.12	0.96	4.53

Table 5.37: Performance of SMH/Z on the Patterson Instances

---

[41] Only the source code of Alvarez-Valdes and Tamarit's truncated branch and bound approach was available.

	SPP[42]	DA[43]	TBB[44]	LS[45]
DEV	5.0	2.60	2.28	1.98
CPU	.01	28.4	.58	56.24

Table 5.38: Performance of Recent Heuristics on the Patterson Instances

Table 5.38 provides the performance of other recent heuristics for the SMPSP on this instance set. Despite the different machines and implementations employed, the methods can be roughly classified as follows: very fast algorithms with a computational effort below a tenth of a second (i.e. SPP and SMH/1), fast algorithms which run no more than a second (i.e. TBB, SMH/10, and SMH/100), and finally algorithms which employ a computational effort of more than a second (i.e. DA, LS, and SMH/500). Each version of SMH outperforms the other heuristics in its class by far.[46] SMH/1, i.e. a single pass of the parallel scheduling scheme with the WCS priority rule, is slightly slower than SPP, i.e. a single pass of the parallel scheduling scheme with the MSLK priority rule, but reveals a far better performance. SMH/10 and SMH/100 - being comparable fast as the truncated branch and bound approach of Alvarez-Valdes / Tamarit (1989a) - outperform the latter. In addition, they show better results than every other heuristic so far presented in the literature. Finally, SMH/500 reveals extremely promising results. While the mean percentage deviation from the optimal objective func-

---

[42] Parallel single-pass procedure with the MSLK priority rule by Davis / Patterson (1974) coded in PASCAL and implemented on an IBM compatible personal computer (80386dx processor with 40 MHz clockpulse).

[43] Disjunctive arc procedure of Bell / Han (1991) coded in Common Lisp implemented on a Macintosh Plus.

[44] Truncated branch and bound by Alvarez-Valdes / Tamarit (1989a) coded in FORTRAN and implemented on an IBM PS/2 Model 70dx (80386dx processor with 25 MHz clockpulse).

[45] Local search technique by Sampson / Weiss (1993) coded in C++ and implemented on a NeXT.

[46] It has to be remarked that only 4 of the 110 instances (i.e. #1 and #10 - #12) have an $RF(R) \leq 0.75$. Hence, for the majority of the problems the parallel scheduling scheme jointly with the WCS priority rule has been employed.

tion value is less than a quarter of the so far best heuristic - the simulated annealing approach of Sampson / Weiss (1993) - the CPU-time averages to only 16% of the latter. SMH has thus been proven to be a viable solution methodology for solving the SMPSP near optimal. The moderate computational requirements (SMH employs only a fraction of the running time which is needed by the so far best heuristic procedures) make it capable for solving even large size problems.

Chapter 6

The Multi-Mode Project Scheduling Problem

This chapter deals with the multi-mode project scheduling problem (MMPSP). As outlined in Chapter 2, the MMPSP is probably the most general and most difficult problem dealt with. A description of the model as well as a 0-1 programming formulation has been provided in Section 2.3. Furthermore, there it has been proven that even the feasibility problem of MMPSP, the so-called mode-assignment problem (MAP), is *NP*-complete. As a consequence, solution procedures proposed so far suffer from severe drawbacks: Exact procedures can only solve very small instances with roughly up to 16 activities to optimality, while heuristic solution approaches fail to generate feasible solutions quite often. Even when feasible solutions are produced, the quality of the latter in terms of the average deviation from the optimum objective function value is rather poor. This discrepancy between applicability of the MMPSP on the one side and the lack of good solution procedures for it on the other side has been the motivation to design a new heuristic capable to solve real-world instances close to optimality.

Chapter 6 is made up as follows: In Section 6.1 a review of the relevant literature is presented. Thereby, Section 6.1.1 is devoted to exact procedures while Section 6.1.2 covers suboptimal approaches. The new heuristic is presented in Section 6.2. Finally, an in-depth computational study is performed in Section 6.3. There, the solution parameters are tuned, the performance of the heuristic w.r.t. problem parameters is evaluated, and finally the heuristic is compared to other suboptimal procedures proposed for the MMPSP.

6.1 Literature Review

6.1.1 Optimal Procedures

Optimal procedures for solving the MMPSP have been presented by Talbot (1982), Patterson et al. (1989), Speranza / Vercellis (1993), and Sprecher (1994). All of them make use of implicit enumeration with branch and bound.

Based on his enumeration scheme proposed for the SMPSP (cf. Talbot / Patterson (1978)), **Talbot** (1982) suggests a two-phase solution approach for the MMPSP. In phase one, activities, modes, and renewable resources are sorted in order to speed up the enumeration procedure applied in phase two. Specifically, maintaining the topological order (cf. Section 2.1.3), activities are sorted w.r.t. one of eight different priority rules. Modes are sorted by non-decreasing duration and renewable resources are ordered w.r.t. non-increasing relative resource usage, where the relative resource usage is calculated as the resource usage divided by the resource availability. In phase two, a subset of the feasible schedules is exhaustively searched for the schedule with the smallest makespan. At the start of the search the time window $[EFT_j, LFT_j]$ is calculated for each activity j, $1 \leq j \leq J$, as described in Sections 2.2.1 and 2.3.1, respectively. Additionally, a lower (LB) and an upper bound (UB) are defined as follows: $LB=EFT_J$ and $UB=T$, where EFT_J denotes the earliest finish time of the unique sink and T the upper bound for the project's makespan, respectively. Beginning with the first activity on the list, it is tried to schedule each activity j, $1 \leq j \leq J$, in the lowest indexed mode as early as possible in its time window. If it is not possible to schedule any mode of activity j in its time window, the algorithm backtracks to activity j-1 and tries to assign to activity j-1 in mode $\mu(j$-1$)$ the earliest feasible finish time in the interval $[FT_{j-1}+1, LFT_{j-1}]$. If the latter interval does not contain a feasible finish time for activity j-1 in mode $\mu(j$-1$)$, then it is tried to schedule the next mode of activity j-1, i.e. $\mu(j$-1$)$+1, as early as possible in the interval $[FT_{j-1}, LFT_{j-1}]$ etc. If a new feasible assignment of mode and start time to activity j-1 could be found, the enumeration procedure is resumed with activity j. Otherwise it backtracks to activity j-2. Whenever a new solution with a makespan lower than UB has been found, the latter one is set to FT_J and the latest finish times LFT_j are updated for all j, $1 \leq j \leq J$. Afterwards, the enumeration procedure is restarted with the first activity on the list. The procedure terminates if (*i*) UB equals LB or if (*ii*) the algorithm backtracks to the first activity on the list, which always is the unique start activity of the project. For both cases, UB equals the optimal solution.

Patterson et al. (1989) and (1990) refined the solution method of Talbot. Most noteworthy is the introduction of a "precedence tree" which allows a systematic enumeration of mode-assignments and start times. In the initialisation phase, modes are sorted as in Talbot (1982), while activities are renumbered w.r.t. the LFT priority rule. Whereas in Talbot (1982) activities are always considered in the order of the priority list, here, relabeling services only the purpose of generating a good (heuristic) solution for the first pass through the enumeration tree. In the latter, associated with each node is exactly one activity which will be scheduled, a partial schedule (including the scheduled activity), and a set of descendant nodes. Each descendant node represents one activity which is eligible for scheduling w.r.t. precedence constraints only. Hence, the number of descendant nodes equals the cardinality of the set of precedence-feasible activities associated with the partial schedule of the ancestor node. The activity associated with the root is the unique dummy source and each leaf of the tree is associated with the unique dummy sink. Thus, each path from the root to one of the leafs is a unique ranking, i.e. a priority list, of the activities of the project such that precedence constraints are maintained. By defining an upper bound for the project's makespan T and restricting the feasible time window of activity j, $1 < j \leq J$, in mode $\mu(j)$ to $[ST_{PPT_j} + d_{j\mu(j)}, LFT_j]$, where PPT_j denotes the immediate predecessor of activity j in the precedence tree, the solution space is fully described. As in Talbot (1982), it is a subset of the set of feasible schedules. Due to the definition of the time windows, the cardinality of the subset is smaller than the one in Talbot (1982). For branching, the node associated with the minimum activity number is selected. Hence, the first path through the enumeration tree is solely determined by the relabeling performed in the initialisation phase. Bounding is performed as in Talbot (1982) implicitly by tightening the time windows. Computational results are given in Patterson et al. (1990). There, 91 instances - similar to the ones of Patterson (1984) - with mainly up to thirty activities were employed. For an imposed time limit of 1 (10) minutes, 30 (33) of the problems were solved on an IBM 4381 mainframe computer.

Sprecher (1994) improved the outlined procedure by introducing the notion of an i-partial schedule which uniquely describes a node i of the enumeration tree and the associated partial schedule (including activity number, assigned mode, and start time of the activity scheduled in node i). Furthermore, Sprecher enhanced the algorithm by applying four dominance criteria and one feasibility bounding rule. The bounding rule has been proposed by Drexl (1991). It checks the feasibility of the current partial schedule by calculating a lower bound for the consumption of nonrenewable resources. Since this can be done very efficiently by preprocessing, the bounding rule shows results superior than each of the dominance criteria, respectively. Amongst the dominance rules, two are worthwhile mentioning: The first rule is due to Drexl (1991). It prunes portions of the enumeration tree if the descendants of a node will lead to the same schedule because, on account of abundant resource availability, start times of eligible activities are not influenced by the order they are considered for scheduling. The second rule is the well-known left-shift dominance rule (cf. Schrage (1970) and Section 5.1.1). Sprecher (1994) performed a computational evaluation on a set of 536 multi-mode test problems with 10 non-dummy activities with three modes each as well as two renewable and two nonrenewable resource types with a resource factor and a resource strength of 0.5 and 1, respectively.[1] The experiment revealed an acceleration factor of approximately hundred in comparison with the originally algorithm of Patterson et al. (1989).

---

[1] The same set of instances will be employed in the computational study of Section 6.3.

Speranza and Vercellis (1993) proposed a depth-first oriented branch and bound procedure which enumerates the set of active schedules.[2] The precedence-based lower bound is employed to prune portions of the enumeration tree. Although Speranza and Vercellis claim the procedure to generate optimal solutions, it has been shown by Hartmann / Sprecher (1993) that for $|R| \geq 2$ and $|N| \geq 0$, i.e. for at least two renewable resource types, the algorithm may not find the optimal solution. Furthermore, for $|R| \geq 0$ and $|N| \geq 1$, i.e. for at least one nonrenewable resource type, the procedure may even fail to find a feasible solution.

6.1.2 Heuristic Procedures

Heuristic solution procedures for the MMPSP have been provided by Slowinski et al. (1991) and Drexl / Grünewald (1993). Solution methods for the MMPSP with $|N|=0$, i.e. without nonrenewable resource types, were addressed in Dell'Amico (1990) and Boctor (1994). Four different solution methodologies can be distinguished: single-pass and multi-pass priority-rule-based scheduling, simulated annealing, and truncated branch and bound.

I. Single-Pass Priority-Rule-Based Scheduling

Boctor (1994) presented a single-pass approach in order to solve the MMPSP with renewable resources only (i.e. by relaxing restriction (2.14) of the 0-1 programming model in Section 2.3.1). He employs a modified parallel scheduling scheme, where an activity is in the decision set if (*i*) all its predecessors are finished and (*ii*) it can be started in at least one of its modes m, $1 \leq m \leq M_j$, at the current schedule time t_n. Out of the decision set an activity is chosen with the MSLK priority rule and the feasible mode with shortest duration is assigned to it. At the beginning, latest start times for the calculation of the MSLK priority values are obtained as described in Section

---

[2] A schedule which belongs to the set of active schedules is termed by Speranza / Vercellis (1993) a "tight" schedule.

2.3.1. Thereafter, every time an activity has been scheduled, latest start times are updated by taking into account the partial mode-assignment. On the basis of 240 instances (50 and 100 activities, 1, 2, and 4 renewable resources) an average deviation from the precedence-based lower bound of 39.2% has been reported. No information w.r.t. running times is given, but from the results of Chapter 5 it can be conjectured that they are quite modest.

Slowinski et al. (1991) proposed a single-pass approach to solve a multiple objective MMPSP. The procedure is an offspring of the branch and bound procedure of Patterson et al. (1989).[3] More precisely, in the first phase a (precedence-feasible) priority list of the activities is derived with one of 12 static priority rules (e.g. LFT, LST, SPT, and GRPW). The second phase, i.e. the scheduling phase, consists of one single pass through the precedence tree as follows: In the order of the priority list, (precedence-feasible) activities are scheduled in the mode with shortest resource-feasible duration at the earliest period possible. Since all decisions in both phases are deterministic, the path in the precedence tree and hence the derived solution is solely determined by the priority list. An import distinction between the exact procedure and the single-pass approach has to be pointed out: Whereas, due to backtracking, the branch and bound algorithm will always derive a feasible solution (if there is one) in the first pass through the precedence tree, this will not be the case for the single-pass approach. Computational results have not been reported.

---

[3] Slowinski et al. do not mention the connection between their heuristic and the exact procedure of Patterson et al. (1989). Instead, they classify the heuristic as a parallel scheduling scheme by referring to the parallel algorithm as outlined by Kelley (1963). Although the formal description of the algorithm is rather vague and bears a lot of ambiguities, the following can be stated: Indeed, the procedure makes use of the schedule time, which is a significant feature of the parallel scheduling scheme. But at the same time the decision set is restricted to activities which are feasible w.r.t. precedence constraints only. Hence, if an activity is selected for scheduling, it might have to be right-shifted in order to start after the current schedule time. Consequently, the solution procedure can neither be characterised as parallel nor as serial.

II. Multi-Pass Priority-Rule-Based Scheduling

On the basis of his single-pass approach, **Boctor** (1994) also suggested a multi-priority rule procedure. Relying on his experimental results he set up a list with five pairs of priority rules for activity and mode selection, respectively. The procedure then performs five passes where pass z, $1 \le z \le 5$, employs the z-th pair of priority rules on the list. Boctor reports an average deviation above the precedence-based lower bound of 35.9% on the same set of instances as employed for the single-pass approach.

Slowinski et al. (1991) extended their single-pass approach to a multi-pass approach by combining elements of a multi-priority rule procedure with sampling. Consequently, priority list λ_l obtained with one of the 12 priority rules employed in their single-pass approach, i.e. l, $1 \le l \le 12$, is used as follows: At each node of the precedence tree, instead of scheduling the next activity on the priority list, one of the first c-ranked precedence-feasible activities is randomly chosen. According to the classification of Hart / Shogan (1987), the approach can be classified as a "cardinality-based semi-greedy heuristic with parameter c". It has to be pointed out that for $c=1$ this equals the deterministic single-pass case, while for $c=J$ random sampling is performed. No computational results have been reported.

Drexl / Grünewald (1993) have proposed a regret-based biased random sampling approach which jointly employs a serial scheduling scheme and the SPT priority rule. Noteworthy is the fact that the start time of a chosen activity is determined w.r.t. precedence constraints only (i.e. within the serial scheduling scheme as described in Section 5.2.1, $ST_{j}*$ is set to $PST_{j}*$ in line 4 of stage n). Feasibility w.r.t. resource constraints is checked only for the final schedule S. The heuristic has been tested extensively on 100 instances with 10 activities, a network complexity of 1.5, three renewable and one nonrenewable resource types as well as different measures of resource scarcity. The best results were obtained with a probability mapping parameter of $\alpha=2$. The sample size - relying on the scarcity of resources - varied between 202 and 3779 in order to generate 100 feasible solutions for each problem, respectively. Depending on the scarcity of resources, an average performance of no more than 3.5% deviation from the optimal objective function value has been documented. The solution time varied between 17 and 321 CPU-seconds on an IBM compatible personal computer (8086 processor with 10 Mhz clockpulse).

III. Simulated Annealing

Slowinski et al. (1991) also suggested simulated annealing for solving the MMPSP. In their approach the three components of a local search technique (cf. Papadimitriou / Steiglitz (1982)) are made up as follows: A *solution* is represented by a (precedence-feasible) priority list λ of the activities j, $1 \leq j \leq J$. As stated above (cf. Subsection I), mode-assignment M and schedule S are uniquely defined by performing the scheduling phase of their single-pass procedure with the priority list λ. The *neighbourhood structure* of λ is defined as follows: Two activities which are not precedence related, i.e. i, j, $1 < i, j < J$, $i \neq j$, $i \not\subseteq \bar{P}_j \cup \bar{S}_j$, $j \not\subseteq \bar{P}_i \cup \bar{S}_i$, are randomly chosen and their positions within λ are interchanged. The *search procedure* is initialised with a priority list λ obtained by the single- or the multi-pass priority rule procedure, respectively. Afterwards, a neighbour λ' of the current priority list λ is generated. If the makespan associated with λ' is smaller than the one associated with λ, λ is replaced by λ', otherwise λ' is accepted with probability $exp(-\delta/p)$,[4] where δ denotes the (positive) difference of the two makespans and p is the control parameter.[5] After a pre-specified number of new solutions λ' have been generated and evaluated, the acceptance parameter p is reduced by 10%. Hence, the probability of accepting a new priority list associated with an inferior objective function value decreases. The heuristic is stopped as soon as the objective function value could not be

---

[4] No information is provided in the case of an infeasible solution associated with λ'.

[5] p is initialised by determining an acceptable deterioration of the objective function (e.g. 20%) and the associated acceptance probability (e.g. 90%) for the first neighbour solution λ' generated.

improved for three consecutive values of the acceptance probability. As for the two other solution procedures proposed by Slowinski et al. (1991), no computational results are reported.

IV. Truncated Branch and Bound

The exact procedures of Talbot (1982), Patterson et al. (1989), and Sprecher (1994) were explicitly recommended by the authors to be used as heuristics by limiting the CPU time. Talbot (1982) reports that activity ordering with the LFT priority rule produced the best results. In their experimental investigation, Patterson et al. (1990) made use of the MSLK priority rule and summarised "our conjecture ... is that additional computer time allowed ... will result in small improvements". Finally, Sprecher (1994) has extensively tested his truncated branch and bound approach on the test instances outlined in Section 6.1.1. Employing four of the five bounding rules and imposing a time limit of 10 seconds on an IBM personal computer with 80486 processor including coprocessor and 25 Mhz clockpulse he solves 524 of the 536 problems to optimality, leaving only one problem unsolved. Despite of these encouraging results, due to the *NP*-hardness of the problem, the number of feasible solutions grows exponentially when the number of activities increases (linearly). Thus, it can be conjectured that the average solution quality will deteriorate dramatically, when solving larger instances. Hence, enumeration-based methods for solving real world project scheduling problems are of only limited use.

6.2 A New Heuristic Solution Methodology for the MMPSP

It was shown in Section 2.3.2 that the feasibility problem corresponding to the MMPSP belongs to the class of *NP*-complete problems. Thus, for heuristics it is severely difficult to generate even feasible solutions for the MMPSP; a fact which has been pointed out by Drexl / Grünewald (1993). This knowledge has been the primary motivation when designing the solution methodology which will be presented in the sequel. Of course, in this research context the solution methodology is based on a priority-rule-based sampling approach. The main idea is to decompose the MMPSP into two problems: the MAP and the SMPSP. As a result of Chapter 5, the SMPSP can be efficiently solved with the procedure proposed therein and thus the problem left is to find in the first place a feasible and in the second place a (w.r.t. to the objective function value of the MMPSP) good solution for the MAP.

Section 6.2.1 is devoted to the first concern: A single-pass procedure is proposed to generate an initial feasible mode-assignment. Section 6.2.2 enhances this procedure by a sampling algorithm which, based on the feasible schedule derived by the SMPSP, will alter the mode-assignment in order to improve the solution. The crucial idea of this approach is to perform only passes which will generate a feasible solution by restricting the set of all mode-assignments to the subset of feasible ones. This bears the benefits of solving more instances and generating better solutions.

6.2.1 Single-Pass Approach

First, the opening mode-assignment scheme (OMA) is presented. OMA consists of J-2 stages, in each of which to exactly one activity one of its modes is assigned. In order to facilitate understanding, two main ideas have to be sketched out: First, within each stage, for every activity the scope is restricted to the mode which consumes the minimum amount of scarce resources, respectively. Resource scarceness is dynamically measured by means of the sum of relative (nonrenewable) resource consumption. Second, in order to reflect resource scarceness properly and hence to avoid infeasibility, activities are chosen for the mode assignment in the order of largest resource consumption. To provide a formal description of OMA, the following notation has to be introduced:

SJ set of activities to which a mode has been assigned, respectively,

πK_r left-over capacity of the nonrenewable resource r,

RC_{jm} relative (nonrenewable) resource consumption of activity j in mode m,

SRC_j smallest relative resource consumption of activity j,

LRC largest relative resource consumption,

where the left-over capacity and the relative resource consumption of non-renewable resources are defined, respectively, as:

$$\pi K_r = K_r - \sum_{j \in SJ} k_{j\mu(j)r} \tag{6.1}$$

$$RC_{jm} = \sum_{r \in N} \frac{k_{jmr}}{\pi K_r} \tag{6.2}$$

Recalling X to be the set of all activities (cf. Definition 5.1), OMA can now be described formally as follows:

OMA

Initialisation: $SJ := \varnothing;\ \pi K_r := K_r\ \forall\, r \in N;$
CALCULATE $RC_{jm}, j \in X, m \in \{1,...,M_j\};$

FOR $n=1$ TO J DO **Stage n**

BEGIN
$SRC_j := \min\{\, RC_{jm} \mid 1 \le m \le M_j \,\}, j \in X \setminus SJ;$
$LRC := \max\{\, SRC_j \mid j \in X \setminus SJ \,\};$
$j^* := \min\{\, j \mid SRC_j := LRC, j \in X \setminus SJ \,\};$
$\mu(j^*) := \min\{\, m \mid RC_{j^*m} = SRC_{j^*}, 1 \le m \le M_{j^*} \,\};$
$SJ := SJ \cup \{j^*\},$ UPDATE $\pi K_r\ \forall\, r \in N, RC_{jm}, j \in X \setminus SJ, m \in \{1,...,M_j\};$
END;

Stop: IF $\pi K_r \ge 0\ \forall\, r \in N,$ a feasible mode-assignment M has been generated;

***

Precisely, OMA works as follows: At the beginning, to none of the activities a mode has been assigned. Consequently the set SJ is empty and the left-over capacity of every nonrenewable resource equals its overall capacity, respectively. At stage n, $1 \le n \le J$, for every activity with a not yet assigned mode, the relative resource consumption for each mode is calculated and the

activity which maximises the minimum relative resource consumption is selected. To this activity the mode with the smallest relative resource consumption is assigned. In case of ties, the lowest labelled activity and mode are
selected, respectively. Finally, the set of activities to which a mode has been
assigned, respectively, and the left-over capacities of nonrenewable resources
are updated. In order to clarify the opening mode assignment, the MMPSP
example of Chapter 2 is recalled in Figure 6.1 and Table 6.1, respectively.

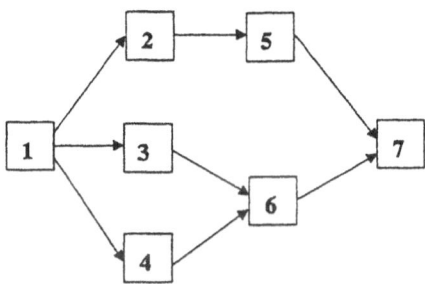

Figure 6.1: Network of the MMPSP Example

j	1	2		3	4		5	6		7
m	1	1	2	1	1	2	1	1	2	1
d_{jm}	0	4	6	2	3	5	2	2	4	0
k_{jm1}	0	2	1	1	3	1	1	2	1	0
k_{jm2}	0	3	1	0	4	2	0	3	2	0
			$R=\{1\}, N=\{2\}, K_1=4, K_2=8$							

Table 6.1: Data of the MMPSP Example

Table 6.2 provides the report of OMA when applied to the example problem. The smallest resource consumption SRC_j, $1 \le j \le J$, is listed by under-
lining the relevant RC_{jm} for each activity, respectively. Note that the only
nonrenewable resource is $r=2$ and that, since the left-over capacity is non-
increasing w.r.t. the stage n, the relative resource consumption is a non-decreasing function of stage n.

Since OMA stops with positive left-over capacity, the derived mode-assignment $M=(1,2,1,2,1,2,1)$ is feasible. Applying SMH/1 (cf. Section 5.5.1) to M gives way to the schedule $S=(0,6,2,5,8,9,9)$ with a makespan of 9 periods which is depicted in Figure 6.2.

				RC_{jm}					SRC_j							
			j	1	2		3	4		5	6		7			
n	SJ	πK_2	m	1	1	2	1	1	2	1	1	2	1	LRC	j^*	$\mu(j^*)$
1	∅	8		0	.37	.12	0	.5	.25	0	.37	.25	0	.25	4	2
2	4	6		0	.5	.16	0			0	.5	.33	0	.33	6	2
3	4,6	4		0	.75	.25	0			0			0	.25	2	2
4	2,4,6	3		0			0			0			0	0	1	1
5	1,2,4,6	3					0			0			0	0	3	1
6	1,...,4,6	3								0			0		5	1
7	1,...,6	3											0		7	1

Table 6.2: Report of OMA for the Example Problem

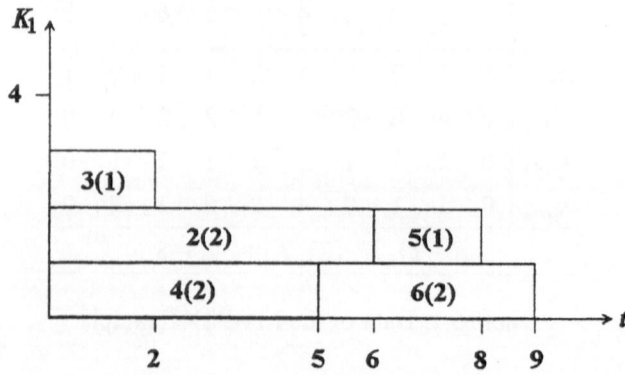

Figure 6.2: Schedule Associated with the Solution Derived by OMA

Since the mode-assignment problem is *NP*-complete OMA is not able to find a feasible solution with certainty. Nevertheless, on the multi-mode instances which will be employed in Section 6.3, it performed very well by deriving a feasible solution for every problem. Additionally, it has to be stressed that OMA is a single-pass approach which thus can be altered to a (regret-based) biased random sampling procedure without much additional effort. From the results gained so far, it can be expected that the latter will produce significantly more feasible solutions than OMA. Also it is quite clear that the following holds:

Theorem 6.1: For $|N|=1$, OMA always creates a feasible mode-assignment if one exists.

Proof: Obvious, since for each activity the mode with smallest resource consumption is chosen.   ∎

To sum it up, OMA usually provides a feasible mode-assignment in the presence of scarce nonrenewable resources. But when the latter are abundant then the mode-assignment at hand might be rather poor because - w.r.t. nonrenewable resources only - modes with shorter duration can be assigned to activities. Ceteris paribus this will yield a schedule with smaller makespan. A quite straightforward way to overcome this deficiency is to allot the left-over capacity of nonrenewable resources to activities in the order of ascending slack.[6] This idea is incorporated in the algorithm "improve mode-assignment" (IMA). In order to describe IMA more detailed, let denote $\Delta k(j,m,r)$ the difference of the resource usage (consumption) w.r.t. resource r, if the mode $\mu(j)$ currently assigned to activity j is changed to the new mode m, $1 \le m \le M_j$, $m \ne \mu(j)$), which can be written formally as:

$$\Delta k(j,m,r) = k_{j\,\mu(j)\,r} - k_{jmr} \qquad m, \mu(j), 1 \le m, \mu(j) \le M_j, m \ne \mu(j) \qquad (6.3)$$

Recalling from Section 2.2.1 the procedures forward recursion (FR) and backward recursion (BR), from Section 5.2.2 the notation for a priority value

---

[6] Throughout the project scheduling literature two synonymous expressions are used: slack (cf. e.g. Levy et al. (1963) and Wiest (1964)) and float (cf. e.g. Elmaghraby (1977, p.145) and Moder et al. (1983, p.78)). In analogy to the well-known minimum slack (MSLK) priority rule (cf. formula 5.9), in here it is referred to slack. The different kinds of slack (float), e.g. total float, free float, interfering float etc., as a result of the time analysis only, are not treated in this study. For details refer to Moder et al. (1983, p. 78) and Ziegler (1985).

$v(j)$, and from Section 5.3.2 the notation $\lambda(j)$ as the ordinal position of activity j within a priority list λ, the formal description of IMA can be stated as follows:

$$\boxed{\text{IMA}}$$

Initialisation: $SJ := \{1,...,J\}$; CALCULATE $\pi K_r \ \forall \ r \in N$;
PERFORM FR and BR (with $T := EFT_J$) on the basis of M;
ASSIGN $\lambda(j)$ according to ascending $v(j) = LFT_j - EFT_j$, $1 \le j \le J$;

FOR $n=1$ TO J DO **Stage n**
BEGIN
  $j := \lambda(n)$; $m := \mu(j)$;
  WHILE $m \ge 1$ DO
  BEGIN
      IF $\pi K_r + \Delta k(j,m,r) \ge 0 \ \forall \ r \in N$ THEN $\mu(j) := m$;
      $m := m-1$;
  END
  UPDATE $\pi K_r \ \forall \ r \in N$;
END;

Stop: A (new) feasible mode-assignment M has been generated;

***

IMA works as follows: On the basis of a feasible mode-assignment M, it performs a forward and backward recursion (with $T = EFT_J$) in order to calculate the traditional precedence-based slack (i.e. the total float) of each activity, respectively. At the end of the initialisation, activities are ranked in the order of ascending slack. The main algorithm consists of exactly $n=1,...,J$ stages, in each of which it is tried to assign to the n-th ranked activity its lowest indexed resource-feasible mode. Generally, this decreases the duration and increases the resource usage (consumption) of the activity under consideration (recall that modes are sorted in the order of non-decreasing duration). If the mode-change is feasible, i.e. there is a lower indexed mode and the (additional) resource consumption induced by the switch does not exceed the left-over capacity of each nonrenewable resource, respectively, the new mode-assignment is stored. Afterwards, the next activity on the list is considered etc. The algorithm stops after stage $n=J$ when each activity has been considered once.

In order to facilitate understanding, IMA will be applied to the mode-assignment $M=(1,2,1,2,1,2,1)$ derived by OMA. Table 6.3 provides the (slack-based) activity ranking as a result of the initialisation phase.

j	1	2	3	4	5	6	7
EFT_j	0	6	2	5	8	9	9
LFT_j	10	17	15	15	19	19	19
LFT_j-EFT_j	10	11	13	10	11	10	10
$\lambda(j)$	1	5	7	2	6	3	4

Table 6.3: Priority List of the IMA Initialisation

n	πK_2	$j=\lambda(n)$	$\mu(j)$	m	$\Delta k(j,m,2)$	$\mu(j)$
1	3	1	1			
2	3	4	2	1	-2	1
3	1	6	2	1	-1	1
4	0	7	1			
5	0	2	2	1	-2	2
6	0	5	1			
7	0	3	1			

Table 6.4: Report of IMA for the Example Problem

Table 6.4 shows the solution report of IMA. The new mode-assignment derived is $M=(1,2,1,1,1,1,1)$. Applying SMH/1 to M results in the schedule $S=(0,6,2,5,8,7,8)$. As can be seen in Figure 6.3, the new solution has an improved makespan of eight periods.

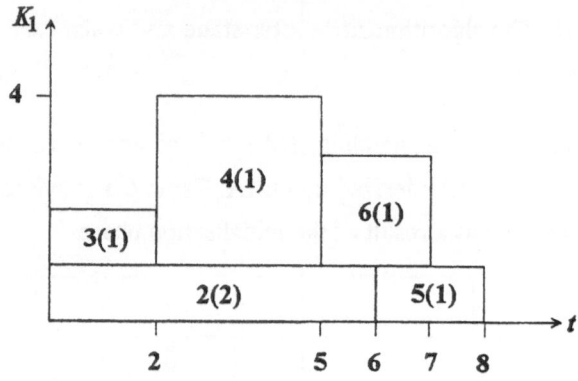

Figure 6.3: Schedule Associated with the Solution of IMA

It should be clear that the following holds:

Theorem 6.2: For a resource strength of $RS(N)=1$, i.e. the nonrenewable un-constrained case, IMA assigns to each activity its mode with shortest duration.

Proof: Obvious.   ■

Remark 6.1: Theorem 6.2 in conjunction with Theorems 5.3 and 5.6 assures that IMA and SMH always derive the optimal solution for the resource-un-constrained case, i.e. $RS(R)=RS(N)=1$.

6.2.2 Multi-Pass Approach

The algorithms so far presented, i.e. OMA, IMA, (and SMH) constitute a classical single-pass approach for solving the MMPSP: A (hopefully) feasible mode-assignment M is generated by OMA and (generally) improved by IMA. On the basis of M, SMH generates a feasible schedule S. Clearly, M and S represent a valid solution for the problem at hand.

This single-pass approach can be extended straightforward to a multi-pass approach in one of two ways:

(*i*) The single-pass is performed several times where probabilistic elements are introduced for the mode-assignment within OMA, IMA, or both.

(*ii*) Instead of starting every time with OMA again, the solution derived by SMH is used to alter the current mode-assignment. This in turn will be the basis for a new schedule to be created by SMH. Proceeding this way has several advantages, to wit: The information contained in the last solution can be exploited in order to (hopefully) create a good new mode-assignment. Furthermore, the alternation of the mode-assignment is much cheaper w.r.t. computational effort than generating a totally new mode-assignment every time. For these reasons, the second option will be followed in the sequel.

The general idea for the mode alternation is as follows: W.r.t. the last schedule generated, for each activity j, $1 < j < J$, a modified slack σ_j which takes into account precedence as well as resource constraints is calculated. Now, if renewable resource constraints are relaxed, associated with a mode-switch for one activity is a chang of the objective function as follows: Let [j,m] denote the tuple of the new mode m, $1 \le m \le M_j$, $m \ne \mu(j)$, which can be assigned to activity j, $1 < j < J$. Then, the duration difference of activity j induced by the mode-switch can be written as:

$$\Delta d(j,m) = d_{jm} - d_{j\mu(j)} \quad m, \mu(j), \ 1 \le m, \mu(j) \le M_j, m \ne \mu(j) \tag{6.4}$$

Under the assumption of relaxed renewable resource constraints the difference for the makespan arises to:

$$\Delta T(j,m) = \begin{cases} \Delta d(j,m), \text{ if } \sigma_j = 0 \\ \max\{0, \Delta d(j,m) - \sigma_j\}, \text{ otherwise} \end{cases} \tag{6.5}$$

with $m, \mu(j), 1 \le m, \mu(j) \le M_j, m \ne \mu(j)$.

Now, the mode-switch associated with the maximum reduction of the makespan is performed. Obviously, a reduction of the makespan can only be obtained by decreasing the duration of the selected activity. Since this enlarges the resource (usage and) consumption, infeasibility of the new mode-assignment might occur. In order to regain feasibility the resource (usage and) consumption of at least one activity has to be decreased. Specifically, activities have to be chosen where a mode-switch frees resources currently causing infeasibility and does not create negative left-over capacity w.r.t. the other nonrenewable resources.

Before presenting a detailed description of the mode alternation procedure the calculation of the modified slack has to be described: The algorithm has been introduced by Wiest (1964) with the aim of extending the operational utility of the (only precedence-based) slack concept to the resource-constrained case. The main idea is to start with a semi-active schedule where none of the activities can be locally right-shifted (cf. Definition 3.7) and to local right-shift activities as far as possible. The difference between the finish time within the new schedule and the finish time in the semi-active schedule does then give a measure of slack in the context of precedence and resource constraints for each activity, respectively. Obviously, the order in which activities are considered for local right-shifting does strongly influence the way the overall slack is allotted to the activities. To obtain an even distribution, Wiest ranks the activities according to four lexicographically ordered priority rules

$$\underline{p}0 = ((\max, FT_j),(\max, ST_j),(\min, RU_j),(\min, j)) \tag{6.6}$$

where $\underline{p}=((\text{extremum}_1, v_1),...,(\text{extremum}_L, v_L))$ denotes the lexicographically ordered priority rules $1,...,L$ and RU_j denotes the renewable resource usage of activity j, which is defined as:

$$RU_j = \sum_{r \in R} k_{jr\mu(j)} \tag{6.7}$$

The priority vector $\underline{p}0$ defines a unique ranking of the activities with the activity number as the final tie breaker. Introducing SL to be the modified slack vector, i.e. $SL = (\sigma_1,...,\sigma_J)$, the "modified slack calculation" (MSC) can formally be put in the following way:

MSC

Initialisation: Given a feasible schedule S, ASSIGN $\lambda(j)$, $1 \leq j \leq J$, according to $p0$;

FOR $n=1$ TO J DO **Stage n**

BEGIN
  $j:=\lambda(n)$;
  Locally right-shift activity j as far as possible;
  Assign to activity j the (new) finish time FT'_j;
  $\sigma_j:=FT'_j-FT_j$;
END;

Stop: The modified slack $SL = (\sigma_1,...,\sigma_J)$ has been calculated;

***

Based on the current solution $M=(1,2,1,1,1,1,1)$ and $S=(0,6,2,5,8,7,8)$, MSC is illustrated by Tables 6.5 and 6.6, respectively. Table 6.5 provides the priority list obtained in the initialisation phase while the report of the modified slack calculation with the resulting slack vector $SL=(0,0,1,0,1,1,0)$ is given in Table 6.6.

j	1	2	3	4	5	6	7
FT_j	0	6	2	5	8	7	8
ST_j	0	0	0	2	6	5	8
RU_j	0	1	1	3	1	2	0
$\lambda(j)$	7	4	6	5	2	3	1

Table 6.5: Priority List of the MSC Initialisation

n	1	2	3	4	5	6	7
$j = \lambda(n)$	7	5	6	2	4	3	1
FT_j	8	8	7	6	5	2	0
FT'_j	8	8	8	6	6	3	0
σ_j	0	0	1	0	1	1	0

Table 6.6: Report of the MSC

After clarifying the calculation of the modified slack, the presentation of the mode alternation procedure can be continued: To provide a precise description of the procedure, the following notation has to be introduced and recapitulated, respectively: Let be

$[j,m]$ an activity-mode tuple,

AJ the set of available activities, i.e. activities to which a new mode has not yet been assigned, respectively,

$AM(j)$ the available modes of activity j,

N' the set of nonrenewable resources currently causing infeasibility,

$JM1$ the activity-mode set 1, i.e. the set of activity-mode tuples $[j,m]$ which can be chosen to reduce the makespan,

$JM2$ the activity-mode set 2, i.e. the set of activity-mode tuples $[j,m]$ which can be chosen to regain feasibility,

$\Delta k(j,m)$ the additionally cumulated resource consumption needed or freed w.r.t. to the nonrenewable resources currently causing infeasibility, if mode $\mu(j)$ assigned to activity j is switched to the new mode m.

Given the integer but not necessarily positive left-over capacity πK_r, $r \in N$, of the nonrenewable resources, $AM(j)$, N', $\Delta k(j,m)$, $JM1$, and $JM2$ are defined as follows:

$AM(j) = \{1,...,M_j\} \setminus \mu(j)$

$N' = \{r \mid r \in N, \pi K_r < 0\}$

$\Delta k(j,m) = \sum_{r \in N'} \Delta k(j,m,r)$

$JM1 = \{[j,m] \mid j \in AJ, m \in AM(j)\}$

$JM2 = \{[j,m] \mid [j,m] \in JM1, \Delta k(j,m,r) \geq 0 \; \forall \; r \in N',$
$$\Delta k(j,m,r) + \pi K_r \geq 0 \; \forall \; r \in N \backslash N'\}$$

The procedure "alter mode-assignment" (AMA) can now be presented formally:

AMA

Initialisation: $AJ := \{1,...,J\}$; CALCULATE $AM(j)$, $1 \leq j \leq J$;
          CALCULATE $\pi K_r \; \forall \; r \in N$; $N' := \varnothing$; CALCULATE $JM1$, $JM2$;

(1) UPDATE $\Delta T(j,m) \; \forall \; [j,m] \in JM1$;
   $\Delta T^{min} := \min\{\Delta T(j,m) \mid [j,m] \in JM1\}$;
   $[j^*,m^*] := \{[j,m] \mid \Delta T(j,m) = \Delta T^{min}, [j,m] \in JM1\}$;
   $\mu(j^*) := m^*$, $AJ := AJ \backslash \{j^*\}$, UPDATE $\pi K_r \; \forall \; r \in N$, UPDATE N', $JM1$, $JM2$;
   IF $N' = \varnothing$, THEN STOP;

(2) IF $JM2 = \varnothing$ THEN Stop;
   UPDATE $\Delta k(j,m) \; \forall \; [j,m] \in JM2$;
   $\Delta k^{max} := \max\{\Delta k(j,m) \mid [j,m] \in JM2\}$;
   $[j^*,m^*] := \{[j,m] \mid \Delta k(j,m) = \Delta k^{max}, [j,m] \in JM2\}$;
   $\mu(j^*) := m^*$, $AJ := AJ \backslash \{j^*\}$, UPDATE $\pi K_r \; \forall \; r \in N$, UPDATE N', $JM2$;
   IF $N' = \varnothing$, THEN Stop ELSE GOTO (2);

Stop: IF $N' = \varnothing$, a new feasible mode-assignment M has been generated;

***

Before continuing the example, a verbally explanation of the above procedure will be provided: AMA starts with every not currently assigned activity-mode tuple as an element of the activity-mode set $JM1$. In step (1) the activity-mode tuple $[j^*,m^*]$ which - under the assumption of relaxed renewable resource constraints - gives way to the largest makespan reduction is chosen out of $JM1$. In case of ties, the lowest activity (mode) number is selected. Activity j^* is removed from the set of available activities AJ. Afterwards, the left-over capacities of the nonrenewable resources πK_r, the set of nonrenewable resources currently causing infeasibility N', and the activity-mode sets $JM1$ and $JM2$ are updated, respectively. If the new mode-assignment is feasible, AMA is finished, otherwise step (2) is performed.

Herein, activity-mode tuples of $JM2$, a subset of $JM1$, are choosable. These are all tuples for which activities have not yet been selected and a mode-change does neither cause an increase of resource consumption w.r.t. nonrenewable resources currently causing infeasibility N' nor does induce infeasibility of the remaining nonrenewable resources $N\backslash N'$. The activity-mode tuple $[j^*,m^*]$ which frees the most resources currently causing infeasibility is selected. Again, in case of ties the lowest activity (mode) number is selected. Activity j^* is removed from AJ and updating of the left-over capacities as well as the sets N', $JM1$, and $JM2$ takes place, respectively. Step (2) is continued until (*i*) feasibility is regained or (*ii*) the set of choosable mode-tuples $JM2$ is empty and hence AMA has to be finished with an infeasible mode-assignment.

For the purpose of clarification the example is resumed: Starting with the last mode-assignment $M=(1,2,1,1,1,1,1)$, the initialisation phase of AMA terminates with $AJ=\{1,...,7\}$, $\pi K_2=0$, $N'=\varnothing$, $AM(j)$ for all j, $1 \le j \le J$, as given in Table 6.7, $JM1=\{[2,1], [4,2], [6,2]\}$, and $JM2=\{[4,2], [6,2]\}$.

j	1	2	3	4	5	6	7
$AM(j)$	$\varnothing$	$\{1\}$	$\varnothing$	$\{2\}$	$\varnothing$	$\{2\}$	$\varnothing$

Table 6.7: Available Modes after the Initialisation Phase of AMA

Step	πK_2	N'	$JM1$ / $JM2$	ΔT / Δk	ΔT^{min} / Δk^{max}	$[j^*,m^*]$
(1)	0	$\varnothing$	[2,1], [4,2], [6,2]	-2, 1, 1	-2	[2,1]
(2)	-2	$\{2\}$	[4,2], [6,2]	2, 1	2	[4,2]

Table 6.8: Report of AMA

Table 6.8 presents the report of AMA. Note that the data provided refers to $JM1$ ($JM2$), ΔT (Δk), and ΔT^{min} (Δk^{max}) for the first (second) step, respectively. In step (1) mode 1 is assigned to activity 2. Since this leads to infeasibility, step (2) has to be proceeded. Herein, one iteration, switching from the 1-st to the 2-nd mode of activity 4, is sufficient to regain feasibility. Hence, AMA stops after both step (1) and (2) have been processed once. The mode-assignment derived is $M=(1,1,1,2,1,1,1)$. Applying SMH/1 to M brings forth the schedule $S=(0,4,2,5,6,7,7)$ with a makespan of seven periods. This schedule equals the optimal solution which is displayed in Figure 6.4.

Introducing M' to be the last feasible mode-assignment and recalling $\underline{M}$ ($\underline{S}$) to be the best mode-assignment (schedule) found so far as well as SL to be the modified slack vector, the entire multi-mode heuristic (MMH) can be summarised as follows:

$$\boxed{\text{MMH}}$$

Initialisation: $y:=0$; COMPUTE M with OMA;
        IF M is infeasible THEN Stop ELSE
        BEGIN
            PERFORM IMA; PERFORM SMH/1; $M'=\underline{M}:=M$; $\underline{S}:=S$;
        END;

FOR $y:=1$ TO Y DO **Pass y**
BEGIN
  COMPUTE SL according to MSC;
  PERFORM AMA on the basis of SL,
  IF M is infeasible THEN $M:=M'$ ELSE $M':=M$;
  PERFORM SMH/1,
  IF $\phi_{SMPSP}(S) < \phi_{SMPSP}(\underline{S})$ THEN DO
  BEGIN
     $\underline{M}:=M$, $\underline{S}:=S$;
  END;
END;

$M:=\underline{M}$; PERFORM SMH/Z;
IF $\phi_{SMPSP}(S) < \phi_{SMPSP}(\underline{S})$ THEN $\underline{S}:=S$;

Stop: IF $y>0$ THEN a feasible solution $(\underline{M},\underline{S})$ for MMPSP has been generated.

***

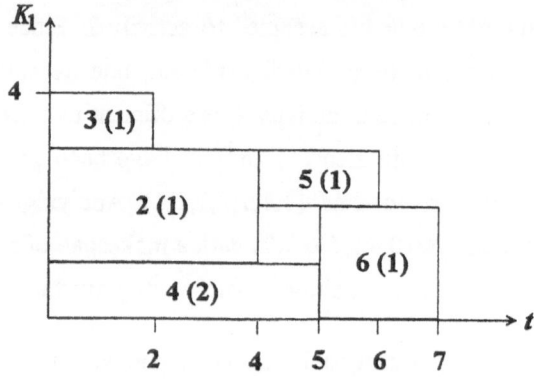

Figure 6.4: Optimal Solution of the MMPSP Example

The initialisation phase of MMH consists of the single-pass approach as outlined in Section 6.2.1: First, OMA is performed to derive the initial mode-assignment. If the latter is infeasible, MMH is stopped without a valid solution for the problem at hand. Otherwise, it is tried to improve the initial mode-assignment by applying IMA. In any case IMA generates a (not necessarily new) feasible mode-assignment for which a feasible schedule is derived by applying SMH/1. Hence, at the end of the initialisation phase, hopefully a feasible solution, i.e. M and S, has been generated deterministically. The multi-pass solution procedure is represented within the passes $y=1,...,Y$. At the beginning of pass y, $1 \le y \le Y$, for each activity the precedence- and resource-based slack, i.e. the modified slack vector SL, is calculated with MSC. Afterwards, AMA alters on the basis of SL the mode-assignment. If this mode-change renders the mode-assignment M infeasible, the latter is set equal to last feasible mode-assignment M'. Pass y is completed by deriving a feasible schedule S with SMH/1. If S has a lower makespan than the so far best schedule $\underline{S}$, the latter is set equal to S. Finally, after Y passes have been performed (and hence $Y+1$ solutions have been evaluated) the multi-pass heuristic for the single-mode project scheduling problem SMH/Z is used in order to improve the so far best schedule $\underline{S}$ on the basis of the so far best mode-assignment $\underline{M}$.

It has been pointed out that within the initialisation of MMH and AMA schedules are derived with the deterministic version of SMH, i.e. a single pass of the tandem "parallel scheduling scheme and worst case slack priority rule". Preliminary computational results, which are not reported here, revealed that improving the quality of intermediate schedules by applying SMH/Z with $Z > 1$ did not render the solutions significantly better. But by applying SMH/Z to the best mode-assignment derived the final solution was improved significantly.

The solution procedure, in the way it has been presented so far, is w.r.t. the mode-assignment a multi-pass approach which is based solely on deterministic decisions. Probabilistic elements are only incorporated by applying SMH/Z to the best mode-assignment. A modification of MMH can now be reached by also introducing stochastic elements within AMA. This is done by employing the regret-based parameterised probability mapping of Section 5.3.2 to the activity-mode tuple selection of step (1) and step (2) with parameters β and γ, respectively. Thus, a solution procedure MMH/Y/Z/β/γ with parameters Y (sample size of mode-assignments), Z (sample size of schedules for the best mode-assignment), β (probability mapping parameter for step (1)), and γ (probability mapping parameter for step (2)) is fully described.

An interesting aspect of MMH is its analogy to local search techniques (cf. Papadimitriou / Steiglitz (1982, p. 454)): The starting point of the search is generated by the initialisation. A *solution* is represented by a feasible mode-assignment vector M. The *cost function* associated with a solution is gained by applying SMH/1 to M. A new neighbour of M is generated in two steps: First, the mode of exactly one activity is changed in step (1) of AMA. Afterwards, in step (2) a new M is derived by changing not yet altered activity-mode tuples until feasibility is derived. The search performed is a Single Neighbourhood Search, i.e. exactly one neighbour solution is created and evaluated within each pass. Finally, applying AMA with stochastic elements renders the deterministic local search probabilistic (cf. Goldberg (1989)).

6.3 Computational Results

The computational study which will be presented in this section has been performed with three goals: First, to tune the parameters of MMH in order to adjust the procedure as good as possible. Second, to assess the performance of MMH w.r.t. different problem parameters, and finally to compare MMH with other heuristics for the multi-mode project scheduling problem. Hence, Section 6.3.1 introduces the statistical model employed, Section 6.3.2 reports on the parameter tuning, while Section 6.3.3 covers the performance of MMH w.r.t. different problem parameters. Finally, Section 6.3.4 provides a comparison of recent suboptimal procedures for the MMPSP.

6.3.1 Statistical Model

For the MMPSP-instances under full factorial design the following statistical model with seven factors can be stated (cf. Section 5.4):

$$DEV_{klmnopqr} = \delta(Y_k, Z_l, B_m, G_n, RF(R)_o, RF(N)_p, RS(R)_q, RS(N)_r) + \varepsilon_{klmnopqr} \quad (6.8)$$

$$CPU_{klmnopqr} = \theta(Y_k, Z_l, B_m, G_n, RF(R)_o, RF(N)_p, RS(R)_q, RS(N)_r) + \varepsilon_{klmnopqr} \quad (6.9)$$

where $DEV_{klmnopqr}$ ($CPU_{klmnopqr}$) denotes the percentage deviation from the optimal objective function value (the average running time in CPU seconds) when the k-th, l-th, m-th, and n-th level of the solution parameters Y, Z, β, and γ, respectively, are applied to the problem with the o-th, p-th, q-th, and the r-th level of the problem parameters $RF(R)$, $RF(N)$, $RS(R)$, and $RS(N)$, respectively. The levels of the solution parameters have been chosen as follows:

$$Y_k \in \{1, 10, 30, 50\} \quad (6.10)$$

$$Z_l \in \{1, 10, 30, 50\} \quad (6.11)$$

$$B_m \in \{0\%, 25\%, 50\%, 75\%, 100\%\} \quad (6.12)$$

$$G_n \in \{0\%, 25\%, 50\%, 75\%, 100\%\} \tag{6.13}$$

The levels of the probability mapping parameters B_m and G_n reflect the amount of bias, respectively (cf. Section 5.4.2).[7] The levels of the problem parameters are:

$$RF(R)_o \in \{0.5, 1\} \tag{6.14}$$

$$RF(N)_p \in \{0.5, 1\} \tag{6.15}$$

$$RS(R)_q \in \{0.2, 0.5, 0.7, 1\} \tag{6.16}$$

$$RS(N)_r \in \{0.2, 0.5, 0.7, 1\} \tag{6.17}$$

As in Chapter 5, instances with the above problem parameters were generated with ProGen (cf. Chapter 4) as follows: Additionally to the levels of the variable parameters given in formulas (6.14) - (6.17), the levels for the constant parameter were adjusted according to Table 6.9. W.r.t. the level of demand generation (cf. Section 4.4.1), the time-resource tradeoff case has been selected. Tolerances were set to 0.05. Generating 10 instances for each combination of $RF(R)$, $RS(R)$, $RF(N)$, and $RS(N)$, a total of $2\cdot4\cdot2\cdot4\cdot10=640$ problems were solved with the exact branch and bound procedure of Sprecher (1994) in order to obtain optimal solutions.[8] Since, as has been pointed out in Remark 4.3, the feasibility of the generated multi-mode problems can not be assured for a low level of the resource strength, only 536 of the 640 instances had a feasible solution. On account of the opening mode-assignment scheme OMA, for all of these 536 instances feasible solutions could be derived with MMH.

---

[7] For the values actually employed in the probability mappings, cf. Table 5.15.

[8] For details of the study refer to Kolisch et al. (1992).

	J	M_j	d_j	$|R|$	U_R	Q_R	$|N|$	U_N	Q_N	S_1	S_j	P_j	P_J	NC
min	10	3	1	2	1	1	2	1	1	3	1	1	3	1.5
max	10	3	10	2	10	2	2	10	2	3	3	3	3	1.5

Table 6.9: Constant Parameter Levels for the MMPSP Instances

6.3.2 Evaluation of Procedure Parameters

As can be seen from Tables 6.10 to 6.13, Y the sample size of mode-assign-ments as well as β the probability mapping parameter of step (1), respec-tively, do have a highly significant influence on the performance (s=0.0000). The sample size of schedules for the best mode-assignment Z is significant (s=0.0727), while γ, the mapping parameter of step (2), does not have sig-nificant effects (s=0.9543).

Y_k	1	10	30	50
DEV_k	17.27	11.94	9.14	7.88
CPU_k	0.35	0.67	1.42	2.17

Table 6.10: Effect of the Sample Size Y on the Performance of MMH

Z_l	1	10	30	50
DEV_l	12.16	11.51	11.29	11.28
CPU_l	0.94	1.08	1.21	1.39

Table 6.11: Effect of the Sample Size Z on the Performance of MMH

B_m	0%	25%	50%	75%	100%
DEV_m	13.63	9.91	10.08	11.24	12.94
CPU_m	1.07	1.30	1.29	1.00	1.11

Table 6.12: Effect of the Mapping Parameter β on the Performance of MMH

G_n	0%	25%	50%	75%	100%
DEV_n	11.29	11.63	11.60	11.62	11.65
CPU_n	1.02	1.18	1.19	1.18	1.20

Table 6.13: Effect of the Mapping Parameter γ on the Performance of MMH

The adjustments for the two probability mappings with the highest performance are 25% and 0% bias for step (1) and step (2), respectively. That is, while step (2) can be performed entirely deterministically, step (1) should be done with a small bias of 25%. Taking into account the trade-off between solution quality and the computational requirement, it can be concluded that the best adjustment of the sample size Z is 30. Larger sample sizes will barely improve the performance but gradually increase the computational effort. The sample size of mode-assignments Y should not be fixed to one of the levels employed, because larger samples seem to produce better solutions.

6.3.3 Evaluation of Problem Parameters

In order to assess the impact of the problem parameters, the procedure parameters were fixed, respectively, to $Y=50$, $Z=30$, $\beta=25\%$, and $\gamma=0\%$. Tables 6.14 to 6.17 show how the resource factor and the resource strength of renewable and nonrenewable resources, respectively, affect the performance for this adjustment of the procedure parameters.

$RF(R)_o$	0.5	1.0
DEV_o	4.23	4.79
CPU_o	2.14	2.37

Table 6.14: Effect of the Renewable Resource Factor

$RF(N)_p$	0.5	1.0
DEV_p	3.55	5.26
CPU_p	2.21	2.30

Table 6.15: Effect of the Nonrenewable Resource Factor

$RS(R)_q$	0.2	0.5	0.7	1.0
DEV_q	7.27	5.52	3.32	2.38
CPU_q	2.51	2.29	2.18	2.10

Table 6.16: Effect of the Renewable Resource Strength

$RS(N)_r$	0.2	0.5	0.7	1.0
DEV_r	4.35	6.51	4.67	2.44
CPU_r	2.42	2.37	2.24	2.09

Table 6.17: Effect of the Nonrenewable Resource Strength

The resource strength of renewable resources and the resource factor of both resource categories influence the performance in the same way as observed for the single-mode problems. That is increasing the resource factor and decreasing the resource strength lowers the performance of the solution procedure. The impact of the resource strength $RS(R)$ is stronger than the one of each resource factor, respectively. The resource strength of the nonrenewable resource category shows a bell-shaped influence on the performance as conjectured by Elmaghraby / Herroelen (1980). That is, the poorest solutions are due to a medium availability of the nonrenewable resource types while very little or plenty nonrenewable resources give way to better solutions. The levels of significance for the problems parameters are $s=0.0000$ for $RS(R)$ and $RS(N)$ as well as $s=0.0341$ and $s=0.0005$ for $RF(R)$ and $RF(N)$, respectively.

6.3.4 Comparison with other Procedures

The heuristics presented by Talbot (1982), Drexl / Grünewald (1993), and Boctor (1994) have been implemented and tested under the same conditions as MMH in order to provide a fair comparison with the latter. For all heuristics the recommendations given by the authors w.r.t. the adjustment of parameters were followed: That is, for the sampling approach due to Drexl / Grünewald (1993) the probability mapping parameter α has been set to 2 and a sample size of Z=100 has been selected. Furthermore, the heuristic has been implemented in two versions: As outlined by the authors, the original version (I) determines the start time of a selected activity subject to precedence constraints only, whereas the improved version (II) calculates a precedence- and resource-feasible start time for the chosen activity. For the single-pass approach of Boctor (1994) the priority rule tandem MSLK / SPT and for the multi-pass approach of Boctor the five best priority rule tandems were employed, respectively.

Table 6.18 shows the performance of MMH for the fixed procedure parameters Z=30, β=25%, and γ=0%, respectively, and different levels of Y. As for SMH, the computational effort increases linearly while the performance measure DEV improves in an (inverse) exponential manner. That is, good solutions can be obtained very quickly, whereas an extensive computational effort has to be undertaken in order to reach (near) optimal solutions.

Y	10	30	50	150	250	350	450
DEV	9.02	5.76	4.53	2.56	1.96	1.72	1.50
CPU	0.72	1.48	2.26	6.16	10.07	13.97	17.87

Table 6.18: Performance of MMH for Different Sample Sizes

Table 6.19 compares the performance of MMH with the heuristics of Talbot (1982), Drexl / Grünewald (1993), Boctor (1994), and the truncated exact method of Sprecher (1994). Additionally to the performance measures DEV and CPU as introduced in Section 6.3.1, SOL denotes the percentage of instances for which a feasible solution could be derived. W.r.t. the limit imposed on the CPU time, two classes of procedures are distinguished: heuristics which run no more than 1 second and 10 seconds, respectively. Within these classes the algorithms are listed in the order of improving performance. In both classes MMH is the only heuristic which solves all 536 problems. Even if the unsolved problems of the other heuristics are not taken into account, MMH outperforms every other heuristic in its class while being comparably fast. An exception holds for the truncated branch and bound procedure of Sprecher (1994) which shows a significant better performance. But it is well known that the performance of truncated optimal procedures collapses when problems become larger.[9] Hence, currently MMH seems to be the only heuristic for (real world) multi-mode project scheduling problems which fulfils three important issues: it derives feasible solutions, the solutions are reasonably close to optimality, and the computational effort is polynomially bounded.

	$CPU_{max} \leq 1$			$CPU_{max} \leq 10$				
	SPP	MPP	MMH/10	TE	BSP/I	BSP/II	TBB	MMH/150
DEV	14.89	10.69	9.02	14.98	11.03	8.46	0.23	2.56
CPU	0.01	0.05	0.72	0.39	4.10	6.00	-	6.16
SOL	51.86	55.4	100	56.34	41.23	82.72	99.81	100

Table 6.19: Performance Comparison of Heuristics for the MMPSP[10]

---

[9] E.g., the CPU time of the exact procedure of Sprecher increases with more than factor 100 when the number of non-dummy activities is increased form 10 to 16 (cf. Sprecher (1994)).

[10] Where SPP (MPP) denotes the single-pass (multi-priority rule) procedure of Boctor (1994), TE the truncated enumeration of Talbot (1982), BSP/I (BSP/II) the original (improved) version of the regret-based biased random sampling procedure of Drexl / Grünewald (1993), and TBB the truncated branch and bound procedure of Sprecher (1994). TBB has been coded in C and implemented on an IBM PS2/70 model with 80486dx processor and 25 MHz clockpulse.

Chapter 7

Project Scheduling with Given Deadline

Chapter 7 deals with the multi-mode project scheduling problem where only renewable resources are taken into account and a given deadline has to be met at the expense of employing additional resources (PSPDL). A motivation of the PSPDL as well as a mixed-integer programming formulation has been provided in Section 2.4. The purpose of this chapter is to demonstrate how the general solution methodologies previously presented, i.e. priority rules, biased random sampling, and problem decomposition, can be made applicable to other project scheduling problems with non-regular performance measures. Therefore, based on a short literature review provided in Section 7.1, Section 7.2.1 introduces an approach to solve the single-mode PSPDL. In Section 7.2.2. this approach is employed within a solution methodology for the multi-mode PSPDL. Finally, Section 7.3 reports on some computational results.

7.1 Literature Review

For solving the project scheduling problem with given deadline (PSPDL), no *specialised* exact or heuristic solution procedures are known from the literature.

Optimal solutions were obtained by Deckro and Hebert (1989) for the single-mode version of the PSPDL. They employed a mixed-integer programming formulation in order to solve one example problem (made up of eight activities and two resource types) with a commercial MIP package. The optimal solution was derived after 6.57 CPU-seconds on a CYBER 760.

Burgess and Killebrew (1962) proposed a heuristic for the related problem of minimising the variance of the resource demand without considering resource constraints (cf. Section 2.4). The heuristic has been originally designed for the AOA notation. For the sake of convenience it is described for the AON convention. In the initialisation phase, Burgess and Killebrew determine the earliest finish schedule (cf. Definition 4.2) by the forward recursion as outlined in Section 2.2.1. Afterwards, $z \geq 1$ passes are performed, where in one pass the schedule is modified by right-shifting every activity j, $1 < j < J$, to its local optimal finish time. Precisely, starting with the highest labelled activity j, $1 < j < J$, the objective function value for each finish time t, $FT_j \leq t \leq \min\{ST_i \mid i \in S_j\}$ is calculated and the (new) finish time is set to the period t inducing the smallest objective function. Passes are repeated until no further improvement of the objective function can be attained. Since the objective function value is non-increasing with the number of passes, the procedure terminates with the actual schedule as the best one found. The outlined heuristic has been extended to the multi-project and multi-resource case by Woodworth and Willie (1975).

7.2 A Heuristic for Solving the PSPDL

While so far only regular measures of performance have been considered (cf. Definition 2.5), the PSPDL has a non-regular performance measure. Hence, the procedures proposed so far, namely SMH and MMH, cannot be employed because depending on the data and the solution parameters they generate active or non-delay schedules. Generally, the latter will not contain the optimal solution when non-regular performance measures are considered. On that account, a solution methodology for the PSPDL is derived as follows: Based on the ideas proposed by Burgess and Killebrew (1962), in Section 7.2.1 a heuristic for the single-mode case of the PSPDL will be provided. This procedure will be employed within Section 7.2.2 in a similar fashion as the SMH within the MMH. That is, for a mode-assignment M, the single-mode procedure is used to generate a schedule, on the basis of which the mode-assignment is modified and so forth. The presentation of the heuristics will be clarified with the following example:

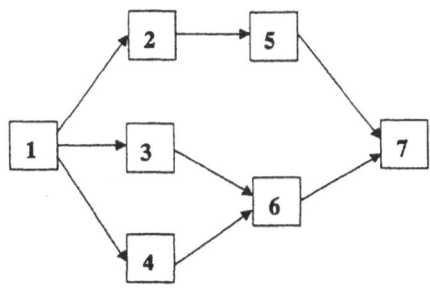

Figure 7.1: Network of the PSPDL Example

j	1	2	3	4	5	6	7
m	1	1	2	1	2	1	2	1	2	1	2	1
d_{jm}	0	3	5	1	5	3	5	1	2	3	5	0
k_{jm1}	0	4	3	5	4	3	1	4	3	4	3	0

$R=\{1\}, K_1=6, o_1=0.5, c_1=1, DL=7$

Table 7.1: Data of the PSPDL Example

7.2.1 Heuristic for the Single-Mode Case

At the beginning the single-mode case of the PSPDL is considered, i.e. M is fixed. Recall $\underline{p}=((\text{extremum}_1, v_1),...,(\text{extremum}_L, v_L))$ to be the lexicographically ordered priority rules $1,...,L$. Hence, the two priority rule vectors[1]

$$\underline{p}1=((\max,FT_j), (\max,ST_j), (\min,RU_j), (\min,j)) \qquad (7.1)$$

$$\underline{p}2=((\min,ST_j), (\min,FT_j), (\min,RU_j), (\max,j)) \qquad (7.2)$$

---

[1] $\underline{p}1$ equals the priority rule vector $\underline{p}0$ as employed within the modified slack calculation MSC (cf. Section 6.2.2). It primarily ranks the activities in the order of descending finish times for right shifting. In contrast, $\underline{p}2$ ranks the activities with increasing start times for left-shifting.

define a unique priority list λ of the activities with the activity number as the final tie breaker, respectively. Furthermore, recalling $\underline{S}$ to be the incumbent best solution, the single-mode deadline heuristic (SMDLH) can be formally stated as follows:

$$\boxed{\text{SMDLH}}$$

Initialisation: PERFORM SMH/1; IF $FT_J > DL$ THEN Stop

ELSE $\underline{S}:=S$; ASSIGN $\lambda(j)$, $1 \leq j \leq J$, according to $\underline{p}1$;

(1) FOR $n:=1$ TO J DO **Right-Shift**

BEGIN

$j:=\lambda(n)$;

$\phi^*_{PSPDL}:=\min\{\phi_{PSPDL}(S') \mid FT'_i=FT_i,\ i\neq j,\ FT'_j \geq FT_j,\ S' \in \mathbf{FS}\}$;

$FT_j:= \max\{FT'_j | \phi_{PSPDL}(S')=\phi^*_{PSPDL}, FT'_i=FT_i,\ i\neq j,\ FT'_j \geq FT_j,\ S' \in \mathbf{FS}\}$;

END;

IF $\phi_{PSPDL}(S) \geq \phi_{PSPDL}(\underline{S})$ THEN Stop

ELSE $\underline{S}:=S$, ASSIGN $\lambda(j)$, $1 \leq j \leq J$, according to $\underline{p}2$;

(2) FOR $n:=1$ TO J DO **Left-Shift**

BEGIN

$j:=\lambda(n)$;

$\phi^*_{PSPDL}:=\min\{\phi_{PSPDL}(S') \mid FT'_i=FT_i,\ i\neq j,\ FT'_j \leq FT_j,\ S' \in \mathbf{FS}\}$;

$FT_j:=\min\{FT'_j | \phi_{PSPDL}(S')=\phi^*_{PSPDL},\ FT'_i=FT_i,\ i\neq j,\ FT'_j \leq FT_j,\ S' \in \mathbf{FS}\}$;

END;

IF $\phi_{PSPDL}(S) \geq \phi_{PSPDL}(\underline{S})$ THEN Stop

ELSE $\underline{S}:=S$, ASSIGN $\lambda(j)$, $1 \leq j \leq J$, according to $\underline{p}1$, GOTO (1);

Stop: If $FT_J \leq DL$, a feasible schedule $S=(FT_1,...,FT_J)$ has been generated;

***

The crucial idea of the SMDLH is to combine two approaches. Based on the heuristic of Burgess and Killebrew (1962), iteratively, activities are right- and left-shifted to a local optimal finish time. Since the shifting of activities has to be accomplished in the presence of scarce renewable resources, it is performed in analogy to the modified slack calculation of Wiest (1964). Hence, the two priority rule vectors $\underline{p}1$ and $\underline{p}2$ are employed to consider the activities for right- and left-shifting, respectively. More precisely, in the initialisation a (not necessarily feasible) schedule S is obtained by SMH/1 for the a priori given mode-assignment M and the resource availabilities $K_r(1+o_r)$, $r \in R$. In case of feasibility, the activities are ranked w.r.t. the priority rule vector $\underline{p}1$, otherwise SMDLH terminates with an infeasible solution. In step (1) the activities are considered according to their ranking for right-shifts. Thereby, each activity is right-shifted to a finish time which is associated with the smallest objective function value of all feasible right-shifts. At the end of step (1), the activities are sorted w.r.t. the priority rule vector $\underline{p}2$. Step (2) corresponds to step (1) with the only difference that activities are now left-shifted. The algorithm terminates as soon as one step could not improve the solution.

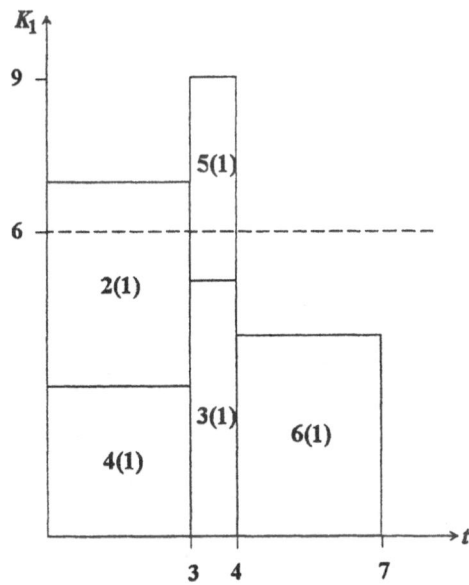

Figure 7.2: Schedule Derived in the Initialisation of SMDLH

In order to clarify SMDLH, the example problem is solved for the mode-assignment $M=(1,1,1,1,1,1)$: Applying SMH/1 to M creates the schedule $S=(0,3,4,3,4,7,7)$ with an objective function value of $\phi_{PSPDL}=6$ which is displayed in Figure 7.2. Since $FT_J \leq DL$ holds, the derived solution is a feasible one for the PSPDL. Table 7.2 gives the associated priority list $\lambda(j)$ derived with $\underline{p}1$.

j	1	2	3	4	5	6	7
$\lambda(j)$	7	6	4	5	3	2	1

Table 7.2: Priority List of the Initialisation

Introducing PFT_j as the precedence-feasible finish time of activity j, $1 \leq j \leq J$, Table 7.3 provides the report of step (1): Only activity 5 is right-shifted by three periods, which results in an improved objective function value of $\phi_{PSPDL}=5$. The derived schedule $S=(0,3,4,3,7,7,7)$ is shown in Figure 7.3. Performing step (2), only activity 5 is left-shifted by two periods which results in the schedule $S=(0,3,4,3,5,7,7)$ and an associated objective function value of $\phi_{PSPDL}=5$. Since there is no improvement of ϕ_{PSPDL}, SMDLH terminates after both step (1) and step (2) have been performed once.

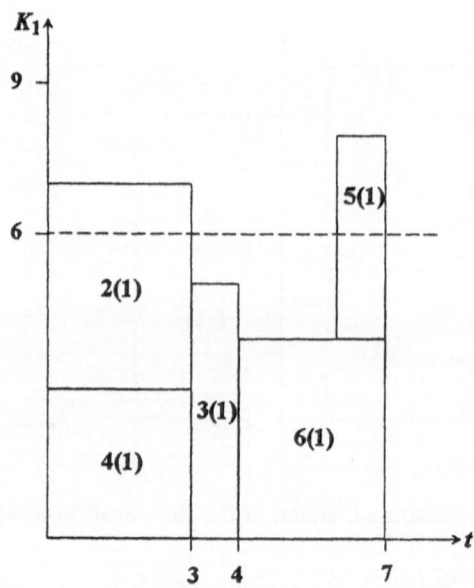

Figure: 7.3: Schedule Derived after Step (1)

n	$j = \lambda(n)$	PFT_j	ϕ^*	FT_j
1	7	7	6	7
2	6	7	6	7
3	5	7	5	7
4	3	4	5	4
5	4	4	5	3
6	2	6	5	3
7	1	0	5	0

Table 7.3: Report of Step (1)

7.2.2 Heuristic for the Multi-Mode Case

In order to tackle the multi-mode case, an initial mode-assignment as well as a scheme for the alternation of modes is required. The aim of the procedure "first mode assignment" (FMA) is twofold: (*i*) it discards infeasible modes and (*ii*) the first labelled mode is assigned to each activity, respectively. This is done in order to obtain a small makespan and hence a feasible solution for the PSPDL. We denote with s_j the precedence-based slack of activity j, $1 \leq j \leq J$, and recall from formula (6.4) $\Delta d(j,m)$ as the difference of the duration when the mode $\mu(j)$ currently assigned to activity j, $1 \leq j \leq J$, is switched to the new mode m, $\mu(j) \neq m$. Now, FMA can be described formally as follows:

$$\boxed{\text{FMA}}$$

Initialisation: $\mu(j):=1$, $1 \leq j \leq J$; PERFORM FR, BR (with $T:=DL$);
$$s_j:=LFT_j-EFT_j, \ 1 \leq j \leq J;$$

FOR $j:=1$ TO J DO **Stage j**
BEGIN
 $m:=M_j$;
(1) IF $(\Delta d(j,m) > s_j)$ THEN DO
  BEGIN
   $m:=m$-1, GOTO (1);
  END;
 $M_j:=m$;
END;

Stop: A mode-assignment M has been generated;

$$***$$

FMA starts by assigning to each activity its lowest labelled mode. Afterwards, the (precedence-based) slack of every activity is calculated on the basis of earliest and latest finish times derived by forward and backward recursion (with $T=DL$), respectively (cf. Section 2.2.1). Note that within the initialisation of the backward recursion, the latest finish time of the unique sink is set to the deadline. The main algorithm compares in stage j, $1 \leq j \leq J$, for activity j, whether modes can be discarded from further consideration because the difference between the duration of the mode with smallest duration and the actual mode exceeds the (precedence-based) slack of the activity under consideration. Recall from Section 2.1.2 that modes are sorted in the order of non-decreasing duration, i.e. $d_{jm} \geq d_{jm-1}$ always holds for $1 < m \leq M_j$. Now, given an activity j, $1 \leq j \leq J$, the duration difference between the highest and the lowest labelled mode is calculated and compared with the slack of the activity. As long as the difference in the duration exceeds the slack the next highest labelled mode is visited. The label of the first mode, the difference in duration of which does not exceed the slack, is set to the number of modes M_j. In order to clarify FMA, Table 7.4 provides a solution report for the examples stated in Figure 7.1 and Table 7.1, respectively. As a result, only activities 2 and 5 can be processed in two modes.

j	1	2	3	4	5	6	7
EFT_j	0	3	1	3	4	6	6
LFT_j	1	6	4	4	7	7	7
s_j	1	3	3	1	3	1	1
$\Delta d(j,2)$	–	2	4	2	1	2	–
M_j	1	2	1	1	2	1	1

Table 7.4: Solution Report of FMA

The final element to be proposed for the PSPDL is a mode-changing scheme. Like for the MMPSP, the general procedure of the scheme is as follows: The current solution derived by the single-mode heuristic is analysed and a priority rule is employed in order to perform a mode-change for exactly one of the activities. The idea is to assign the overall cost associated with the current solution, i.e. ϕ_{PSPDL}, to the activities. Afterwards, the activity causing the highest cost is chosen and its currently not chosen mode with smallest (cost) weighted resource usage is assigned to it. More precisely, recalling $A_t(S)$ (cf. Definition 3.1) to be the set of activities of schedule S being in progress in period t, the analysis of the current solution is as follows: Let C_{rt} be the cost incurred by resource r within period t, which is calculated as:

$$C_{rt} = c_r \max\{0, \sum_{j \in A_t(S)} k_{j\mu(j)r} - K_r\} \qquad\qquad r \in R, 1 \le t \le T \qquad (7.3)$$

Further, let PC_j be the cost associated with each activity j, which is computed according to:

$$PC_j = \sum_{r \in R} \sum_{t=1}^{T} C_{rt} \frac{k_{j\mu(j)r}}{\sum_{i \in A_t(S)} k_{i\mu(i)r}} \qquad\qquad 1 \le j \le J \qquad (7.4)$$

Now, the "change mode-assignment" (CMA) can be put formally as follows:

$$\boxed{\text{CMA}}$$

Initialisation: CALCULATE C_{rt}, $r \in R$, $1 \le t \le T$; CALCULATE PC_j, $1 \le j \le J$;

Main:

$PC_{max}:=\max\{PC_j \mid 1 \le j \le J\}$;

$j^*:=\min\{j \mid 1 < j < J, PC_j = PC_{max}\}$;

$C_{min}:=\min\{d_{j^*m} \sum_{r \in R} c_r\, k_{j^*mr} \mid 1 \le m \le M_{j^*}, m \ne \mu(j^*)\}$;

$\mu(j^*):=\min\{m \mid 1 \le m \le M_{j^*}, m \ne \mu(j^*), d_{j^*m} \sum_{r \in R} c_r\, k_{j^*mr} = C_{min}\}$;

Stop: A new mode-assignment M has been generated;

***

In order to clarify CMA, the solution visualised in Figure 7.3 is considered.[2] Table 7.5 and Table 7.6 report the costs associated with the periods and the activities, respectively.

t	1	2	3	4	5	6	7
C_{1t}	1	1	1	0	0	0	2

Table 7.5: Cost Associated with the Periods

j	1	2	3	4	5	6	7
PC_j	0	1.71	0	1.29	1	1	0

Table 7.6: Cost Associated with the Activities

On account of the activity costs, activity 2 is selected. Then, mode $m=2$ is assigned to activity 2, since only the modes one and two are available and the

---

[2] It has to be noted that not $S=(0,3,4,3,7,7,7)$ as displayed in Figure 7.3, but $S=(0,3,4,3,5,7,7)$ is the last solution derived by SMDLH. Nevertheless, both schedules cause the same costs PC_j for the activities j, $1 \le j \le J$, and hence both schedules lead to the same (new) mode-assignment.

current mode is $\mu(2)=1$. This gives way to the new mode-assignment $M=(1,2,1,1,1,1,1)$.

Recalling $\underline{M}$ ($\underline{S}$) to be the incumbent best mode-assignment (schedule) and SMDLH/1 to be the deterministic version of the single-mode deadline heuristic with sample size "1", the entire deadline heuristic (DLH) can be formally summarised as follows:

> **DLH**

Initialisation: PERFORM FMA; PERFORM SMDLH/1; ASSIGN $\underline{M}:=M$, $\underline{S}:=S$;

FOR $y:=1$ TO Y DO **Pass y**
BEGIN
  PERFORM CMA, PERFORM SMDLH/Z;
  IF $\phi_{PSPDL}(S) < \phi_{PSPDL}(\underline{S})$ THEN DO
  BEGIN
     ASSIGN $\underline{M}:=M$, $\underline{S}:=S$;
  END;
END;

Stop: A solution $(\underline{M},\underline{S})$ for the PSPDL has been generated;

***

Within the deterministic version of DLH the sample size Z for the SMDLH is 1, i.e. $Z=1$. A regret-based biased random sampling heuristic on the basis of DLH is attained by introducing χ as the probability mapping parameter for the choice of the finish time within the SMDLH as well as ξ and ζ as the probability mapping parameters for the activity and mode selection within CMA, respectively. Finally, the number of sample sizes for SMDLH and DLH is Z and Y, respectively.

7.3 Preliminary Computational Results

In order to test the efficiency of the outlined solution procedure, two sets of PSPDL instances were generated with ProGen (cf. Chapter 4): Set 1 with a tight deadline and a medium-level of renewable resources ($\delta_{fac}=0.1$,

$RS(R)$=0.5) and set 2 with a medium-level deadline and a scarce availability of renewable resources (δ_{fac}=0.3, $RS(R)$=0.1). For both sets, the additional resource factor o_r and the cost for an additional resource unit c_r were set to "1", respectively. Table 7.7 summarises the set-dependent parameter levels, while Table 7.8 provides the parameter levels which are the same for both instance sets.

	set 1	set 2
δ_{fac}	0.1	0.3
$RS(R)$	0.5	0.1

Table 7.7: Set-Dependent Parameters Levels for the PSPDL Instances

	J	M_j	d_j	S_1	S_j	P_j	P_J	NC	$|R|$	U_R	Q_R	$RF(R)$
min	5	2	1	1	1	1	1	1.2	2	1	1	1
max	5	2	5	3	3	3	3	1.2	2	10	2	1

Table 7.8: Constant Parameter Levels for the PSPDL Instances

For each set 40 instances were generated with ProGen, respectively. Optimal solutions were obtained by solving the mixed-integer programming model (2.19) - (2.25) with the industrial version of LINDO (cf. Schrage (1991)) on an IBM RS 6000/550 at the computer laboratory of the Christian-Albrechts-Universität zu Kiel. The computation took for both instance sets a couple of seconds.

Since some of the problems had an optimal objective function of ϕ^*_{PSPDL}=0, the average percentage deviation from the optimal objective function could not be employed as performance measure. Instead, the overall percentage deviation $ODEV$ has been utilised which is calculated as follows:

$$ODEV = \frac{\sum \phi_{PSPDL} - \phi^*_{PSPDL}}{\sum \phi^*_{PSPDL}} \cdot 100 \qquad (7.5)$$

That is, ODEV is calculated by summing up the difference between the heuristic and optimal objective function value over all instances and dividing it by the sum of the optimal objective functions values.

In order to assess the significance of the procedure parameters Z, Y, χ, ξ, and ζ, a first computational study was performed as follows. DLH was used with each combination of the sample sizes Z and $Y \in \{1,5\}$, respectively, as well as the probability mapping parameters χ, ξ, and $\zeta \in \{0\%, 75\%, 100\%\}$, respectively. I.e., all 80 problems were solved with $2 \cdot 2 \cdot 3 \cdot 3 \cdot 3 = 108$ differently adjusted versions of DLH.

As a result, only the sample size Y ($s=0.0000$), i.e. the number of generated mode-assignments, and the probability mapping parameter of the activity selection ξ ($s=0.0107$) showed a significant influence. All other solution parameters were not significant, i.e. Z ($s=0.8829$), χ ($s=0.9991$), and ζ ($s=0.2543$).

Hence, the solution parameters were fixed as follows: $Y=20$, $Z=5$, $\chi=0\%$, $\xi=75\%$, and $\zeta=0\%$. Table 7.9 shows the performance for the thus tuned DLH.

	set 1	set 2
ODEV	31.0	189.2
CPU	1.91	2.47
SOL	100%	100%

Table 7.9: Performance of the DLH

As can be seen in the last row, DLH could derive feasible solutions for all 80 instances. The quality of the solutions is acceptable for the instances of set 1, i.e. problems with a tight deadline and a medium availability of renewable resources. On average the cost of a heuristically derived project schedule exceeded the minimal cost by 1.57 units. Based on an average cost of 5.05 units this equals 31%. Unfortunately, the performance deteriorates drastically for problems of set 2 (with a medium-level deadline and scarce renewable resources). On average the cost exceeded the optimal cost of 6.95 units by more than 13.15 units which results in an overall percentage deviation of 189%.

On account of these results the following can be stated: While the mode changing scheme CMA seems to work properly, it is obviously the single-mode deadline heuristic which - in the case where deadlines are not very tight - fails to shift activities properly in order to derive a low cost schedule. Hence, further efforts have to be undertaken to improve DLH or to design a new approach for the single-mode PSPDL. An idea might be to solve the SMPSP subject to different levels of resource availability as pointed out by Demeulemeester (1992) for the total resource(-cost) minimisation problem (cf. Section 2.4).

Chapter 8

Project Scheduling with Setup Times

This chapter deals with the project scheduling problem when setup times are explicitly considered (PSPST). The motivation of the problem and a mixed-integer programming formulation have been given in Section 2.5. In this chapter, it is shown how the methods derived for the single-mode project scheduling problem without setup times (cf. Chapter 5) can be properly adapted, in order to solve the more general PSPST. The remainder of the chapter is organised as follows: First, with the work of Kaplan (1991) the related literature is reviewed. Then, Section 8.1 introduces the solution procedure for the PSPST. Finally, Section 8.2 provides - on the basis of a small computational study - insight into the performance of the proposed algorithm.

The only publication so far dealing with setup times in the context of project scheduling is the one by Kaplan (1991). Kaplan considers the single-mode problem with preemption allowed. Whenever a preempted activity has to be restarted, a setup time is incurred. The problem is modelled via a unit-time-duration SMPSP (cf. Chapter 3), where each activity j, $1 < j < J$, is split into d_j unit-time-duration activities. A dynamic programming procedure is proposed to solve the problem to optimality. Unfortunately, Demeulemeester (1992) has pointed out that due to an incorrect theorem the algorithm might fail to find the optimal solution.

8.1 Solution Methodology

Since the PSPST is a generalisation of the SMPSP, one of the heuristics suggested for the latter, i.e. the parallel or serial scheduling scheme, should be applied as a solution approach. A careful look at the problem structure reveals that at a stage n, $1 \leq n \leq J$, each setup-resource r, $r \in R^S$, is in a definite setup-state. Consequently, each of the activities in the decision set requesting a setup-resource can be scheduled at stage n in only one mode. Hence, it is sufficient to employ one of the scheduling schemes as suggested in Chapter 5 for the single-mode project scheduling problem and additionally keep track of the setup-states.

Principally, both schemes can be used. Within the serial scheme for every activity j in the decision set, $j \in D_n$, which requests a setup-resource the earliest precedence- and resource-feasible start time EST'_j has to be calculated in order to inquire the state of the setup-resource requested and consequently the mode activity j has to be performed in. Since this is rather time consuming, the parallel scheme provided in Section 5.2.1 is selected as a framework for a heuristic to solve the PSPST.

In addition to the parallel scheduling scheme as already presented in Chapter 5, at stage n with the schedule time t_n let SP_{ru} be the setup-state u of setup-resource r, where SP_{ru} is defined as follows:

$$SP_{ru} = \begin{cases} 1, \text{ if setup-resource } r \text{ is in setup-state } u \\ 0, \text{ otherwise} \end{cases} \tag{8.1}$$

The initialisation phase is then extended to

Initialisation: $n:=1$; $t_n:=0$; $D_n:=\{1\}$; $A_n:=C_n:= \varnothing$; $\pi K_r:=K_r \ \forall \ r \in R \cup R^S$,
$\qquad \qquad SP_{ru}:=0 \ \forall \ r \in R^S$, $u=1,...,U_r$; GOTO Step (2); $\qquad\qquad$ (8.2)

That is, each setup-resource is initialised to be not set up at the end of period 0. Of course, in a rolling planning horizon setup-resources have to be initialised appropriately.

In stage n, at the beginning of step (2), i.e. the selection of an activity of the decision set, the mode of each activity in the decision set is assigned according to the setup-state of the setup-resource requested:

$$\mu(j) := M_j - \sum_{r \in R^S} \sum_{u=1}^{U_r} k_{jru} SP_{ru} \qquad\qquad \forall\, j \in D_n \qquad (8.3)$$

In order to clarify the mode assignment, Figure 8.1 and Table 8.1 recall the example originally provided in Chapter 2.

Now, consider activity $j=3$ requesting setup-resource $r=2$ in setup-state $u=1$ ($k_{321}=1$). Besides activities 2 and 4, respectively, activity 3 is in stage $n=2$ with the associated schedule time $t_2=0$ in the decision set D_2. Furthermore, at the schedule time $t_2=0$, none of the two setup-resources has been set up, respectively, i.e. $SP_{ru}=0 \ \forall\, r \in R^S$, $u=1,...,U_r$. Now, the mode is assigned to activity 3 as follows: $\mu(3) = M_3 - (k_{311} SP_{11} + k_{321} SP_{21} + k_{322} SP_{22}) = 2 - (0\cdot0 + 1\cdot0 + 0\cdot0) = 2$. That is, activity 3 has to be performed in mode 2 (i.e. with setup) when started at the schedule time $t_2=0$.

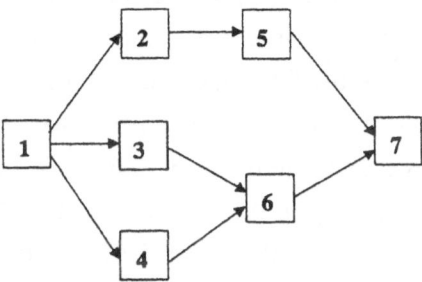

Figure 8.1: Network of a Project Scheduling Problem

j	1	2	3	4	5	6	7
m	1	1 2	1 2	1 2	1 2	1 2	1
d_{jm}	0	3 4	1 2	2 3	1 2	1 2	0
k_{j11}	0	1	0	0	0	1	0
k_{j21}	0	0	1	0	1	0	0
k_{j22}	0	0	0	1	0	0	0

$R^S=\{1,2\}$, $U_1=1$, $U_2=2$, $K_1=K_2=1$

Table 8.1: Example for the PSPST

Finally, after activity j^* has been scheduled, setup-states of the setup-resources have to be updated within step (2) as follows:

$$SP_{ru}=\phi(k_{j^*r},\, k_{j^*ru},\, SP_{ru}) \qquad\qquad \forall\, r \in R^S,\, u=1,...,U_r \qquad (8.4)$$

Table 8.2 shows the update mapping ϕ. Since each of the three independent variables can be "0" or "1", altogether $2\cdot2\cdot2=8$ different cases have to be distinguished, where the first six cases correspond to columns 2 - 7 in Table 8.2, respectively. Cases 1 and 2 are interpreted as follows: If the selected activity j^* does not request the setup-resource r, then the setup-state u does not change. For cases 3 and 4 the following holds: If the selected activity j^* requests the setup-resource r in a setup-state $u'\neq u$, then the setup-state is set (back) to zero. Cases 5 and 6 term: If the selected activity j^* requests the setup-resource r in setup-state u, then the setup-state is 1. Finally, the cases 7 and 8 are not relevant, since the selected activity j^* cannot request the setup-resource r in setup-state u while not requesting the setup-resource r.

The update of the setup-states is clarified by resuming the example presented above. Consider activity $j^*=3$ has been scheduled, then the setup-states of the two-setup resources are updated as follows: $SP_{11} = \phi(k_{31}, k_{311}, SP_{11}) = (0, 0, 0) = 0$, $SP_{21} = \phi(k_{32}, k_{321}, SP_{21}) = (1, 1, 0) = 1$, and $SP_{22} = \phi(k_{32}, k_{322}, SP_{22}) = (1, 0, 0) = 0$.

SP_{ru}	0	1	0	0	1	1
k_{j*r}	0	0	1	1	1	1
k_{j*ru}	0	0	0	0	1	1
SP_{ru}	0	1	0	1	0	1

Table 8.2: Update of Setup-States

With the three extensions made above, i.e. formulas (8.2) - (8.4), the setup time heuristic (STH) can now be put formally as follows:

$$\boxed{\text{STH}}$$

Initialisation: $n:=1$; $t_n:=0$; $D_n:=\{1\}$; $A_n=C_n:=\varnothing$; $\pi K_r:=K_r$ $\forall$ $r \in R \cup R^S$; $SP_{ru}:=0$ $\forall$ $r \in R^S$, $u=1,...,U_r$; GOTO Step (2);

WHILE $|PS_n| < J$ DO **Stage n**

BEGIN

(1) $t_n := \min \{ FT_j \mid j \in A_{n-1} \}$;
$A_n := A_{n-1} \setminus \{ j \mid j \in A_{n-1}, FT_j = t_n \}$;
$C_n := C_{n-1} \cup \{ j \mid j \in A_{n-1}, FT_j = t_n \}$;
UPDATE R_n, πK_r $\forall$ $r \in R$, and D_n;

(2) $\mu(j):= M_j - \sum\limits_{r \in R^S} \sum\limits_{u=1}^{U_r} k_{jru} SP_{ru}$, $\forall j \in D_n$;

$j^* := \min\limits_{j \in D_n} \{ j \mid v(j) = \text{extremum}\limits_{i \in D_n} v(i) \}$;

$ST_{j^*} := t_n$;
$FT_{j^*} := ST_{j^*} + d_{j^*}$;
$A_n := A_n \cup \{ j^* \}$;
$SP_{ru}:=\phi(k_{j*r}, k_{j*ru}, SP_{ru})$ $\forall$ $r \in R^S$, $u=1,...,U_r$;
UPDATE πK_r $\forall$ $r \in R$, PS_n, D_n, and R_n;
IF $D_n \neq \varnothing$ THEN GOTO Step (2), ELSE $PS_{n+1} := PS_n$, $n:=n+1$;

END;

Stop: A feasible schedule $S =(FT_1,...,FT_J)$ has been generated;

$$***$$

In order to clarify the solution procedure, Table 8.3 shows the report of STH when the WCS priority rule is applied deterministically to the example problem presented above. The columns with $\mu(j)$ and $v(j)$ contain the mode and the priority value of each activity in the decision set, respectively. For the sake of shortness, the column with the remaining activities has been omitted. The schedule obtained represents the optimal solution which is displayed in Figure 8.2.

n	t_n	πK_1	πK_2	SP_{11}	SP_{21}	SP_{22}	A_n	C_n	D_n	$\mu(j)$	$v(j)$	j^*	FT_{j^*}
1	0	1	1	0	0	0	∅	∅	1	1	7	1	0
2	0	1	1	0	0	0	∅	1	2,...,4	2,2,2	3,7,5	2	4
	0	0	1	1	0	0	2	1	3,4	2,2	7,5	4	3
	0	0	0	1	0	1	2,4	1	∅				
3	3	0	1	1	0	1	2	1,4	3	2	4	3	5
	3	0	0	1	1	0	2,3	1,4	∅				
4	4	1	0	1	1	0	3	1,2,4	∅				
5	5	1	1	1	1	0	∅	1,...,4	5,6	1,1	5,5	5	6
	5	1	0	1	1	0	5	1,...,4	6	1	5	6	6
	5	0	0	1	1	0	5,6	1,...,4	∅				
6	6	1	1	1	1	0	∅	1,...,6	7	1	6	7	6

Table 8.3: Report of the STH

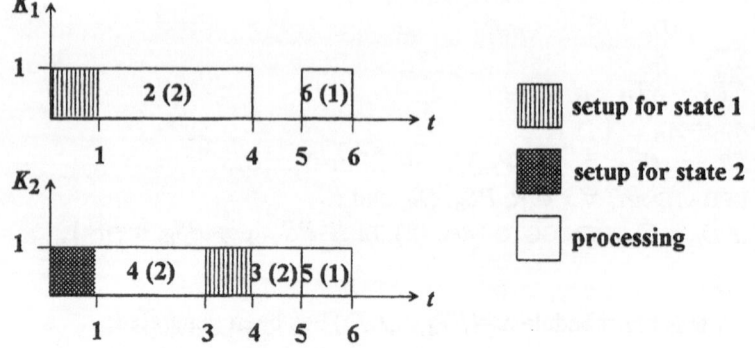

Figure 8.2: Optimal Solution of the PSPST Example

8.2 Preliminary Computational Results

In order to test the efficiency of the STH, two sets of PSPST instances have been generated with ProGen (cf. Chapter 4): "small" instances with five non-dummy activities and one renewable resource type ($J=5$, $|R|=1$) and "medium" size instances with ten non-dummy activities and two renewable resource types ($J=10$, $|R|=2$). The constant parameter levels which are the same for both instance sets are provided by Table 8.4 while the variable parameter levels are given in Table 8.5 for each set, respectively. Processing and setup times were derived, respectively, as follows: $p_j = d_j$ and $s_j = \mathrm{TRUNC}(d_j/2)$. Finally, tolerances were set to 0.05.

	M_j	d_j	$S_1{=}S_j{=}P_j{=}P_J$	U_R	$Q_R{=}Q_{RS}$	$RF(R){=}RF(R^S)$	$|R^S|$	U_{RS}	$U_1{=}U_2$
min	2	2	1	1	1	1	2	1	2
max	2	5	3	3	1	1	2	1	2

Table 8.4: Constant Parameter Levels for the PSPST Instances

	small			*medium*		
NC	1.0	1.25	1.5	1.25	1.5	1.75
RS(R)	0.0	0.5	1.0	0.0	0.5	1.0

Table 8.5: Variable Parameters Levels for the PSPST Instances

Generating 5 instances for each combination of *NC* and *RS(R)*, a total of $3 \cdot 3 \cdot 5 = 45$ problems emerged for the "small" and "medium" size instances, respectively. Optimal solutions have been derived by solving the mixed-integer programming model (2.26) - (2.34) with the industrial version of LINDO (cf. Schrage (1991)) on an IBM RS 6000/550. In order to make the medium size instances amenable for general problem solvers, the horizon-varying solution technique of Patterson / Huber (1974) as outlined in Section 5.1.1 has been employed as follows: A lower bound (*LB*) was derived by setting $M_j{=}1$, $1 < j < J$, i.e. neglecting setups by considering processing times only, and

solving the resulting SMPSP with the optimal procedure of Demeulemeester
/ Herroelen (1992a). The upper bound (*UB*) was deduced by setting $M_j=2$,
$1 < j < J$, i.e. always performing a setup, and solving the resulting problem to
optimality. Nevertheless, although for all small problems the minimum
makespan was derived, only 15 of the medium size instances were solved to
optimality. The computation time required for the solvable medium size instances was in the range of hours, while for the non-solvable problems even
within days of running time no optimality has been ensured.

The heuristic results were derived with a regret-based biased random
sampling heuristic on the basis of the tandem "STH / WCS" as described in
the last section. Adjustments of the probability mapping, the mapping parameter, and the lower bounds were done as already presented within Section 5.5. Furthermore, the same programming language and computer as described in Section 5.4 were employed.

Tables 8.6 and 8.7 provide the results of the computational study: In the
second column the average deviation of the upper bound *UB* from the optimal solution is given. The 3-rd to the 5-th column present the results derived
with STH, where the number behind the slash represents the number of
schedules *Z* generated.

	UB	STH/1	STH/10	STH/30
DEV	11.59	1.14	0.11	0.00
CPU		0.00	0.04	0.11

Table 8.6: Computational Results for the (45) Small Instances

	UB	STH/1	STH/10	STH/30
DEV	13.52	4.37	0.82	0.00
CPU		0.01	0.11	0.31

Table 8.7: Computational Results for the (15) Medium Size Instances

As can be seen in the second column, not explicitly considering setup times is disadvantageous: When solving the SMPSP with the setup time included in the duration of each activity, both instance sets are solved with more than 10% deviation from the optimal solution. On the other hand, the STH performed remarkably good. Employing a sample of 10 schedules, the small instances were almost solved to optimality, while for the medium size instances less than 1% deviation from the optimal solution was obtained. Increasing the sample size to 30, all instances were solved to optimality. The computational effort was for all cases far below a second.

One observation is noteworthy: The deterministic single-pass as well as the sampling approach (with $Z < 30$) revealed a distinct lower performance for medium size instances than for small instances. In other words, to obtain the same performance the number of samples has to be increased with ascending problem size. The rationale is that the solution space, i.e. the number of non-delay schedules, rapidly grows when the number of activities is enlarged. Hence, with constant sample size, the probability of finding a good solution decreases. Note that this holds for one deterministic pass, too.

Thus, it can be conjectured that for (project) scheduling problems, ceteris paribus, the performance of deterministic priority-rule-based heuristics as well as of sampling approaches decreases with ascending problem size. Fortunately, sampling heuristics have the potential of a constant performance by appropriately increasing the sample size Z. Obviously, this can only be achieved at the cost of a growing computational effort.

Chapter 9

Applications to Production Management

As outlined in Chapter 1, the main emphasis of this work has been on models and (heuristic) methods for planning projects in the presence of scarce resources. In Section 2.2.2 it has been shown that the single-mode project scheduling problem is a general case of most production scheduling problems, i.e. the job shop problem, the (permutation) flow shop problem, the open shop problem as well as single and parallel machine problems. Additionally, in the two subsequent sections it will be demonstrated how the models and methods of project scheduling play a vital role for two important modules of (short-term) computer integrated manufacturing (CIM): Production planning and control (PPC) systems and so-called "electronic leitstand" or "Fertigungsleitstand" systems.

9.1 The Planning Process of Production Management

According to the addressed planning horizon, three decision levels can be distinguished within production management (cf. Silver / Peterson (1985)): the strategic, the tactic, and the operational level. Within the operational level, production management has to make decisions on the short-term production program, the required resources, and the way of processing (cf. Drexl et al. (1994b)). Generally, the decisions are derived in the following four-stage planning concept (cf. Zäpfel / Missbauer (1993) and Drexl et al. (1994b)):

(*i*) With the master production schedule (MPS) the quantities of the final products are specified.

(*ii*) The **material requirements planning** (MRP) determines the quantities
and times for all component parts and raw materials which go into the final
products.

(*iii*) Within **scheduling and capacity planning** it is tried to consider the resource constraints by balancing the resource demand with the availability of
resources.

(*iv*) Finally, jobs are released to the shop floor, where they have to be
scheduled and controlled subject to scarce resources.

Today, these decisions are usually derived by electronical-data-based systems. More precisely, stages (*i*) to (*iii*) are pursued by production planning
and control (PPC) systems, while stage (*iv*) is handled by electronic leitstand
systems.

9.2 Applications within PPC Systems

PPC systems are made of a data-base for the management of the relevant
information and a set of methods to perform the tasks associated with stages
(*i*) to (*iii*). Roughly, these methods proceed in the following way:

To obtain the master production schedule, PPC systems give the decision
maker relevant information such as data about orders, stock levels, etc.
Sometimes the systems propose MPS's by making use of more elaborate
tools, e.g. linear programming models.

The material requirements planning is usually performed as follows: On the
basis of the bill of materials (BOM) and estimated lead times, quantities and
(latest) periods for all components (including the raw material) which go into
the final products are calculated. Afterwards they are aggregated to lot sizes
(to be referred to as jobs in the sequel).

Finally, the task of scheduling and capacity planning is done in two steps:
First, time windows, i.e. earliest and latest start times (cf. Section 2.2.1), for

the jobs are calculated. Starting with an earliest finish schedule (cf. Definition 4.2), resource skylines are compared with the resource availabilities and it is tried to harmonise resource demand and availability by shifting jobs or taking overtime into consideration. Obviously, these tasks are very similar to the problems encountered when scheduling projects in the presence of precedence and resource constraints. The balancing of resource demand and availability is performed automatically by methods proposed for solving resource-constrained project scheduling problems, e.g. by the algorithms outlined in Chapter 5. In the case where tight deadlines have to be met considering overtime, the models and methods of Chapter 8 can be utilised. Hence, the not very elaborated procedures currently employed within PPC systems could be substituted or enriched by relevant models and algorithms from the field of project scheduling.

9.3 Applications within Leitstand Systems

After jobs have been released to the shop floor by the PPC system, the task of short-term assignment, scheduling, and control of the jobs subject to scarce resources is performed by the leitstand (cf. Adelsberger / Kanet (1991)). A leitstand is the computerised version of the manual Gantt-chart. The latter represents the oldest, simplest, and most widely used method for scheduling jobs. A Gantt-chart is made up as follows: Each resource of a type is listed as a row, while periods correspond to columns. For each period a job is processed in, the job is plotted in every row corresponding to a re-source employed. Despite its simplicity and visual appeal, a Gantt-chart is very limited in evaluating alternative schedules. Hence, users must rely on trial and error for improvements. This process becomes quite complicated and unreliable as the number of jobs increases.

The leitstand automates the tasks of the Gantt-chart by offering the follow-ing five components (cf. Adelsberger / Kanet (1991) and Drexl / Kolisch (1993b)):

(*i*) A data-base system for managing the information needed.

(*ii*) A schedule generation component.

(*iii*) A schedule editor for the manual rework of schedules.

(*iv*) A graphical component for providing a visual representation of the precedence relations and the Gantt-chart.

(*v*) Finally, an evaluation component for the calculation of different performance measures.

Clearly, the problems encountered within the schedule generation component are of the type as addressed by the four different models in Chapter 2, namely the SMPSP, the MMPSP, the PSPST, and the PSPDL. Hence, the methods proposed in Chapters 6 to 8 can be incorporated in order to derive schedules with close to optimal performance measures. In fact, the PRISMA Leitstand (cf. Drexl et al. (1994a)) has a schedule generation component which is based on the heuristic proposed by Drexl / Grünewald (1993). The latter has been introduced in Section 6.1.2.

Chapter 10

Concluding Remarks

In this final chapter, the results of the foregoing chapters are briefly sum-marised and an outlook for further directions of research is provided.

In the second chapter two new models, the project scheduling problem with given deadline (PSPDL) and the project scheduling problem with setup times (PSPST), have been presented. Furthermore, it has been proven that the feasibility problem of the (very general) multi-mode project scheduling problem (MMPSP) turns out to be *NP*-complete as soon as there is more than one nonrenewable resource type. Finally, cutting and packing problems, i.e. the bin-packing as well as the 2-dimensional cutting-stock problem, have been derived as special cases of the single-mode project scheduling problem (SMPSP). Nevertheless, further efforts should be directed at modelling general applicable project scheduling problems.

Chapter 3 has provided a formal schedule classification for project schedul-ing problems which made it possible to classify the heuristics introduced in this work. Beyond that, a general classification of optimal and approximate algorithms for project scheduling problems - as outlined in Sprecher et al. (1994) - should be undertaken.

In Chapter 4 problem parameters and their incorporation into a general problem generator have been presented. On account of the results a discus-sion has been started on the impact and the proper parameter of the network structure of a project (cf. Kolisch et al. (1995) and De Reyck / Herroelen (1993)). Hence, further improvements in characterising project scheduling problems are about to come. Beyond the scope of project scheduling, the three essential concepts of the generator, i.e. the network construction procedure, the resource factor as a measure of the density of the coefficient matrix, and the resource strength expressing the degree of availability of the resources, should be made applicable to the construction of other optimisation problems as well.

Chapter 5 has provided a precise presentation of (single-pass) priority-rule-based scheduling schemes and their application within multi-pass (biased random sampling) procedures. The detailed analysis of the so-called RSM priority rule has been the stepping stone for the development of two new priority rules. An in-depth computational study showed that the latter outperformed all other rules tested. Furthermore, the study provided detailed recommendations for the general use of priority rules, scheduling schemes, and ways of sampling. On account of these findings, a new (hybrid) single-mode heuristic with bounding schemes has been designed which outperforms all other suboptimal procedures available in the open literature. Despite these encouraging results a question still open is the influence of the problem size on the performance of heuristics in general and the parameter-dependent superiority of one of the scheduling schemes in particular.

Chapter 6 has brought up a general framework for solving the MMPSP. In analogy to the problem decomposition of the MMPSP into the mode-assignment problem (MAP) and the SMPSP, the heuristic consists of two parts: a local search procedure which derives feasible solutions for the MAP and the single-mode heuristic (SMH) as presented in Chapter 5 for solving the (resulting) SMPSP. The search of mode-assignments is guided by the solutions derived with the SMH. An in-depth computational study revealed that the aim of deriving feasible, close-to-optimal solutions was met. Nevertheless, as for the single-mode case, a matter of further investigations should be the performance of the heuristic for larger benchmark problems. Furthermore, the general solution methodology could be streamlined for distinctive subclasses of the MMPSP, e.g. multi-mode problems with renewable resource types only. Finally, it seems worthwhile to employ the heuristic together with new local search techniques. An example might be tabu search (cf. Glover (1990)) in order to temporary exclude specific mode-assignments from further considerations.

Chapter 7 has provided a first attempt to tackle the important problem of deadlines. While the results for instances with a tight deadline were acceptable, the heuristic failed to provide good results for instances with a medium-level deadline. Hence, further efforts are necessary.

In Chapter 8 it has been shown that the parallel scheduling scheme can be extended straightforwardly for solving the project scheduling problem with explicit consideration of setup times. Further investigations should be directed towards the design of tailored priority rules which make use of problem specific knowledge. One idea is to appropriately consider unscheduled activities which require the same setup.

Finally, Chapter 9 has emphasised the significance project scheduling plays for production management. In particular, it has been outlined how the models and methods presented can be put to work within two new concepts of short term production planning, i.e. production planning and control and leitstand systems.

List of Notations

$r \in R$	set of renewable resource types	2.1.1
$r \in N$	set of nonrenewable resource types	2.1.1
K_r	per period (overall) availability of renewable (nonrenewable) resource type r	2.1.1
$j=1,...,J$	activities of a project	2.1.2
$j=1$ $(j=J)$	unique dummy source (sink)	2.1.2
$m=1,...,M_j$	modes of activity j	2.1.2
d_{jm}	(nonpreemptable) duration of activity j performed in mode m	2.1.2
k_{jmr}	per period usage (overall consumption) of renewable (nonrenewable) resource r required to perform activity j in mode m	2.1.2
G	graph (network)	2.1.3
V	node set	2.1.3
A	arc set	2.1.3
P_j	set of immediate predecessors of activity j	2.1.3
$\bar{P}_j$	set of all predecessors of activity j	2.1.3
S_j	set of immediate successors of activity j	2.1.3
$\bar{S}_j$	set of all successors of activity j	2.1.3
FT_j	finish time of activity j	2.1.4
$S=(FT_1,...,FT_J)$	schedule	2.1.4
$M=(\mu(1),...,\mu(J))$	mode-assignment	2.1.4
ϕ	function (mapping)	2.1.4
ST_j	start time of activity j	2.2.1
EST_j	earliest start time of activity j	2.2.1
EFT_j	earliest finish time of activity j	2.2.1
T	upper bound for the project's makespan	2.2.1
DL	deadline of the project	2.4
O_{rt}	number of additional (renewable) resources of type r used in period t	2.4

o_r	factor limiting the amount of additional resources of type r to o_r percent of the regular per period availability of the (renewable) resource r	2.4
c_r	cost per additional unit of the (renewable) resource r	2.4
R^S	set of renewable resources where a setup is necessary	2.5
$u=1,...,U_r$	setup-states of setup-resource r	2.5
$k_{jru}=1$	activity j has to be performed on setup-resource r in setup-state u	2.5
$A_t(S)$	activities of schedule S being in progress in period t	3.2
S_{UTD}	unit-time-duration schedule	3.2
$j1$	first activity emanating from activity j in the unit-time-duration schedule	3.2
S	set of schedules	3.2
FS	set of feasible schedules	3.2
SAS	set of semi-active schedules	3.2
AS	set of active schedules	3.2
NDS	set of non-delay schedules	3.2
ROUND	function, rounds a real argument to an integer	4.1
TRUNC	function, truncates the decimal fraction of a given real	4.1
RAND	function, draws a uniformly distributed integer out of a specified interval	4.1
<u>RAND</u>	function, draws a uniformly distributed real out of a specified interval	4.1
J^{min} (J^{max})	minimal (maximal) number of non-dummy activities	4.1
M^{min} (M^{max})	minimal (maximal) number of modes per activity	4.1
d^{min} (d^{max})	minimal (maximal) duration of an activity-mode tuple	4.1
δ_{fac}	deadline factor	4.1
A^{min} (A^{max})	minimal (maximal) number of non-redundant arcs of a network	4.3
ε_{NET}	tolerated deviation from the network complexity	4.3
NC	network complexity	4.3

S_j^{min} (S_j^{max})	minimal (maximal) number of successors of activity j	4.3
$P_j^{min}(P_j^{max})$	minimal (maximal) number of predecessors of activity j	4.3
$[j,m]$	activity-mode tuple	4.4.1
τ	resource category	4.4.1
$RF(\tau)$	resource factor of resource category τ	4.4.1
ARF	current resource factor	4.4.1
$Rq[j,m,r]$	resource-request of activity j in mode m w.r.t. resource type r	4.4.1
Q_τ^{min} (Q_τ^{max})	minimal (maximal) number of resources of category τ used by activity-mode tuple $[j,m]$	4.4.1
$U_\tau^{min}(U_\tau^{max})$	minimal (maximal) demand for a resource type of category τ	4.4.1
$RS(\tau)$	resource strength of resource category τ	4.4.1
εRF	tolerated deviation of the resource factor	4.4.1
$Q[j,m]$	current number of resources requested by activity-mode tuple $[j,m]$	4.4.1
CT	set of currently choosable triplets	4.4.1
Q_j	number of resources requested by activity j	4.4.1
LB	lower bound for the project's makespan	5.1.1
UB	upper bound for the project's makespan	5.1.1
$\lceil u \rceil$	unique integer in the interval $[u,u+1[$	5.1.1
PS	partial schedule	5.1.1
X	set of the activities $j=1,...,J$	5.1.1
S_{EFT}	earliest finish (time) schedule	5.1.2
F	forbidden set	5.1.2
$\mathbf{F}$	set of all forbidden sets	5.1.2
MF	minimal forbidden set	5.1.2
$\mathbf{MF}$	set of all minimal forbidden sets	5.1.2
V	shift vector	5.1.2
C_n	complete set at stage n	5.2.1
D_n	decision set at stage n	5.2.1
R_n	remaining set at stage n	5.2.1
πK_{rt}	left-over capacity of the renewable resource type r in period t	5.2.1
PST_j	the precedence feasible start time of activity j	5.2.1
$v(j)$	priority value of activity j	5.2.1
t_n	schedule time at stage n	5.2.1
A_n	active set at stage n	5.2.1

πK_r	left-over period capacity of the renewable resource type r at the schedule time	5.2.1
EST_j	earliest precedence and resource feasible start time of activity j	5.2.2
$\underline{w}$	weighting vector	5.2.2
$\succ$	ranking (of alternatives)	5.2.2
AP_n	set of activity pairs in the decision set at stage n	5.2.2
GFP_n	set of generally forbidden pairs in the decision set at stage n	5.2.2
TFP_n	set of temporarily forbidden pairs in the decision set at stage n	5.2.2
CSP_n	set of currently schedulable pairs in the decision set at stage n	5.2.2
$\Pi^r_{(i,j)}$	the earliest time the temporarily forbidden activity pair (i,j) can be processed simultaneously w.r.t. resource type r	5.2.2
$\Pi_{(i,j)}$	the earliest time to process two activities (i,j) of a temporarily forbidden activity pair simultaneously w.r.t. to all resource types	5.2.2
$\overline{\Pi}_{(i,j)}$	the earliest time for any activity pair (i,j) to be scheduled simultaneously	5.2.2
$E_{(j,i)}$	the earliest time to schedule activity i if activity j is started at the schedule time t_n	5.2.2
$E_{(i,j)}$	the earliest time to schedule activity j if activity i is started at the schedule time t_n	5.2.2
$\psi(j)$	probability of selecting activity j	5.3.2
λ	priority list	5.2.2
$\lambda(j)$	ordinal position of activity j in a priority list	5.3.2
α	probability mapping parameter	5.3.2
ρ_j	regret value of activity j w.r.t. to the worst consequence in the decision set	5.3.2
DEV	percentage deviation from the optimal solution	5.4
CPU	CPU-time in seconds	5.4
$\succ\succ$	significant ranking (of alternatives)	5.4
$E[]$	expected value	5.4
s	level of significance	5.4.1
PM	probability mapping	5.4.1
MP	mapping parameter	5.4.1
SS	scheduling scheme	5.4.1
PR	priority rule	5.4.1
z	counter of the actual sample size	5.5.1

Y_k	level of sample size for mode-assignments	6.3.1
Z_l	level of sample size for schedules	6.3.1
B_m	levels of probability mapping parameter β	6.3.1
G_n	levels of probability mapping parameter γ	6.3.1
PFT_j	the precedence feasible finish time of activity j	7.2.1
s_j	precedence based slack of activity j	7.2.2
C_{rt}	cost incurred by resource r within period t	7.2.2
PC_j	cost associated with activity j	7.2.2
χ	probability mapping parameter for the choice of the finish time	7.3
ξ	probability mapping parameter for the activity selection	7.3
ζ	probability mapping parameter for the mode selection	7.3
$ODEV$	overall percentage deviation	7.3
SP_{ru}	setup-state of setup-resource r at stage n with schedule time t_n	8.1

List of Abbreviations

PERT	program evaluation and review technique	1.1
GERT	graphical evaluation and review technique	1.1
CPM	critical path method	1.1
PSP	project scheduling problem	1.3
SMPSP	single-mode project scheduling problem	1.3
MMPSP	multi-mode project scheduling problem	1.3
PSPDL	project scheduling problem with given deadline	1.3
PSPST	project scheduling problem with setup times	1.3
CIM	computer integrated manufacturing	1.3
PPC	production planning and control	1.3
AON	activity-on-node network	2.1.3
AON	activity-on-arc network	2.1.3
FR	forward recursion	2.2.1
BR	backward recursion	2.2.1
JSP	job shop problem	2.2.2
FSP	flow shop problem	2.2.2
PFSP	permutation flow shop problem	2.2.2
ALB	assembly line balancing problem	2.2.2
BP	bin packing problem	2.2.2
MAP	mode assignment problem	2.3.2
FMS	flexible manufacturing system	2.5
PSPUTD	project scheduling problem with unit-time-duration activities	3.2
BAG	Brooks algorithm	5.1.2

SSS	serial scheduling scheme	5.2.1
PSS	parallel scheduling scheme	5.2.1
SPT	shortest processing time (priority rule)	5.2.2
MIS	most immediate successors (priority rule)	5.2.2
LST	latest start time (priority rule)	5.2.2
GRD	greatest resource demand (priority rule)	5.2.2
MSLK	minimum slack (priority rule)	5.2.2
GRPW	greatest rank positional weight (priority rule)	5.2.2
WRUP	weighted resource utilisation ratio and precedence (priority rule)	5.2.2
MTS	most total successors (priority rule)	5.2.2
LFT	latest finish time (priority rule)	5.2.2
RSM	resource scheduling method	5.2.2
IRSM	improved RSM (priority rule)	5.2.2
WCS	worst case slack (priority rule)	5.2.2
ANOVA	analysis of variance	5.4
ALV	probability mapping due to Alvarez-Valdes / Tamarit	5.4.2
BAK	probability mapping due to Baker	5.4.2
COP	probability mapping due to Cooper	5.4.2
DRE	probability mapping due to Drexl	5.4.2
SMH	single-mode heuristic	5.5.1
GPB	general precedence-based bound	5.5.2
GRB	general resource-based bound	5.5.2
PPB	parallel precedence-based bound	5.5.2
PRB	parallel resource-based bound	5.5.2
SPB	serial precedence-based bound	5.5.2
SPP	single-pass procedure	5.5.3
DA	disjunctive arc procedure	5.5.3
TBB	truncated branch and bound procedure	5.5.3
LS	local search procedure	5.5.3
OMA	opening mode-assignment (scheme)	6.2.1
IMA	improved mode-assignment (scheme)	6.2.1
MSC	modified slack calculation	6.2.3
AMA	alter mode-assignment (scheme)	6.2.3
MMH	multi-mode heuristic	6.2.3
MPP	multi-pass procedure	6.3.4
TE	truncated enumeration	6.3.4
BSP	biased sampling procedure	6.3.4

MIP	mixed integer program	7.1
SMDLH	single-mode deadline heuristic	7.2.1
FMA	first mode-assignment (scheme)	7.2.2
CMA	change mode-assignment (scheme)	7.2.2
STH	setup time heuristic	8.1
MPS	master production schedule	9.1
MRP	material requirements planning	9.1
BOM	bill of materials	9.1

References

Adelsberger, H.H. and J.J. Kanet (1991): The leitstand - A new tool for computer-integrated manufacturing, Production and Inventory Management Journal, Vol. 32, pp. 43-48.

Ahn, J. and A. Kusiak (1991): Scheduling with alternative process plans, in: Fandel, G. and G. Zäpfel (Eds.): Modern production concepts, Springer, Berlin, pp. 386-403.

Alvarez-Valdes, R. and J.M. Tamarit (1989a): Heuristic algorithms for resource-constrained project scheduling: A review and an empirical analysis, in: Slowinski, R. and J. Weglarz (Eds.): Advances in project scheduling, Elsevier, Amsterdam, pp. 113-134.

Alvarez-Valdes, R. and J.M. Tamarit (1989b): Algoritmos heuristicos deterministas y aleatorios en secuenciacion de proyectos con recursos limitados, Qüestiio, Vol. 13, pp. 173-191.

Arora, R.K. and R.K. Sachdeva (1989): Distributed simulation of resource constrained project scheduling, Computers & Operations Research, Vol. 16, pp. 295-304.

Badiru, A.B. (1988): Towards the standardization of performance measures for project scheduling heuristics, IEEE Transactions, Vol. 35, pp. 82-89.

Baker, K.R. (1974): Introduction to sequencing and scheduling, Wiley, New York.

Balas, E. (1969): Machine sequencing via disjunctive graphs: An implicit enumeration algorithm, Operations Research, Vol. 17, pp. 941-957.

Balas, E. (1971): Project scheduling with resource constraints, in: Beale, E.M.L. (Ed.): Applications of mathematical programming techniques, English University Press, London, pp. 187-200.

Ball, M. and M. Magazine (1981): The design and analysis of heuristics, Networks, Vol. 11, pp 215-219.

Barker, J.R. and G.B. McMahon (1985): Scheduling the general job shop, Management Science, Vol. 31, pp. 594-598.

Bartusch, M., R.H. Möhring and F.J. Radermacher (1988): Scheduling project networks with resource constraints and time windows, Annals of Operations Research, Vol. 16, pp. 201-240.

Bedworth, D.D. and J.E. Bailey (1982): Integrated production control systems - Management, analysis, design, Wiley, New York.

Bedworth, D.D. (1973): Industrial systems: Planning, analysis, control, Ronald, New York.

Bell, C.E. and J. Han (1991): A new heuristic solution method in resource-constrained project scheduling, Naval Research Logistics, Vol. 38, pp. 315-331.

Bell, C.E. and K. Park (1990): Solving resource-constrained project scheduling problems by A* search, Naval Research Logistics, Vol. 37, pp. 61-84.

Blazewicz, J., W. Cellary, R. Slowinski, and J. Weglarz (1986): Scheduling under resource constraints - Deterministic models, Baltzer, Basel.

Blazewicz, J., K. Ecker, G. Schmidt, and J. Weglarz (1993): Scheduling in computer and manufacturing systems, Springer, Berlin.

Blazewicz, J., J.K. Lenstra, and A.H.G. Rinnooy Kan (1983): Scheduling subject to resource constraints: Classification and complexity, Discrete Applied Mathematics, Vol. 5, pp. 11-24.

Bock, D.B. and J.H. Patterson (1990): A comparison of due date setting, resource assignment, and job preemption heuristics for the multiproject scheduling problem, Decision Sciences, Vol. 21, pp. 387-402.

Boctor, F.F. (1990): Some efficient multi-heuristic procedures for resource-constrained project scheduling, European Journal of Operational Research, Vol. 49, pp. 3-13.

Boctor, F.F. (1994): Heuristics for scheduling projects with resource restrictions and several resource-duration modes, International Journal of Production Research, Vol. 31, pp. 2547-2558.

Bowman, E.H. (1959): The schedule-sequencing problem, Operations Research, Vol. 7, pp. 621-624.

Brucker, P., B. Jurisch, and A. Krämer (1992): The job shop problem and immediate selection, Osnabrücker Schriften zur Mathematik, Fachbereich Mathematik, Universität Osnabrück.

Burgess, A.R. and J.B. Killebrew (1962): Variation in activity level on a cyclical arrow diagram, The Journal of Industrial Engineering, Vol. 8, pp. 76-83.

Carlier, J. and B. Latapie (1991): Une methode arborescente pour resoudre les problemes cumulatifs, Recherche operationnelle, Vol. 25, pp. 311-340.

Carruthers, J.A. and A. Battersby (1966): Advances in critical path methods, Operational Research Quarterly, Vol. 17, pp. 359-380.

Christofides, N., R. Alvarez-Valdes, and J.M. Tamarit (1987): Project scheduling with resource constraints: A branch and bound approach, European Journal of Operational Research, Vol. 29, pp. 262-273.

Conway, R.W., W.L. Maxwell, and L.W. Miller (1967): Theory of scheduling, Addison-Wesley, Reading, Massachusetts.

Cooper, D.F. (1976): Heuristics for scheduling resource-constrained projects: An experimental investigation, Management Science, Vol. 22, pp. 1186-1194.

Cooper, D.F. (1977): A note on serial and parallel heuristics for resource-constrained project scheduling, Foundations of Control Engineering, Vol. 2, pp. 131-134.

Crowder, H., R.S. Dembo, and J.M. Mulvey (1979): On reporting computational experiments with mathematical software, ACM Transactions on Mathematical Software, Vol. 5, pp. 193-203.

Davies, E.M. (1973): An experimental investigation of resource allocation in multiactivity projects, Operational Research Quarterly, Vol. 24, pp. 587-591.

Davis, E.W. (1966): Resource allocation in project network models - A survey, The Journal of Industrial Engineering, Vol. 17, pp. 177-188.

Davis, E.W. (1973): Project scheduling under resource constraints - Historical review and categorization of procedures, AIIE Transactions, Vol. 5, pp. 297-313.

Davis, E.W. (1975): Project network summary measures constrained-resource scheduling, AIIE Transactions, Vol. 7, pp. 132-142.

Davis, E.W. and G.E. Heidorn (1971): An algorithm for optimal project scheduling under multiple resource constraints, Management Science, Vol. 17, pp. 803-816.

Davis, E.W. and J.H. Patterson (1975): A comparison of heuristic and optimum solutions in resource-constrained project scheduling, Management Science, Vol. 21, pp. 944-955.

Deckro, R.F. and Hebert, J.E. (1989): Resource constrained project crashing, OMEGA International Journal of Management Science, Vol. 17, pp. 69-79.

Dell'Amico, M. (1990): Un algoritmo euristico per la pianificazione delle risorse nei progetti software, in: Proceedings of the annual conference of the operational research society of Italy, pp. 211-226.

Demeulemeester, E. (1992): Optimal algorithms for various classes of multiple resource-constrained project scheduling problems, Dissertation, Katholieke Universiteit Leuven, Belgium.

Demeulemeester, E. and W.S. Herroelen (1992a): A branch-and-bound procedure for the multiple resource-constrained project scheduling problem, Management Science, Vol. 38, pp. 1803-1818.

Demeulemeester, E. and W.S. Herroelen (1992b): A branch-and-bound procedure for the generalized resource-constrained project scheduling problem, Working Paper, Departement of Applied Economic Sciences, Katholieke Universiteit Leuven, Belgium.

Demeulemeester, E. and W.S. Herroelen (1992c): An efficient optimal solution procedure for the preemptive resource-constrained project scheduling problem, Working Paper, Departement of Applied Economic Sciences, Katholieke Universiteit Leuven, Belgium.

Demeulemeester, E., B. Dodin, and W. Herroelen (1993a): A random activity network generator, Operations Research, Vol. 41, pp. 972-980.

Demeulemeester, E., S.E. Elmaghraby, and W. Herroelen (1993b): The discrete time / cost trade-off problem in project networks, Working Paper, Departement of Applied Economic Sciences, Katholieke Universiteit Leuven, Belgium.

Dervitiotis, K.N. (1981): Operations Management, McGraw-Hill, Tokyo.

De Reyck, B. and W. Herroelen (1993): On the use of the complexity index as a measure of complexity in activity networks, Working Paper, Departement of Applied Economic Sciences, Katholieke Universiteit Leuven, Belgium.

Domschke, W. and A. Drexl (1991a): Einführung in Operations Research, 2-nd edition, Springer, Berlin.

Domschke, W. and A. Drexl (1991b): Kapazitätsplanung in Netzwerken - Ein Überblick über neue Modelle und Verfahren, OR Spektrum, Vol. 13, pp. 63-76.

Drexl, A. (1990): Fließbandaustaktung, Maschinenbelegung und Kapazitätsplanung in Netzwerken, Zeitschrift für Betriebswirtschaft, Vol. 60, pp. 53-70.

Drexl, A. (1991): Scheduling of project networks by job assignment, Management Science, Vol. 37, pp. 1590-1602.

Drexl, A., W. Eversheim, H. Esser, and R. Grempe (1994a): CIM im Werkzeug-maschinenbau: Der PRISMA-Montageleitstand, Zeitschrift für betriebswirtschaftliche Forschung, Heft 3, pp. 279-295.

Drexl, A., B. Fleischmann, H.-O.Günther, H. Stadtler, and H. Tempelmeier (1994b): Konzeptionelle Grundlagen kapazitätsorientierter PPS-Systeme, Zeitschrift für betriebswirtschaftliche Forschung, to appear.

Drexl, A. and J. Grünewald (1993): Nonpreemptive multi-mode resource-constrained project scheduling, IIE Transactions, Vol. 25, No. 5, pp. 74-81.

Drexl, A. and R. Kolisch (1993a): Produktionsplanung und -steuerung bei Einzel- und Kleinserienfertigung: Grundlagen, Wirtschaftswissenschaftliches Studium, Jg. 22, pp. 60-66, 102-103.

Drexl, A. and R. Kolisch (1993b): Produktionsplanung und -steuerung bei Einzel- und Kleinserienfertigung: Leitstandskonzepte, Wirtschaftswissenschaftliches Studium, Jg. 22, pp. 137-141.

Dyckhoff, H. (1990): A typology of cutting and packing problems, European Journal of Operational Research, Vol. 44, pp. 145-159.

Elmaghraby, S.E. (1977): Activity networks: Project planning and control by network models, Wiley, New York.

Elmaghraby, S.E. and W.S. Herroelen (1980): On the measurement of complexity in activity networks, European Journal of Operational Research, Vol. 5, pp. 223-224.

Elsayed, E.A. (1982): Algorithms for project scheduling with resource constraints, International Journal of Production Research, Vol. 20, pp. 95-103.

Fehler, D.W. (1969): Die Variationen-Enumeration - Ein Näherungsverfahren zur Planung des optimalen Betriebsmitteleinsatzes bei der Terminierung von Projekten, Elektronische Datenverarbeitung, Vol. 10, pp. 479-483.

Figge, S. (1992): Kapazitätsplanung in Netzwerken: Eine vergleichende Untersuchung von prioritätsregelbasierten Einplanungsstrategien, Master Thesis, Christian-Albrechts-Universität zu Kiel, Germany.

Fisher, M.L. (1980): Worst-case analysis of heuristic algorithms, Management Science, Vol. 26, pp. 1-17.

Fisher, H. and G.L. Thompson (1963): Probabilistic learning combinations of local job-shop scheduling rules, in: Muth, J.F. and G.L. Thompson (Eds.): Industrial scheduling, Prentice-Hall, New Jersey, pp. 225-251.

French, S. (1982): Sequencing and scheduling: An introduction to the mathematics of the job-shop, Wiley, New York.

Garey, M.R., R.L. Graham, D.S. Johnson, and C.C. Yao (1976): Resource constrained scheduling as generalized bin packing, Journal of Combinational Theory, Vol. 21, pp. 257-298.

Garey, M.R. and D.S. Johnson (1979): Computers and intractability - A guide to the theory of NP-completeness, Freeman, San Francisco.

Giffler, B. and G.L. Thompson (1960): Algorithms for solving production scheduling problems, Operations Research, Vol. 8, pp.487-503.

Giffler, B., G.L. Thompson, and V. Van Ness (1963): Numerical experience with the linear and monte carlo algorithm for solving production scheduling problems, in: Muth, J.F. and G.L. Thompson (Eds.): Industrial scheduling, Prentice-Hall, New Jersey, pp. 21-38.

Glover, F. (1990): Tabu Search: A Tutorial, Interfaces, Vol. 20, pp. 74-94.

Goldberg, D.E. (1989): Genetic algorithms in search, optimization and machine learning, Addison-Wesley, Reading, Massachusetts.

Golden, B.L. and W.R. Steward (1985): Empirical analysis of heuristics, in: Lawler, E.L, J.K. Lenstra, A.H.G. Rinnooy Kan, and D.B. Shmoys (Eds.): The traveling salesman problem, Wiley, New York, pp. 207-249.

Gonguet, L. (1969): Comparison of three heuristic procedures for allocating resources and producing schedules, Lombaers, H.J.M. (Ed.): Project planning by network analysis, North-Holland, Amsterdam, pp. 249-255.

Hart, J.P. and A.W. Shogan (1987): Semi-greedy heuristics: An empirical study, Operations Research Letters, Vol. 6, pp. 107-114.

Hartmann, S. and A. Sprecher (1993): A note on "Hierarchical models for multi-project planning and scheduling", Manuskripte aus den Instituten für Betriebswirtschaftslehre der Universität Kiel No. 338, Christian-Albrechts-Universität zu Kiel, Germany.

Hastings, N.A.J. (1972): On resource allocation in project networks, Operational Research Quarterly, Vol. 23, pp. 217-221.

Haupt, R. (1989): A survey of priority rule-based scheduling, OR Spektrum, Vol. 11, pp. 3-16.

Hax, A.C. and D. Candea (1984): Production and inventory management, Prentice-Hall, New Jersey.

Heller, J. and G. Logemann (1962): An algorithm for the construction and evaluation of feasible schedules, Management Science, Vol. 9, pp.168-183.

Herroelen, W.S. (1972): Resource-constrained project scheduling - The state of the art, Operational Research Quarterly, Vol. 23, pp. 261-275.

Herroelen, W.S. and E. Demeulemeester (1992): Recent advances in branch-and-bound procedures for resource-constrained project scheduling problems, Working Paper, Departement of Applied Economic Sciences, Katholieke Universiteit Leuven, Belgium.

Jackson, R.H.F., P.T. Boggs, S.G. Nash, and S. Powell (1991): Guidelines for reporting results of computational experiments. Report of the ad hoc committee, Mathematical Programming, Vol. 49, pp. 413-425.

Johnson, T.J.R. (1967): An algorithm for the resource-constrained project scheduling problem, Dissertation, Massachusetts Institute of Technology, USA.

Kamburowski, J., D.J. Michael, and M. Stallmann (1993): On the minimum dummy-arc problem, Recherche operationnelle, Vol. 27, pp. 153-168.

Kaplan, L. (1991): Resource-constrained project scheduling with setup times, Working Paper, Departement of Management Science, University of Tennessee, Knoxville, USA.

Kelley, J.E. Jr. (1961): Critical-path planning and scheduling: Mathematical basis, Operations Research, Vol. 9, pp. 296-320.

Kelley, J.E., Jr. (1963): The critical-path method: Resources planning and scheduling, in: Muth, J.F. and G.L. Thompson (Eds.): Industrial scheduling, Prentice-Hall, New Jersey, pp. 347-365.

Kim, S.-Y. and R.C. Leachman (1993): A hierarchical approach to multi-resource multi-project scheduling with explicit lateness costs, IIE Transactions, Vol. 25, pp. 34-44.

Kolisch, R., A. Sprecher, and A. Drexl (1995): Characterization and generation of a general class of resource-constrained project scheduling problems, Management Science, to appear.

Kurtulus, I.S. and E.W. Davis (1982): Multi-project scheduling: Categorization of heuristic rules performance, Management Science, Vol. 28, pp. 161-172.

Kurtulus, I.S. and S.C. Narula (1985): Multi-project scheduling: Analysis of project performance, IIE Transactions, Vol.17, pp.58-66.

Krishnamoorthy, M. and N. Deo (1979): Complexity of the minimum-dummy-activities problem in a PERT network, Networks, Vol. 9, pp. 189-194.

Lawrence, S.R. (1985): Resource-constrained project scheduling - A computational comparison of heuristic scheduling techniques, Working Paper, Graduate School of Industrial Administration, Carnegie-Mellon University, Pittsburgh, USA.

Lawrence, S.R. and T.E. Morton (1993): Resource-constrained multi-project scheduling with tardy costs: Comparing myopic, bottleneck, and resource pricing heuristics, European Journal of Operational Research, Vol. 64, pp. 168-187.

Levy, F.K., G.L. Thompson, and J.D. Wiest (1962): Multiship, multishop, workload-smoothing program, Naval Research Logistics Quarterly, Vol. 9, pp. 37-44.

Levy, F.K., G.L. Thompson, and J.D. Wiest (1963): Introduction to the critical-path method, in: Muth, J.F. and G.L. Thompson (Eds.): Industrial scheduling, Prentice-Hall, New Jersey, pp. 331-346.

Li, R.K.-Y. and J. Willis (1991): Alternative resources in project scheduling, Computers & Operations Research, Vol. 18, pp. 663-668.

Li, R.K.-Y. and J. Willis (1992): An iterative scheduling technique for resource-constrained project scheduling, European Journal of Operational Research, Vol. 56, pp. 370-379.

Li, R.K.-Y.and J. Willis (1993): Resource constrained scheduling within fixed project durations, Journal of the Operational Research Society, Vol. 44, pp. 71-80.

Malcolm, D.G., J.H. Roseboom, C.E. Clark, and W. Fazar (1959): Applications of a technique for research and development program evaluation, Operations Research, Vol. 7, pp. 646-669.

McClain, J.O. and L.J. Thomas (1985): Operations management - Production of goods and services, 2-nd edition, Prentice-Hall, New Jersey.

Moder, J.J. and C.R. Phillips (1964): Project management with CPM and PERT, 1-st edition, Van Nostrand Reinhold, New York.

Moder, J.J., C.R. Phillips, and E.W. Davis (1983): Project management with CPM, PERT and precedence diagramming, 3-rd edition, Van Nostrand Reinhold, New York.

Möhring, R.H. (1984): Minimizing costs of requirements in project networks subject to a fixed completion time, Operations Research, Vol. 32, pp. 89-120.

Mohanty, R.P. and M.K. Siddiq (1989): Multiple projects-multiple resources-constrained scheduling: Some studies, International Journal of Production Research, Vol. 27, pp. 261-280.

Monma, C.L. and C.N. Potts (1989): On the complexity of scheduling with batch setup times, Operations Research, Vol. 37, pp. 798-804.

Müller-Merbach, H. (1967): Ein Verfahren zur Planung des optimalen Betriebsmitteleinsatzes bei der Terminierung von Großprojekten, Zeitschrift für wirtschaftliche Fertigung, Vol. 62, pp. 83-88, 135-140.

Neumann, K. (1975): Operations Research Verfahren Band III, Carl Hanser Verlag, München.

Neumann, K. (1990): Stochastic project networks - Temporal analysis, scheduling and cost minimization, Springer, Berlin.

Norbis, M.I. and J.M. Smith (1986): Two level heuristic for the resource constrained scheduling problem, International Journal of Production Research, Vol. 24, pp. 1203-1219.

Panwalkar, S.S. and W. Iskander (1977): A survey of scheduling rules, Operations Research, Vol.25, pp. 45-61.

Papadimitriou, C.H. and K. Steiglitz (1982): Combinatorial optimization - Algorithms and complexity, Prentice-Hall, New Jersey.

Pascoe, T.L. (1966): Allocation of resources C.P.M., Revue Francaise Recherche Operationelle, No. 38, pp. 31-38.

Patterson, J.H. (1973): Alternate methods of project scheduling with limited resources, Naval Research Logistics Quarterly, Vol. 20, pp. 767-784.

Patterson, J.H. (1976): Project scheduling: The effects of problem structure on heuristic performance, Naval Research Logistics Quarterly, Vol. 23, pp. 95-123.

Patterson, J.H. (1984): A comparison of exact approaches for solving the multiple constrained resource, project scheduling problem, Management Science, Vol. 30, pp. 854-867.

Patterson, J.H. and W.D. Huber (1974): A horizon-varying, zero-one approach to project scheduling, Management Science, Vol. 20, pp. 990-998.

Patterson, J.H. and G.W. Roth (1976): Scheduling a project under multiple resource constraints: A zero-one programming approach, AIIE Transactions, Vol. 8, pp. 449-455.

Patterson, J.H., R. Slowinski, F.B. Talbot, and J. Weglarz (1989): An algorithm for a general class of precedence and resource constrained scheduling problems, in: Slowinski, R. and J. Weglarz. (Eds.): Advances in project scheduling, Elsevier, Amsterdam, pp. 3-28.

Patterson, J.H., F.B. Talbot, R. Slowinski, and J. Weglarz (1990): Computational experience with a backtracking algorithm for solving a general class of precedence and resource-constrained scheduling problems, European Journal of Operational Research, Vol. 49, pp. 68-79.

Pearl (1984): Heuristics: Intelligent search strategies for computer problem solving, Addison-Wesley, Reading, Massachusetts.

Potts, C.N, D.B. Shmoys, and D.P. Williamson (1991): Permutation vs. non-permutation flow shop schedules, Operations Research Letters, Vol. 10, pp. 218-284.

Pritsker, A.A.B. and W.W. Happ (1966): GERT: Graphical evaluation and review technique, Part I: Fundamentals, Journal of Industrial Engineering, Vol. 17, pp. 267-274.

Pritsker, A.A.B. and G.E. Whitehouse (1966): GERT: Graphical evaluation and review technique, Part II: Probabilistic and industrial engineering applications, Journal of Industrial Engineering, Vol. 17, pp. 293-299.

Pritsker, A.A.B. and G.E. Whitehouse (1966): GERT: Graphical evaluation and review technique, Part II: Probabilistic and industrial engineering applications, Journal of Industrial Engineering, Vol. 17, pp. 293-299.

Pritsker, A.A.B., L.J. Watters, and P.M. Wolfe (1969): Multiproject scheduling with limited resources: A zero-one programming approach, Management Science, Vol. 16, pp. 93-107.

Radermacher, F.J. (1985 / 86): Scheduling of project networks, Annals of Operations Research, Vol. 4, pp. 227-252.

Rinnooy Kan, A.H.G. (1976): Maschine scheduling problems: Classification, complexity and computations, Nijhoff, The Hague, The Netherlands.

Sampson, S.E. and E.N. Weiss (1993): Local search techniques for the generalized resource constrained project scheduling problem, Naval Research Logistics, Vol. 40, pp. 365-375.

Schrage, L. (1970): Solving resource-constrained network problems by implicit enumeration - nonpreemptive case, Operations Research, Vol. 18, pp. 263-278.

Schrage, L. (1979): A more portable Fortran random number generator, ACM Transactions on Mathematical Software, Vol. 5, pp.132-138.

Schrage, L. (1991): LINDO - An optimization modelling system, 4-th edition, Scientific Press, San Francisco.

Shaffer, L.R., J.B. Ritter, and W.L. Meyer (1965): The critical-path method, McGraw-Hill, New York.

Silver, E.A. and R. Peterson (1985): Decision systems for inventory management and production planning, 2-nd edition, Wiley, New York.

Slowinski, R. (1978): A node ordering heuristic for network scheduling under multiple resource constraints, Foundations of Control Engineering, Vol. 3, pp. 19-27.

Slowinski, R. (1980): Two approaches to problems of resource allocation among project activities - A comparative study, Journal of the Operational Research Society, Vol. 31, pp. 711-723.

Slowinski, R. (1989): Multiobjective project scheduling under multiple-category resource constraints, in: Slowinski, R. and J. Weglarz (Eds.): Advances in project scheduling, Elsevier, Amsterdam, pp. 113-134.

Slowinski, R., B. Soniewicki, and J. Weglarz (1991): DSS for multiobjective project scheduling subject to multiple-category resource constraints, submitted to European Journal of Operational Research.

Slowinski, R. and J. Weglarz (Eds.): Advances in project scheduling, Elsevier, Amsterdam.

Smith-Daniels, D.E. and V.L. Smith-Daniels (1987): Optimal project scheduling with materials ordering, IIE Transactions, Vol. 19, pp. 122-129.

Sprecher, A., R. Kolisch, and A. Drexl (1994): Semi-active, active, and non-delay sched-ules for the resource-constrained project scheduling problem, European Journal of Op-erational Research, to appear.

Stinson, J.P. (1976): A branch and bound algorithm for a general class of multiple re-source-constrained scheduling problems, Dissertation, Graduate School of Business Administration, University of North Carolina, USA.

Stinson, J.P., E.W. Davis, and B.M. Khumawala (1978): Multiple resource-constrained scheduling using branch and bound, AIIE Transactions, Vol. 10, pp. 252-259.

Storer, R.H., S.D. Wu, and R. Vaccari (1992): New search spaces for sequencing problems with application to job shop scheduling, Management Science, Vol. 38, pp. 1495-1509.

Syslo, M.M. (1984): On the computational complexity of the minimum-dummy-activities problem in a PERT network, Networks, Vol. 14, pp. 37-45.

Talbot, B. (1982): Resource-constrained project scheduling with time-resource tradeoffs: The nonpreemptive case, Management Science, Vol. 28, pp. 1197-1210.

Talbot, B. and J.H. Patterson (1978): An efficient integer programming algorithm with network cuts for solving resource-constrained scheduling problems, Management Sci-ence, Vol. 24, pp. 1163-1174.

Thesen, A. (1976): Heuristic scheduling of activites under resource and precedence re-strictions, Management Science, Vol. 23, pp. 412-422.

Thesen, A. (1977): Measures of the restrictiveness of project networks, Networks, Vol. 7, pp. 193-208.

Tsubakitani, S. and R.F. Deckro (1990): A heuristic for multi-project scheduling with limited resources in the housing industry, European Journal of Operational Research, Vol. 49, pp. 80-91.

Ulusoy, G. and L. Özdamar (1989): Heuristic performance and network / resource charac-teristics in resource-constrained project scheduling, Journal of the Operational Re-search Society, Vol. 40, pp. 1145-1152.

Valls, V., M.A. Perez, and M.S. Quintanilla (1992): Heuristic performance in large re-source-constrained projects, Working Paper, Departament D'Estadistica I Investigacio Operativa, Universitat De Valencia, Spain.

Weber, K. (1990): Probabilistische Analyse von Heuristiken der kombinatorischen Op-timierung - Ein Überblick, Optimization, Vol. 21, pp. 965-989.

Wee, T.S. and M.J. Magazine (1982): Assembly line balancing as generalized bin pack-ing, Operations Research Letters, Vol. 1, pp. 56-58.

Weglarz, J. (1981): Project scheduling with continuously divisible, doubly-constrained re-sources, Management Science, Vol. 27, pp. 1040-1053.

Weglarz, J. (1989): Project scheduling under continuous processing speed vs. resource amount activity models, in: Slowinski, R. and J. Weglarz (Eds.): Advances in project scheduling, Elsevier, Amsterdam, pp. 273-295.

Whitehouse, G.E. and J.R. Brown (1979): Genres: An extension of Brooks algorithm for project scheduling with resource constraints, Computers & Industrial Engineering, Vol 3, pp. 261-268.

Wiest, J.D. (1964): Some properties of schedules for large projects with limited resources, Operations Research, Vol. 12, pp. 395-418.

Wiest, J.D. (1967): A heuristic model for scheduling large projects with limited resources, Management Science, Vol. 13, pp. B359-B377.

Woodworth, B.M and C.J. Willie (1975): A heuristic algorithm for resource leveling in multi-project, multi-resource scheduling, Decision Sciences, Vol. 6, pp. 525-540.

Ziegler, H. (1985): Minimal and maximal floats in project networks, Engineering Costs and Production Economics, Vol. 9, pp. 91-97.

Zäpfel, G. and H. Missbauer (1993): New concepts for production planning and control, European Journal of Operational Research, Vol. 67, pp. 297-320.